1971

MERRILL JENSEN
Vilas Research Professor of History
University of Wisconsin
ADVISORY EDITOR TO DODD, MEAD & COMPANY

THE HERITAGE AND CHALLENGE
OF HISTORY

THE HERITAGE
AND CHALLENGE
OF HISTORY

BY PAUL K. CONKIN AND
ROLAND N. STROMBERG

DODD, MEAD & COMPANY
NEW YORK   1971   TORONTO

ISBN 0-396-06316-0

Library of Congress Catalog Card Number: 73-145395

Printed in the United States of America

PREFACE

Historians today feel more disquietude than at any time in our recent past. The historical profession is severely fragmented, in definition, methods, purpose. Rarely has our youth so lightly valued historical knowledge. Perhaps most people sense an almost complete discontinuity between past and present concerns. Yet, the very stresses and strains of contemporary life suggest the pressing need for historical mindedness, for a recognition of continuities. This is equally true whether most of our past merits our celebration or deserves only our condemnation.

Any profession can succumb to myopia, particularly in times of prosperity. Until recently, historians often relaxed in the comfort and security of an old, well-established profession. They rarely questioned the legitimacy or the long-range usefulness of their inquiry. Much more than social scientists, they remained aloof from definitional and methodological controversies. But no more. Gentility and decorum still grace their conferences and soften their controversies. But the decorum is forced. No true community of historical scholars exists. Strident voices question the utility of all our deliberations.

One result of such a crisis of confidence is the increasing self-consciousness of historians. They are now willing to embark upon the most subtle philosophical investigations. An unprecedented contemporary interest in history by professional philosophers has not only helped stimulate the historian's concerns, but has also provided him with the intellectual resources needed for such disciplined self-analysis.

The most basic question for the historian has always been: What is history? The answer to this implicates all the other controverted issues: Is history a science? How does it relate to other disciplines? Does historical inquiry require a unique pathway to truth? Is historical explanation different from other types of explanation? Can a history be true? Can it be objective? What role does value play in historical writing? What is the place of causation in history? What are the proper tools for dealing with historical evidence? And, perhaps the most tantalizing of all, what is history for, or what social role does it play?

These questions, and others of the same type, are not new ones. Perhaps some of the answers are new. Since the Greeks, both historians and philosophers have asked, and proffered answers, to such questions. Thus, in Part I of this book, Roland N. Stromberg presents a brief account of the history of history in the West, seeking to focus on the most notable epochs, the greatest historians, and even more particularly on developing conceptions about history. In this sense, he has written a brief history of historical self-consciousness, and in the process uncovered the knotty problems of subject, method, and purpose that Western historians have faced through the centuries.

In Part II, Paul K. Conkin turns from history to analysis. In topical chapters, he tries to bare the theoretical issues of greatest contemporary concern for historians. He is particularly anxious to clarify some of the unending problems of definition, and to reveal at least the range and subtlety of philosophical issues that attend historical inquiry. For each major problem, he presents his own tentative resolution. These can be compared to other, contending views referred to in the text or identified in his bibliography.

For each of the two sections of the book there is, at the end of the book, a bibliography which can guide the dedicated student to more intensive study, and which can also assist the teacher of a course in historiography in his assignment of student reports on special topics. The authors believe that such a course ought to be taught more commonly than it is at present. Graduate students often take something of the sort, though, reflecting perhaps the historians' conceptual confusion, procedures vary widely from college to college. Undergraduates seldom do, yet it is increasingly clear that both the history and the theory of history are essential in preparing for the more profitable study of history itself.

The two authors believe the two Parts of this book complement

each other, and the more so because they represent two very different but equally necessary approaches to an understanding of history.
The authors completely divided their responsibilities, according to
their interests, teaching experiences, and greatest competence. Except
for mutual editorial assistance, Roland Stromberg alone wrote the
historical section; Paul Conkin all the analytical chapters. The authors collaborated on parts of the transitional chapter VII of Part I,
and on the final, brief "Epilogue: Some Practical Advice."

In such a joint effort they recognize the difficulty of a proper
acknowledgment of all the varied assistance received, from helpful
libraries all the way to excellent typists. But they do want, especially,
to note the contributions of their students, in Stromberg's Historiography Seminar at the University of Wisconsin-Milwaukee, and in
Conkin's Proseminar in the Philosophy of History at the University
of Wisconsin, Madison.

PAUL K. CONKIN
ROLAND N. STROMBERG

CONTENTS

Preface   v

PART I. THE HERITAGE OF HISTORY   1
1. The Roots of Western History: The Ancient World   3
2. Medieval Historical Writing   19
3. History in the Early Modern Period: From Renaissance
   and Reformation to Enlightenment   31
4. The Enlightenment Contribution to Historical Thought
   and Method   45
5. The Nineteenth Century: Golden Age of History   57
6. History in Our Own Time: The Twentieth Century   82
7. Recent Trends in History   105

PART II. THE CHALLENGE OF HISTORY   127
8. Introduction and Definition   129
9. History and the Generalizing Sciences   151
10. Causation   174
11. Objectivity and Value   197
12. Use   220
Epilogue: Some Practical Advice   245

Bibliographies:
   1. Bibliography on the Heritage of History   253
   2. Bibliography on the Challenge of History   269
Index   273

THE HERITAGE AND CHALLENGE
OF HISTORY

PART I

THE HERITAGE
OF HISTORY

Profitable philosophical discussion of any science depends
on a thorough familiarity with its history and its present state.

—NORWOOD HANSON, *Patterns of Discovery*

C hapter 1

THE ROOTS OF WESTERN HISTORY: THE ANCIENT WORLD

THE HISTORICAL-MINDEDNESS OF WESTERN CIVILIZATION

The place of history in Western civilization has been a uniquely great one—a legacy of the dual tradition of Hebraism and Hellenism, of the Judaic-Christian sense of time and the Greek critical spirit. Few if any other civilizations have possessed this sort of historical-mindedness.

It may be thought that no society can "escape history," and this is in some sense true. The past lies around us everywhere we look, in the form of physical mementos such as buildings, monuments, objects of art and utility; and in the legends and tales preserved about memorable deeds in the past, such as even savages relate. It is a gigantic fact almost comparable to physical nature in its presence. "Teaching about the past is a constant element found in all societies," some have asserted. Certain forms of historical consciousness doubtless exist even in primitive societies. Nevertheless, primitive man and some of our most highly developed civilizations, above all the Oriental ones, have not endowed time with the kind of value that Western man has always ascribed to it. In his interesting book *Cosmos and History: The Myth of the Eternal Return* (and elsewhere), the distinguished historian of religions Mircea Eliade pointed out that traditional or "archaic" societies, which are what most men have lived in through most of humanity's time on earth, typically "refuse history." Though he believed in a golden age in the past (the oldest and most ubiquitous of all human myths), primitive or archaic man lived in a timeless dimension, ritualized around primordial acts in a way that seems determined to deprive time of any real meaning.

And, if we turn to a very sophisticated and old civilization, that of India, we see clearly that its modes of thought ascribe no significance or "ontological content" at all to time. It is without meaning. The Indian tradition posits huge time cycles of millions of years which always come back to the same place. Creation, destruction, and new creation go on endlessly, rather like the explosion of the primeval atom followed by its eventual contraction back into that atom, in a cycle of some eighty billion years, which present-day astronomical science tells us is the pattern of the physical cosmos. There is no progress and no goal, only the endless turning of the wheel of time around and around. Under such conditions history can have no importance. Indian philosophy and religion—whether Brahman, Buddhist, or Jainist—have aimed steadily at escaping from the wheel of existence by transcending entirely the time-bound human condition, the goal being to attain nirvana, a realm of pure being unbounded by time and space.[1]

Great-cycle theories were familiar to the ancient Greeks, as readers of Plato know. Eliade seems right in urging that an annihilation of history rather than an acceptance of it has been typical of mankind, and Western civilization has been atypical in its intense historical-mindedness. Western time has been rectilineal rather than cyclical and thus has been meaningful rather than meaningless. This idea came from the unique religion of the Jews, taken over by Christianity (and later by Islam), which saw God's hand in the events of history and perceived a final goal of history. Western history has, moreover, usually been seen as at least partly determined by man himself rather than as externally determined by an inscrutable external will or fate. This idea came from the unique philosophy of the ancient Greeks, who invented rational and scientific thought. Just as the combination of Greek and Hebraic elements formed Western civilization in general, the combination of the two elements produced the Western sense of history: in origin, the meaningfulness of time was Judaic-Christian; the self-determination of man, Hellenic.

In the early kingdoms of the ancient Near East which were the first human civilizations—Egyptian, Sumerian, Babylonian—no history

---

1. The Chinese, a rather more this-worldly people than the Indians, kept elaborate official records (political, administrative). Still, their cyclical, non-progressive view of history made them relatively unhistorical by Western standards.

was written, really. Events were recorded, and genealogies were kept, and kings boasted of their deeds. But we do not find any sense of history as it was later understood because no plan or pattern was discerned in the flow of events; things happened because of the "incalculable whims of the Gods."[2] The creation of large unified empires run by efficient states helped in some ways to prepare the way for written history. In the first place, they provided significant units of history. No units exist to *have* a significant history if men are dispersed in numerous small tribes or villages; a certain size and importance is necessary. We need only recall the extent to which history has flourished in modern times around the nation-state unit, telling the story of the birth, rise, and growth of England, France, Germany, the United States, and so on. Power becomes centralized, and the story of this power takes on importance. The deeds of Nebuchadnezzar and Ramses II in ancient times *were* worth recording and boasting about, since these potentates were rulers of mighty kingdoms. Such recording of major action was a beginning of history. But the ancient kingdoms seldom carried the matter any further; they never sought to analyze and explain these deeds, to discern their meaning, or to see them as a *process*.

By the time of the Assyrians, the Chaldeans, the Hittites, and the Egyptian New Kingdom (from c. 1500 B.C.), there was extensive preservation of documents in official archives. These were highly developed states, now fully in possession of the art of writing. No governmental bureaucracy is able to resist the impulse to preserve its records—a practical necessity as well as a badge of dignity. Yet it remained true that little or nothing that could be called "history" was written: there were no works of literature undertaking to narrate, describe, or analyze the happenings of the past in coherent form. With all our recent upgrading of the achievements of these ancient peoples, as our knowledge about them has grown (a veritable revolution since 1900, brought about by archaeological excavation), we still cannot make them historians. We must agree that critical inquiry into man's affairs began with the Greeks and that the Jews were indeed a "peculiar people" in attaching so much importance to the events of human history.

2. Jacquetta Hawkes and Sir Leonard Woolley, UNESCO History of Mankind, vol. I, *Pre-History and the Beginnings of Civilization* (New York: Harper and Row, 1963), p. 815.

Once regarded by Christians and Muslims as well as by themselves
as a people chosen by divine Providence for a unique and wondrous
revelation, the ancient Hebrews came to seem less "peculiar" in the
light of modern historical research. In the nineteenth century the first
wave of higher criticism stressed the many similarities between Judaic
beliefs and those of the more powerful peoples who surrounded the
tiny Jewish state—Babylonians, Egyptians, Assyrians, and others. But
if this is true in some details, it is not true in their larger outlook.
They broke away from the prevalent pattern in their religion, one of
the greatest in world history. For our purposes, the significance of
this spiritual revolution lies in its intense consciousness of history—its
charging of temporal events with the greatest possible amount of
"ontological content." And this vision of history was planted deeply
into the consciousness of Western man by its expression in the Bible,
constantly read, recited, and meditated on for so many centuries.

The Bible has been called a "story-telling masterpiece" and the first
"truly historical narrative of considerable scope and high relative
accuracy" (Harry Elmer Barnes). It is much nearer to popular folk
history than to scientific or critical history. It is mixed with myth; it
is not critical or "conceptual"; it is passionate and imaginative; and
it contains its share of errors and oversimplifications. But it is more
than a chronicle, usually more than the bare record of occurrences
without context or interpretation which Babylonian and Egyptian
kings left behind. It finds a purpose in history; it has a theme. This
was part and parcel of the religion of Israel; the Jews "clothed their
faith in historical dress," they believed that each event of history
testified to the will of God. They were the children of Yahweh, the
one God. Why did He raise them up and then cast them down? The
Prophets explained this as a result of Israel's sins and made it the
basis of a call to repentance and atonement. What lay ahead? A
"history religion" like that of the Jews must see in the historical
process some purposeful direction and a final goal. History would
come to a grand climax. A Messiah would come to redeem the Jewish
people and restore their kingdom and power. Or perhaps this final
triumph would bring this world to an end and usher in another and
better one. Perhaps Israel would have to suffer, a martyr to humanity,
but she would at least serve a providential purpose. The Jewish messianic and eschatological consciousness was of course handed on to

the Christians, who were also Jews. The Incarnation and the future Apocalypse or Last Judgment were specific historic phenomena which made time, to the Christian, a linear dimension, charged with meaning and divided into significant epochs. All history before the birth of Christ led up to this climax; afterward, one looked forward to that Last Day, which might come any time. (Certain hints and clues in the Bible provided generations of Christians with the absorbing game of figuring out just when it might come—a game played in almost every decade down to quite recent times.) It should be noted also that, for the Christian, this was a universal plan, tying all mankind together in the same providence, since Christ's message of salvation was offered to all and all should learn of it and accept it.

"The Christian religion is a daily invitation to study history," a modern scholar, F. M. Powicke, has written. Rooted in concrete happenings, it has caused even its foes to share that historical interest. What actually did happen in that Jewish city some two thousand years ago? And had the event been foretold? Is the Bible true and of divine origin, as Christians claimed, or could it be convicted of falsity? An incredible amount of research energy has been devoted to such questions; it once was the chief concern of scholarship. In later years Protestants and Roman Catholics disputed the history of the early Church, too. More recently, beyond the specific concern for the biblical narratives, this framework of reference has passed into the consciousness of many who had left Christianity as such behind them. "Many of them live by what they choose to forget," Jacques Maritain has remarked, concerning modern secular versions of the millennial and eschatological vision of history. Atheistic socialists and agnostic liberals silently adopted it. They wrote schemes of history marked by progress toward a final goal without realizing that the structure of their history came originally from Judaic-Christian sources. Even after deserting Christianity, one cannot escape its vision of history, for that vision continues to shape the structure of modern secular ideologies.

Yet something else was needed to produce a satisfactory historical viewpoint. Despite their concern with aspects of historic time, devout Christians did not usually make the best historians. Not only were they often credulous, as some of the early Christian chronicles well demonstrate, but their range of interest was narrow and they lacked principles of explanation and selection. They recorded their troubles;

they waited for the day of judgment; they invoked the wrath of God against pagan empires. While insisting (against the Greeks) that no event was the result of chance or blind fate but was part of a providential order, they found this principle historically insufficient. If one thinks that all events are equally providential, he will attach significance to them and perhaps record them; but on what basis will he select and order them? No historian goes far in his work without realizing that he must select some events, from the inexhaustible supply of them, because these are for some reason more important; then he must order these according to some scheme of relationship. Precisely because it attached so much importance to each and every event—the fall of a sparrow comes before God's eyes as clearly as the fall of a kingdom—Judaic-Christian history found it hard to select and tended to lack organization.

After toying in the nineteenth century with the idea that secular history is virtually the same as the divine purpose, in our day Christian theology has tended to return proudly to an older view, asserting that we cannot discern God's will in secular history. The latter is deserving of respect, but it is not the path to salvation. The Christian has faith that at the end of the road, somehow, there will sound the last trumpet which brings life everlasting; but we cannot see at all clearly the road that leads there. Truly Christian historiography has tended to find in each day fresh miracles, evidence of God's will, and yet no plan or pattern that merely human intelligence can decipher. For we see through a glass darkly, and only in another world will we see clearly. The Christian rejoices in the mystery and is content to believe that all will come well despite the evidences of disorder in the world. If we must concede that the Bible lies at the heart of all Western consciousness of human time, we must also admit that biblical history is nothing like the modern kind of history, which wrests, or tries to wrest, from the past its secrets of cause and effect, sequence and orderly process. The Christian regards such a claim as blasphemous.

For an example of this, one might glance at Edward Johnson's "Wonder-Working Providence," an American colonial work which, though a tribute to the devout piety of the Puritan New Englanders, is a curiosity as history. Eusebius of Caesarea, the first significant Christian historian, did not organize well; his first work was a bare chronicle, and his deservedly praised *Ecclesiastical History* lacked a plan of development. Perhaps because he was a Greek, he was critical (though there is no reason why Christian historiography should not be critical and accurate; that the early ones often were not probably reflects only that they were written by poor and uneducated people). He was certainly industrious. But as a historian Eusebius cannot compare with Herodotus and Thucydides. Subsequently Christian historians found a great theme in the expansion of Christianity—the work of the missionaries. It could be argued that Christians lacked sufficient sympathy with merely secular questions to have much interest in careful examination of them. Faced with a war of rival kingdoms, a Christian might simply dismiss it as a judgment on the pagans; could he have analyzed it as exhaustively as Thucydides did the Peloponnesian War? A pronounced moralizing cast and a powerful prejudice operated on the Christian. So they do, arguably, on most historians. But some things were lacking to make the best history, and those things, provided by the Greeks, were a more critical spirit, a more open mind, and a belief in more human freedom.

Maritain has observed that coherent historical writing requires freedom within a pattern of providence. If there is only chance and caprice, there can be no meaningful structure; if there is complete determinism, there is no drama or interest. Christianity does leave man the dignity of being a free agent within the framework of a general providence (at least most versions of Christianity do); in contrast, as an eighteenth-century English critic observed of Homer, "there is hardly a stone or javelin thrown, or an arrow shot, that is not either directed or turned aside by some god." So the Greeks did not always exceed the Christians in this respect. Nevertheless, Greek classical thought about man and fate, as developed in the great Athenian tragedies of the zenith of Hellenic civilization in the sixth and fifth centuries B.C., shows a remarkable balance between the two. Though accused by Christians of believing in blind fate and at times strongly addicted to the cyclical view (there is little notion of progress in classical thought),[3] the Greeks nevertheless "had a lively and

3. Ludwig Edelstein, in *The Idea of Progress in Classical Antiquity* (Baltimore: Johns Hopkins Press, 1967), seeks to show that this traditional view is wrong. There are admittedly some exceptions to it; few if any ideas were totally unknown to those eager and wide-ranging inquirers, the ancient Greeks. Still, beyond question the progressivists were a distinct minority, and—more important —their outlook did not survive.

indeed a naive sense of the power of man to control his own destiny."[4]
It is exactly this tension between remorseless fate and proud human
will that gives Greek drama its power. Strong men face the inscrutable
necessity of things (not a divine providence in the Christian sense,
but a fate bound up in the laws of existence) and are usually beaten,
but they are often the victims of their own blindness or arrogance.
They *could* have beaten fate had they known just a little more or had
they overcome their tragic flaw of character. It is typical of Greek
tragedy that a fatal flaw of this sort in an otherwise strong and noble
person finally defeats him. Life is hard and searches out every human
weakness. Heroes go to their doom. Yet man is great even in defeat.
Nor is his doom inevitable; it is conceivably within his power to overcome fate and evade his tragic destiny; though this does not happen
on the stage, the effect of the drama on the spectators is not to depress
but to exhilarate them.

Sophocles and Aeschylus are not irrelevant to Herodotus and
Thucydides, for the dramatists and the historians shared the same
closely integrated Athenian culture and were even personal friends.
Many a commentator has discerned in Thucydides' great *History of
the Peloponnesian War,* one of the supreme masterpieces of all historical literature, something akin to the structure of Greek tragedy.
But the miracle of Athens in the Periclean age included more than its
art and drama. Science and philosophy were the greatest Greek contributions to mankind. They were born as one in the Ionian isles on
the shores of Asia Minor in the seventh century B.C., as a critical,
inquiring, and above all conceptual way of thinking (putting things in
terms of abstract ideas rather than of mythological tales). Critical
history was born about the same time. "The origin of Greek historiography, like Greek philosophy, lies in Ionic thought," writes
Momigliano.[5] Herodotus was not the first Greek historian. Behind
him was Hecataeus, behind him Xenophanes, and behind him probably some pioneer whose name has been lost—it is an irony that
history does not know its own founder. The word "history" itself
comes from the Greek word meaning "inquiry," and unquestionably
we must credit the Greeks, who invented so many things intellectual,

4. R. G. Collingwood, *The Idea of History* (London: Oxford University Press,
1946), p. 24; also, p. 41.
5. Arnaldo Momigliano, "The Place of Herodotus in the History of Historiography," *Studies in Historiography* (New York: Harper and Row, 1966).

with the founding of history as an autonomous inquiry rather than as a branch of religion or as a byproduct of mythology. It was a part of that skeptical and critical Ionic revolt against traditional mythology which was the birth of philosophy, of science, virtually of "thought" itself. By the time it reached fifth-century Athens, this intellectual growth had ripened and was ready to give birth to Socrates and Plato as well as to Aeschylus, Sophocles, and Euripides, to Hippocrates the doctor, to the Parthenon and the sculpture of Praxiteles, and to all the other glories of classical Greece. Herodotus and Thucydides represented the muse Clio in this amazing gallery of genius.

THE GREAT GREEK AND ROMAN HISTORIANS

Our short account of the development of history down through the ages will seldom if ever have time to present individual historians in any detail. Among the Greek and Roman historians, Herodotus, Thucydides, Polybius, Tacitus, and Livy are still widely read, being available in many editions, and presumably always will be read as long as there are literate people. They are "classic." Others, such as Xenophon, Sallust, Procopius, and Suetonius, as well as the Romanized Jew Josephus, are not far behind in popularity. Students of Greek and Roman history are familiar with many others, most of whose works have been lost or exist only in fragments. Indeed, we have portions only of most of the above greats—only 35 of Livy's 142 books, for example. All of the "big five" deserve individual attention in even a brief survey, and in addition we will seek to appraise the qualities and the deficiencies of the Graeco-Roman school of historians as a whole.

Herodotus, "the father of history," an inquisitive and much-traveled Greek from Asia Minor whose major work was on the Persian Wars of the Greeks, was ridiculed by the irreverent Aristophanes and was long regarded as the father of lies as well as of history; yet he was held in deep respect throughout ancient times. Today the essential accuracy of Herodotus in most matters has been vindicated. There were few documents in Greece and Herodotus could not read those of the East; he had to rely mainly on oral tradition and testimony, as did most of the ancient historians, which makes his high level of accuracy the more impressive. Less systematic and structured than Thucydides, who is generally regarded as the greater of the two,

Herodotus, writing in the middle of the fifth century B.C., has always
appealed more to some because of his "wider humanity" (Herder).
Herodotus wrote in happier times than those in which Thucydides
took up a pen dipped in tragedy to analyze the bitter civil war of the
Greek cities a generation later. He wrote to "preserve from oblivion
the memory of men's deeds, and to prevent the great and wonderful
actions of the Greeks and the Barbarians from losing their proper
share of glory; and to record the grounds of their quarrel." Herodotus
tried to be critical and gives naturalistic explanations of events. He
did not often refer to divine intervention as Homer had so often done
in his poetic account of the Trojan Wars several centuries earlier. He
does not always avoid this, and today we must smile at some of his
explanations. He was essentially a narrative historian, and he was
a most skillful one. He had a far-ranging curiosity about peoples and
places, and his Greekness emerged in his concern to separate truth
from falsehood by careful inquiry; he knew the value of first-hand
testimony and sought, though in no very systematic way, to devise
tests for the authenticity and credibility of witnesses.

Unlike the Hebrews, the Greeks usually saw no long-range plan or
purpose to the course of history. In the main, they had no idea of
progress. They studied particular events which revealed tragedy and
human interest. The war between Athens and Sparta and their allies
which broke out in 431 B.C. had both. Thucydides' great masterpiece
was a study in contemporary history, as for the most part Herodotus'
was too. It went far to establish the whole canon which ancient historical writing followed. An austere standard of accuracy, objectivity,
and analytical quality was exhibited; the immortal preface declares
proudly that "I have written my work not as an essay which will win
the applause of the hour, but as a possession for all time." The style
was brilliant, if rather tightly woven. Thucydides made up the
speeches with which his work is liberally sprinkled, models of ora-
torical skill. This practice puzzles and sometimes repels modern
scholars, but the speeches add to the effect; and they were, Thucydides
claimed, essentially if not literally correct. They helped him in his
examination of men's motives and dilemmas. "The longest and most
decisive step that has ever been taken by a single man towards making history what it is today," as J. B. Bury declared, this book of a
retired Athenian general (exiled about 420 B.C. for a military failure)
could be criticized, perhaps, because it concentrates on politics alone,

but this concentration gives it unity and strength, too. Perhaps never have narrative power, rigorous analysis, and dramatic power been so effectively combined. Behind this effort, which occupied Thucydides some thirty years of his life and which he never finished, lay the burning goal of seeking to understand in order to learn. This is an anatomy of war and revolution, of the internal and external breakdown of order, written in the belief that future men might avoid such tragedies if only they could learn from history. It leaves divine intervention and miraculous happenings wholly out of the picture. Thucydides hoped "it may be judged useful by those who desire an exact knowledge of the past as an aid to the interpretation of the future, which in human affairs must resemble if it does not duplicate the past."

Herein he probably erred. The hope that one might extract laws from the study of the past which could be applied profitably to the future was destined to prove illusory. The future not only fails to duplicate the past; it does not even resemble it. There are always too many differences between the past and the present to make past experiences wholly applicable to present ones. The unhistorical outlook of the Greeks, in not seeing much development or progress, is revealed here. We can expect to apply past lessons to future problems only if we assume that nothing changes very much, that men and circumstances stay substantially the same. Despite this fundamental criticism, which applies to almost all of classical historiography, Thucydides' work has indeed remained a possession for all time, and it dominated the entire ancient tradition of historical writing. Every future historian wrote in the shadow of the two great Athenians, no less than all philosophers were disciples of Plato and Aristotle for many centuries.

The names of a number of Greek historians after Thucydides are known, but the writings of only a few, including Xenophon and Diodorus, survived. The next important one was Polybius, the Greek who brought history to the Romans. He was the last great classical Greek historian, one who can bear comparison with Herodotus and Thucydides and bear it very well. Captured in 168 B.C. and taken to Rome, Polybius became the friend and tutor of prominent Romans. He was one of the first who brought Greek literature and learning to the city on the Tiber which, though engaged in conquering the world, was still almost barbarous in its thought. His imagination was struck by the meteoric rise of Rome, as well it might be: "Can anyone be so indifferent or idle as not to care to know by what means and under what policy almost the whole of the inhabited world was conquered and brought under the rule of a single city, and that within a period of not quite 53 years?" Such extraordinary occurrences are what stimulate historical inquiry, and of all rises and falls the greatest was that of the Roman Empire. Polybius watched its rise and wanted to know why it rose.

Such causal factors are extraordinarily difficult to establish with precision, and it cannot be said that Polybius succeeded in finding them. But his search was both stimulating and productive. Highly critical, admirably impartial, a man of affairs himself with much experience of the world, and a splendid writer, Polybius is one of the greatest of all historians. The apprentice historian can perhaps learn more from him than he can from any other model. He had an extraordinarily keen eye for selecting the apt illustration, the telling incident. But Polybius never quite solved the riddle of causes. His most notable answer to the question of why the empire flourished pointed to the balance of the Roman constitution, in which he found a happy blend of the classic types of government, democracy, aristocracy, and monarchy, allowing scope for common people, nobility, and a single ruler. He believed this balance enabled the empire to avoid the cycle of decay which the Greeks thought inevitably afflicted each of these orders in turn.

Polybius looked at republican Rome in its days of youth and success and admired the character qualities of this sturdy people. The other outstanding Roman historians chronicle the process of decay. Titus Livy (59 B.C.–A.D. 17) wrote, it is true, at the beginning of the imperial era, in the Augustan age, and told in patriotic vein a story of success. But he was aware of deterioration in Roman character and institutions and wrote in part to revive morale by showing Romans the stuff of which their forefathers were made. Livy may seem less of a historian than the others we have mentioned partly because he was unable to draw on documentary sources. He purveyed legends about the early history of Rome. But not only was he a gifted stylist, he also sought explanations and had the Roman reverence for the past. Hannah Arendt has remarked that this was a trait the Romans possessed far more than the Greeks. Neither Herodotus nor Thucydides was particularly concerned with tradition. It is clear that Livy was widely read and played a large part in that temporary Augustan recovery of morale to which Virgil's *Aeneid* also contributed. This points to one of the practical functions history can provide: pride in one's race, nation, or other group. Noteworthy also is the fact that Rome's unification of the ancient world enabled Livy to adopt a global perspective, to see all the various local histories as part of one great stream.

For many, the greatest Roman historian, and perhaps their all-time favorite, is the scintillating Tacitus, who wrote from about A.D. 85 to 115, a time when the empire was reaching a peak of power and glory but was already beginning its process of internal decay and revealing its persistent problem of the imperial succession. It is difficult to praise Tacitus' style too highly, and this above all is what we can learn from him. He is compulsively readable; the brilliance of his writing leaves one breathless. It varies from epigrammatic brevity to full description, from sober narrative to poetic lyricism. His subject matter was largely court politics. The period between A.D. 30 and 112, about which he wrote (essentially the history of his own time, once more), though we may think of it as Rome's silver if not golden age, was, he says, "rich in disasters, frightful in its wars, torn by civil strife, and even in peace full of horrors." Tacitus presents a devastating record of human weakness and depravity that is rivaled only by the verse of his near-contemporaries, Horace and Juvenal. We have entered a different moral universe, which is very nearly that of the artist-intellectual alienated from his society. Tacitus is a moralizing historian, famous for his statement that "History's highest function is to ensure that noble actions are not left unrecorded and that evil words and deeds are held up to the reprobation of posterity." His criteria of selection are those deeds which were either "conspicuous for excellence or notorious for infamy." He found more of the latter than the former. Tacitus is known also for his work on the Germans; in his praise of these uncorrupted barbarians one can read a reproach against his own civilization. Of the *Histories* and the *Annals,* it was once thought that the literary quality exceeded the factual reliability; James Westfall Thompson, author of an older history of historical writing, even said we should read Tacitus "as a great writer . . . but not as an historian." But the monumental researches of one of the greatest of modern classicists, Sir Ronald Syme, have gone far to vindicate his integrity. Within his range, Tacitus is now accorded high honors.

WEAKNESSES OF ANCIENT HISTORIOGRAPHY

It will be observed that Tacitus' range, like that of the other ancient historians, was a narrow one. They wrote almost exclusively political history, and that was almost exclusively of their own time or not far from it. The reasons for this lay mainly in the nature of the materials on which they could draw for their sources. Livy had to rely on legends about early Rome because very few documents had been preserved. Thucydides excluded on principle any topic except one about which the historian could interview living witnesses. There were then no great collections of manuscripts in archives, nor were there learned journals and numerous professional scholars to sort these out. This, by modern standards, considerably limited the scope of ancient historians both in time and in subject matter. On the other hand, one cannot legitimately criticize a writer for not writing another book than the one he did, nor can one deny the high significance of the subjects chosen: the Greek wars, the rise of Rome, the moral decline of the Roman ruling class.

Ancient historiography has been criticized on more serious grounds. "Livy and Tacitus stand side by side as the two great monuments to the barrenness of Roman historical thought," R. G. Collingwood wrote in his important *Idea of History*. He also turned thumbs down on Thucydides. These are extreme judgments, but Collingwood made some valid points. Despite Thucydides, the Greeks did not value historical work highly. Although there were other views, the dominant school of classical philosophy was rooted in what Collingwood called "substantialism," or essentialism; that is, it searched for substances and essences, which were regarded in the Platonic manner as changeless and eternal, not transitory and evolutionary. Thus, Greek thought was not truly historical; it did not see the present as a product of the past, nor did it see anything as a product of its experience. Human nature itself was seen substantialistically: men and peoples had a given nature, which is their essence, and which does not change; to suppose that such natures are shaped in history was an idea little congenial to the ancients. The school of Thucydides, rooted in a belief in the changelessness of things, believed that past and present situations could be exactly compared, as we have noted. Their inveterate habit of looking for the general in specifics made the Greeks good scientists but poor historians, for history is not a generalizing science. Aristotle, who made the decisive pronouncements on Greek thought, ranked history below both philosophy and poetry, since it approaches neither perfect truth nor perfect beauty. It is the realm of probability and conjecture.

That history was accorded no place in the medieval universities, not being deemed anywhere near the equal of philosophy and mathematics, was a legacy of this bent of mind. History was regarded as a practical subject, like engineering; it was thought to be of much value to politicians but of no philosophical interest. Or it was regarded as a subordinate branch of ethics, its function being to supply the examples of those principles discovered by reason. The Romans, more so perhaps than the Greeks, certainly respected it highly on this level. In Cicero's famous definition, history is "the light of truth, the witness of time, the mistress of life." The first reflected the very worthy and very pronounced ancient belief that the historian must be unbiased, impartial, and critical. "History's first law is that an author must not dare to tell anything but the truth; its second is that he must make bold to tell the whole truth," Cicero declared. Lucian, a Greek in Roman service, whose manual "How to Write History" is about the only such formal treatise of methodology surviving from the ancient world, gave the same advice. His work says just about all any such manual has ever said on the need to examine sources critically, to use original sources, and to watch out for biased witnesses. Like Ranke seventeen hundred years later, Lucian advises the historian to "tell it like it is"—exactly as it happened—without intruding his own prejudices: "The historian's one task is to tell the thing as it happened. . . . He has to make his brain a mirror, unclouded, bright, and true of surface. . . . Historians are not writing fancy school essays."

Cicero's second maxim about history meant that, as "the witness of time," it had pietistic value in keeping alive great deeds and great ideas, which otherwise would be lost to view. The Jews, like the Romans a people with a deep sense of the national community, expressed this in the "Let us now praise famous men" passage in Ecclesiasticus: "Their seed shall remain forever, and their glory shall not be blotted out." We can hear Tacitus adding that neither should the memory of *in*famous men be forgotten, as a warning and a lesson to posterity. As "the mistress of life," history was "an instruction for the present and a warning for the future," as a later humanist put it. We can learn lessons of conduct and polity from it. In these maxims Cicero summed up most of the classical thinking about

history. It was hardly an ignoble testament. We seek truth; we preserve the best of the past to build civilization; we profit from the
"lessons of the past."

Yet the fact remains that the ancient historians were all very
unhistorical by modern standards, for they did not understand the
reality of change. They did not see any over-all direction in history
and believed events happened in a kind of eternal present. They did
not sense process, evolution, organic change taking place. Perhaps
this is why, despite the great genius of a few, the run-of-the-mill
historical writing of the ancient world seems to have been pretty poor
stuff. It was inclined to be rhetorical and bombastic. In fact, as a
school subject it was placed under rhetoric; its function was teaching
moral philosophy by example. In lesser hands, the Thucydidean set
speech became an excuse for writing history by making up imaginary
orations. Didactic history, which we see in Plutarch, reduced it to
polite essays in how "lives of great men all remind us we can make
our lives sublime." The dangers of the Tacitus approach are obvious:
history becomes indignant moralizing or the relating of mere scandal.
(There is none of the latter in Tacitus, but there is some in Suetonius.)
There was an obvious inconsistency in vowing, on the one hand, to
write history *sine ira et studio* (without anger or prejudice—Tacitus)
and, on the other, declaring its highest purpose to be that of inculcating sound morals and denouncing vice.

At its best both critical and philosophical, searching for deeper
causes, aware that "it is not sufficient to proclaim fact; we have to
set forth the purposes and reasons which underlie events" (Sempronius Asellio), eager in its quest for truths to lighten man's load
in the future by diligent study of his past experiences, written with
rare gifts of style and a keen sense of drama, ancient historical writing with all its blind spots was a magnificent heritage. Like other
phases of the Greco-Roman intellectual tradition, it dominated
Western civilization for many centuries. Renaissance humanists will
revive and disseminate these same concepts hundreds of years later.
With delight, Machiavelli and Guicciardini will rediscover and read
Polybius and Livy. In most respects, this classical view of history
lasted down into the eighteenth century, not to be transformed until
the most recent era of history.

C hapter 2

MEDIEVAL HISTORICAL WRITING

EARLY MEDIEVAL HISTORY

At one time a tendency existed to see the Middle Ages as a long cultural desert which Western man traversed in agony, dragging with him a little of the civilization that remained after the Fall of Rome but jettisoning ever more of it until at one point, deep in the heart of the Dark Age wilderness, he clutched but two or three battered books. At the end of the trail lay the fountains of the Renaissance, just in time to save the weary traveler from intellectual death. What little there was of literary creation during this eight- or nine-hundred-year period was nasty, poor, brutish, short, and monkish, the last adjective meaning much the same as the others. Therefore, we might dismiss the entire period in any account of serious historical work, save for, admittedly, a certain amount of quite primitive chronicling of battles, crusades, and feudal feuds. As against this obviously distorted picture we might place a different one, that of a most lively and interesting age, disorderly but creative, in which Christianity developed fully, the Germanic barbarians brought their own culture into contact with that of Latin Christianity, and a good deal of ancient classical culture was preserved and gradually added to, especially during the twelfth-to-fourteenth-century revival of intellectual life. Or, we might protest that so long a period has little unity and choose to divide it up into several different parts. How to handle those ambiguously titled Middle Ages still presents problems and is an object lesson in historical interpretation. On any showing, much history was written during this era or eras, though it perhaps cannot be said that a genuinely historical outlook prevailed. Western historiography owes a decisive debt to the greater medieval historians for

19

keeping alive a great tradition, even if they added little to the existing Christian and classical conceptions of history.

It might be argued that some of this "monkish" history was an improvement on the Romans in some respects. The Venerable Bede, who lived in Northumbria from about 675 to 735, wrote his much-admired *Ecclesiastical History of the English People* in what was at that time a rare center of cultural convergences. It drew on that rich though abortive Irish civilization of early medieval times as well as on the zeal of the Roman Church in the missionary age and on the remnants of classical culture. Greek was known at Jarrow, Bede's famous monastery, where there was a large library. He was acquainted with a wide range of writers, including among historians Eusebius and Josephus; the late Roman-Christian savants Marcellinus, Cassiodorus, Gregory of Tours (author of a fine sixth-century history of the Franks, indispensable to our knowledge of this obscure period); and Isidore of Seville, a great scholar in Visigothic Spain. Eusebius was his chief historical model; but Bede meditated, like all literate Christians, on the brilliant writings of the Church Fathers, Ambrose, Augustine, Jerome, and Gregory the Great (Gregory I), who set forth the grand role of the Church and Christianity, the City of God that survived the ruin of Rome, that Earthly City which a remorseless Providence had laid low in the most exciting of all historical events. It was this tremendous change that had drawn from Saint Augustine his *City of God*—weak, no doubt, as history, but throbbing with the excitement of a great theme: how the spiritual kingdom, entangled here below with terrestrial empires, would march inevitably toward its eternal destiny. Bede imitated the great African's division of historic time into six ages corresponding to the days of the week and of God's creation—the seventh, equaling the Sabbath, being the final Great Day of Judgment and eternal rest.

Bede sent away to Rome for copies of documents in the papal archives and drew widely on other monastic libraries as well as on oral testimony. He was a fine historian. He had, E. W. Watson has said, "the statesmanship to know what was of permanent importance, and the skill to record it clearly and fully."[1] There is a suspicion that he had a touch of English patriotic pride, too. A predilection for the miraculous, some factual slips, and a robust Christian prejudice against

---

1. In A. Hamilton Thompson, ed., *Bede: His Life, Times, and Writing* (New York: Russell and Russell, 1966), p. 59 (first printed 1932).

pagans and heretics may remind us that we are in the Middle Ages; but no one can doubt that Bede had a vigorous, sharp mind and a fine style. His historical writing obviously represents a fruitful amalgamation of Christian and classical heritages. As a Christian, Bede was moved by a vision of the Judgment Day and by a desire to learn how much time remained until the great moment: he began as a chronologer. He also approached history by way of that common medieval exercise, the lives of the saints. Hagiography led to historiography.

If to the devout Christian "History is a record of God's incessant supervision of men's affairs" every event however seemingly trivial may be charged with the highest significance. But, as we previously observed, the Christian's general interest in history, as the theater of divine Providence, seems often to have difficulty translating itself into effective historical writing. E. H. Harbison observed in this connection that "It is easier to say that God acts constantly in history than to say when and where."[2] The Christian's disgust (in this age, at least) with a corrupt and confusing world of political power made him inclined, like Augustine, to turn away from profane history after sketching an outline of its decay.

The worldly minded Greeks wrote better history, even if the Christians had the more historical vision. In Bede's case, the Church itself and the record of holy men provided him with his subject. It is obvious, though, that he had learned something from the pagan historians. Care, thoroughness, the critical method, exactness of analysis, and clarity of organization came from that source. Bede also stressed the moral effect of historical learning, in good classical manner: the past provides us with examples of virtue, and the concrete example drives the lesson home. ("Sive enim historia de bonis bona referat, ad imitandum bonum auditor sollicitus instigatur. . . .") To Bolingbroke, as late as the eighteenth century, history was "philosophy teaching by example"; to Bede it was Christian virtue taught by example, but the concept of history in both cases was a classical one. He also made use of the famous Thucydidean device of the speech.

Bede was admittedly a rarity even in 730: "there was nothing to be compared with him on the Continent at this time," an English scholar boasts. Gregory of Tours, the only early medieval historian to rank with Bede in stature, was really a remnant of Roman culture living on

2. In his *Christianity and History* (Princeton, N. J.: Princeton University Press, 1964), p. 118.

for a time in southern France. In Bede's last years the Muslim tide swept across the Pyrenees. It was turned back but dominated Spain and southern Italy and controlled the Mediterranean, thus dooming Christian Europe to economic stagnation. The Northumbrian flowering showed what could have happened had it not been for these grave economic and political developments. There were to be other occasional flowerings as Europe struggled through the next few centuries. The great Irish and English monasteries were devastated by the Norse raids, but Boniface and Charlemagne's advisor, Alcuin, carried Northumbrian learning to the Continent. There were to be many lesser Bedes, monks who chronicled the affairs of their locality or monastery. There was to be a continuation of his work in the *Anglo-Saxon Chronicle,* which set down the main events of English history through the twelfth century, and in the work of Geoffrey of Monmouth (d. 1152) and the more philosophical John of Salisbury (d. 1180).

In Charlemagne's circle, too, was Einhard, born about 770 and educated at the influential abbey of Fulda which Boniface had founded in Franconia, where his tomb is still lovingly preserved. A talented craftsman in all the arts, Einhard, perhaps about 817–21, after Charles's death, wrote a fine life of the emperor to whom he was so devoted. Carolingian annalists, in the *Royal Annals* of Lorsch, kept a faithful record of each year's chief events in the manner of the *Anglo-Saxon Chronicle.* There are other biographies of kings and popes, and there is a flood of hagiography. The falsest of the bromides about the "Dark Ages" is that they lacked literary culture. There is almost too much of it. "Every monk his own historian" seems almost to have been the rule. Subject matter tended to be too local, reflecting the fragmentation of the age. But when Charlemagne temporarily restored political unity, a renaissance in all the arts eagerly burst forth, indicating that cultural resources were abundantly present and needed only some degree of public order to allow them scope for growth. The emperor himself, an eager and omnivorous reader, tried to learn Latin literature as well as astronomy and, indeed, everything else in this naïve infancy of the European mind. We know that he especially liked both Augustine's *De civitate Dei* and stories of *antiquorum res gestae.* This Germanic barbarian delight in tales of noble deeds done in the past should be added to the list of factors conditioning the historiographical tradition. The epics and sagas of the Middle Ages expressed and perpetuated that instinct which loves and strives to keep alive good stories, filled with heroes and battles, and the memory of mighty deeds done in former times. Would-be historians concerned to trace the history of their profession ought to spend at least some time reading the medieval epics, for these, like Homer before them, bear something of that childish delight in sheer narrative which is probably an essential part of any historical work, even if it is not the only part.

THE LATER MIDDLE AGES

When, after nearly two centuries of anguish, medieval Europe returned to the task of reconstructing a civilization, it must be conceded that it followed the Greek path in placing history well outside the charmed circle of the highest learning. Its interests were in logic, law, and pure philosophy. It seized onto these unchanging things because it had known too much disorder and fragmentation, and it wanted something purer than the muddy political affairs of the world. (Perhaps Clio's reputation had been even further impaired by the association of historical research with the industry of forging false documents, practiced by certain very sophisticated adepts of historical methodology.) "The scholastic method as it developed in the Middle Ages was an utterly unhistorical, if not anti-historical method," wrote E. H. Harbison. "History had little if any real interest for the profoundest thinkers of this age."[3] There were no chairs of history in the universities. Thomas Aquinas wrote nearly one hundred books, in which he had something to say not only about philosophy but about almost every subject, including ethics, science, psychology, politics, government, and law; about the only thing on which nothing can be found is history. He "had little sense of history, at least as we understand the word," remarks his editor, Thomas Gilby, in an understatement. "He treats his great forerunners as though they were speaking to him then and there."[4] Truth, to Saint Thomas, was not historically conditioned, not relative. He sought it in a timeless dimension. His powerful mind was completely without a feeling for the dialectic of thought in history.

Of course, the apocalyptic spirit continued to exist. Popularly, sects like the Joachites (followers of Joachim of Flora) and others carried

3. *Christianity and History,* pp. 271–72.
4. *Saint Thomas Aquinas: Philosophical Texts,* selected and translated by Thomas Gilby (New York: Oxford University Press, 1960), pp. xxi–xxii.

on the "pursuit of the millennium" with unflagging (if sometimes flagellant) zeal, as poor men poured their hopes for a better life somewhat pathetically into these expectations of a great "New Deal" to come suddenly at any moment. The rich would be cast down and the humble raised up, all would be equal, and there would be paradise on earth. The often arid logical analysis carried on by the Schoolmen in the universities found its opposite in this highly emotional popular chiliasm. But such unlettered enthusiasts were seldom capable of writing any history; their significance for history lies in their perpetuation of that lively Judeo-Christian sense of a time-goal in history to which we previously referred. Most of these cults arose in the later Middle Ages. As Norman Cohn notes,[5] such Joachite versions of the Millennium were contrary to the teachings of the Church, since Augustine had made it clear that the Church itself was the realization of the Kingdom of God on earth and that there was no place for a further messianic fulfillment. And some of them went far beyond any possible version of Christianity to anticipate, in Cohn's words, "those latter-day philosophies of history which are most emphatically anti-Christian." Joachim divided history into several ages, each characterized by distinctive features, in an ascending order, much as Condorcet and Comte and Marx would do. The Middle Ages here bore within itself a whole school of "modern" revolutionary messianism which has deeply influenced present conceptions of history.

Though the temples of learning were in the possession of metaphysicians and logicians, Clio was not so easily dismissed. History managed to survive. Biography continued to provide a point of entry; Joinville's life of Saint Louis had to be history as well as biography. The other most frequently reprinted and read historical writings of the high medieval period include the descriptions of the Crusades by Villehardouin and others; Bishop Otto of Freising's *Two Cities,* a twelfth century work which obviously suggests Augustine's influence; and Froissart's *Chronicles of England, France, and Spain,* most notable for its accounts of the Hundred Years' War.

Let us glance at the last, or almost the last, of this lineage, Froissart. This fourteenth-century Frenchman was steeped in the romances and poetry which were so notable a flowering of the Age of Chivalry:

5. Norman Cohn, *The Pursuit of the Millennium: Revolutionary Messianism in Medieval and Reformation Europe . . .* (New York: Harper Torchbooks, 1961), pp. 100–102.

those tales of knights who became not merely bold and brave but courteous and gentle and frequently amorous as well. He was a composer of chivalric tales and amorous songs. The later Middle Ages civilized the feudal warrior into a high-minded idealist and a well-groomed lover, at least in song, and we have reached the decadence of a ruling class in some respects. But in Froissart's time the great war of England and France broke out, and Froissart, as a Frenchman in the service of England, was in a good position to observe it and to appreciate its drama. (Later he returned to France and served French patrons.) He was a good war reporter and accumulated a great deal of battlefront information. A cosmopolitan writer and diplomat, he traveled back and forth between France and England, in a way typical of those prenationalistic days. He also traveled to Spain where he wanted to learn what was going on in the war between Aragon, Castile, and Portugal. He wrote in French, but that language was still well understood by the English upper classes. In chronicling the events of the Hundred Years' War, Froissart was remarkably objective. However, this objectivity becomes less remarkable when we understand that he had friends on both sides. In addition, there was a relative lack of national feeling in this war, which has indeed been called the first of the wars of modern nationalism but was more nearly the last of the feudal wars. He was not concerned, as a modern doubtless would be, to justify or favor the cause of one side or the other. He was, in quite a singular way, concerned with the nobility of the actions, with the extent to which they met chivalric standards, rather than with the cause itself. It matters not whether one wins or loses, it is how one plays the game, Froissart thinks. He admires warriors who lose gracefully as well as those who win nobly, without regard for which side they are fighting on. In this respect, Froissart reflected his age and class and intellectual training. He is the historian of chivalry.

Every history reflects in part the intellectual outlook of its time. The aristocratic and chivalric aspect of Froissart's book, which may not appeal to all modern tastes, was a dominant interest in his time, and it commanded his enthusiasm. (He was a devotee of that somewhat sentimental type of late chivalry which created the Order of the Garter and the Knights of the Golden Fleece.) It seems odd to us, no doubt, if not downright sinful, that he looked at the Peasant Revolt of 1381 largely in this light, not approving of it because it was led by rather lowbrow and uncourteous types. He was not interested in revolution or in social change in its own right. His work is an interesting study in the preconceptions of historians. This period saw the birth of modern nationalism and of a new social and economic order, which is what present historians are interested in. Froissart was interested—not quite entirely, but predominantly—in noble deeds done on the field of battle.

"It is of little value to criticize him for not being what he never intended to be," a recent writer about him sighs—nor, we should add, what he could not have been. Historians are themselves products of history. Froissart could paint a scene and describe a battle splendidly. He sought to get at the truth as critically as he could, in which he expressed the perennial quality of the historian. Because he did not have enough evidence he often failed, but whenever he had observed the action himself or could get first-hand accounts, he turns out, when checked, to be reasonably accurate. He supplies a good deal of colorful incident in his excellent prose. Ironically, later historians found him a mine of information about things he put in only as background for knightly battles. They were not interested in the battles but *were* interested in the incidental detail because it sheds light on life and work in his time. This would certainly have surprised Froissart.

A source of knowledge to later historians, as were Bede and Einhard and Gregory of Tours and a large number of medieval chroniclers—a great, invaluable source—Froissart was not quite a historian himself. He was more a romantic war correspondent, offering superb vignettes of battle and of other dramatic events of his time. He did not put them together in any connected way to supply a single sustained account of a process or a period. He could not have understood what that meant, in all likelihood; if he had been able to understand, he would not have been interested in doing it. Enough for him to have found a chivalrous action, a knightly encounter, a glorious deed! He expressed one of the Middle Ages' basic themes, as did Bede (the Church), Joachim (the Apocalypse), the Scholastic Doctors, and others. Each age must deal with the past in its own way.

BYZANTINE AND ARABIC HISTORICAL WRITING

As nearly every schoolboy knows, learning and the arts in the Middle Ages were far superior in areas adjacent to backward Europe

Terry Cook – "HAND in YOU

When: June 15th, 16th and 17th   **(Deadline for sign-**

Who: The first 75 boys and girls (6th -12th grade)

Where: Decatur Indoor Sports Center (DISC)

Time: 9:00 a.m – 2:00 p.m

Cost: $110 **(Send payment to Future Shot – P.O Box**

Lunch: 12:00 – 12:45 (Campers may bring there lunc
Subway. They must have and be responsible for thei

COMPLETE AND RETURN THE REMAINING PORTION

Contact Coach Cook – (217) 855-0993

Participant Name: _____

Age: _____ **D.O.B:** _____ **En

School: _____

Phone: 1) _____   2)

with her poverty, her feudalism, and her lack of populous cities. We are perhaps fonder of this poor old person because she is our direct ancestor in the line of civilization and because she was after all rather endearing despite her faults. But historiography, like other branches of knowledge, did much better elsewhere. A prominent student of Byzantine studies declared that "No other nation, with perhaps the exception of the Chinese, has such a rich historical literature as the Greeks."[6] At a time when most of the people of western Europe were living in mud huts, the Roman Empire withdrew to the banks of the Bosporus, became fully Greek (its intellectual side had always been primarily Greek), and carried on the ancient classical traditions there at the great city of Constantinople for a number of centuries. The Byzantine historians were more numerous and more sophisticated than were those of Western Christendom. They had access to great libraries and were supported by a powerful state, while Europeans were being terrified by barbarian bands and scarcely knew what lay beyond their village or monastery. Yet this Byzantine ghost of the Roman Empire was remarkably conservative and tradition-bound and scarcely aspired to break new ground in cultural affairs. It produced both chronicles and histories. The latter dealt with contemporary or near-contemporary subjects, were written in classical Greek, and were highly stylized. In brief, they were well within the Thucydidean tradition. Professor Vyronis, in his *Readings in Medieval Historiography,* chooses three of them to reprint: Procopius, sixth-century historian of Justinian's memorable reign; Michael Psellus, a versatile eleventh-century professor, author, and politician, evidently the John Kenneth Galbraith of his age, rather superficial but brilliant; and Anna Comnena, a woman historian, daughter of the emperor Alexius, who wrote in the twelfth century amid signs of the empire's final decline. The lady historian is a good storyteller. She avows her dedication to her parents from earliest infancy, even from the womb, and although she tells us that she labored to make her account objective, she makes her failure to achieve this goal quite evident. She writes to preserve from oblivion the memory of actions which otherwise would be drowned in Lethe's gulf—a fine traditional motive for historical writing and, as we know, one shared by all literate peoples. "The tale of history forms a very strong bulwark against the stream of time, and

6. Carl Krumbacher, quoted in Speros Vyronis, ed., *Readings in Medieval Historiography* (Boston: Houghton Mifflin, 1968), p. 130.

to some extent checks its irresistible flow." Hers is an appealing personal history, but it is in no way more than that.

This may be an appropriate place to observe that there is nothing wrong with straight narrative history. We may inquire why our historian does not go beyond the events themselves to tell us the "causes," perhaps the "underlying causes," implying for this function both a more useful and a more philosophical status. But the full story itself is one way of presenting the "causes." If we ask why team A defeated team B in last week's football game, perhaps there were general factors involved such as the better conditioning, the superior ability, the greater enthusiasm, or the abler coach of team A; but then the game itself, all that happened in it, is part of the explanation, too. The luck of the game, the dropping of a pass at a crucial moment, an injury to a key player—everything that happened during the game is part of the reason why one team won. (For a further discussion of causation and explanation, see Part II, Chapter 10 of this book.)

But the problem of selection always stares the historian in the face. He cannot possibly put everything in. He must extract the *significant* elements from the infinite abundance of human experience. So even a descriptive account must focus carefully on the crucial events, leaving out the less important and showing why that which is included was important. In its exuberance of detail and its fondness for events on purely personal grounds, Miss Comnena's history falls short of this ideal.

As it happens, we have from an only slightly later period an outstanding example of quite a different kind of history, one which aspired to interpretation at the highest level. The Arabic historian Ibn Khaldun (1332–1406) was a ripe product of that brilliant Islamic civilization which in his era was in rapid decline both in Spain and in the Middle East, its twin axes, before the advance of Christians and Turks, respectively. It had, however, far surpassed the civilization of Western and even Eastern Christendom for the previous several centuries. It produced many other historians, though Khaldun's fame has much overshadowed that of the others. In its great cities with their magnificent libraries, it had preserved and added to the ancient classical heritage. The Arabs were the teachers of Europe in the twelfth century; both Scholastic philosophy and the literature of chivalry owed a large debt to them, as is well known. Ibn Khaldun was born in northern Africa of a family that had once lived in Spain

but was pushed out by the Christian reconquest. He spent most of
his life, which he described in an autobiography, in active political
work in the Arab principalities of north Africa and southern Spain,
even venturing as far as Syria where he met the great conqueror
Timur the Lame. He found time to compose a preliminary volume
and six main volumes of his *Universal History*. Arnold J. Toynbee,
the contemporary creator of an attempt at comparative world history,
declared that the *Muqaddimah*, or introductory volume to Ibn Khaldun's *Universal History*, is "the greatest work of its kind that has
ever been created by any mind in any time or place." Ibn was certainly interested in a very sweeping assault on nothing less than the
causes of the rise and fall of civilizations, as Toynbee has been. He
had experienced the decline of an Arab empire that had expanded
fabulously in the seventh and eighth centuries to embrace most of the
Mediterranean shores, only to decline and fall like Rome's. He was
aware that there had been other empires that rose and fell in Asia.
Ibn Khaldun's deeply inquiring mind was impatient of most earlier
historiography. Muslim historians there had been; but he remarks
that not only were they uncritical, failing to reject nonsensical stories,
but above all "they did not look for, or pay any attention to, the causes
of events and conditions." History, he tells us, is popular; both kings
and common folk aspire to know it. But what kind of history? Gossip
about political leaders, "elegantly presented and spiced with proverbs."
There is another dimension, "the inner meaning of history," which
is truly philosophical and involves going behind the events to discern
their significance.

Every historian worth his pay has realized this. But Ibn Khaldun
was perhaps the first to seek the *ultimate* meaning of history by comparing various civilizations in search of nothing less than the laws
which govern the origins, growth, and decay of institutions and cultures. The idea was taken up by Vico and Montesquieu in the European Enlightenment, by a number of nineteenth-century theorists, and
more recently in a more extensive way by Arnold Toynbee. It is a
task fraught with difficulties and is perhaps inherently impossible
despite its allure. It is a measure of Khaldun's stature that he was
aware of all the dimensions of the problem—physical, geographic,
psychological, social, and economic. His work was almost grotesquely
incomplete; yet it was for centuries a giant pioneering effort without
a parallel. The work became known to Europe only in the early

nineteenth century, but indirectly it may have seeped in earlier to influence Montesquieu.[7] If Ibn Khaldun arrived at any one explanation for the growth and decay of societies, it was a psychocultural cycle, in which success spoils a people; originally hardy, they are rendered effete, corrupt, and selfish by wealth and power, and they fall to a fresh barbarian conquest. (This is something like the dynastic-cycles theory of the Chinese historians, it would seem.) But his work is far subtler than this crude statement would suggest. It touches strongly on intellectual history and on economic history as well; the speculations are those of a far-ranging, deeply inquisitive mind. Perhaps it is only in the twilight of a distinguished civilization that such works are possible. Ibn Khaldun's work was almost lost in the darkness that settled over the Arab world not long after his death.

7. Such is the conjecture of an article in the *Journal of the History of Ideas* (July–September, 1967), by Warren E. Gates.

C hapter 3

HISTORY IN THE EARLY MODERN PERIOD: FROM RENAISSANCE AND REFORMATION TO ENLIGHTENMENT

THE RENAISSANCE

That time-honored division of Western history which puts "Renaissance and Reformation" together in one basket might perhaps be questioned, for purposes of general history, though it seems as good as any, since all periodizations are arbitrary. If modern man was born in this general period, this deliverance of a novelty was certainly not the intention of either of these movements. One wanted to go back to ancient Greece and Rome; the other wanted to go back to the earliest Christianity. They were not much connected with each other, except in a chronological overlap: it is difficult to imagine minds more different than Machiavelli's and Luther's. For the purposes of a history of history, they stand in the same ambiguous light. Both have been credited with bringing to birth "modern historical scholarship"; yet neither intended anything like this. If they performed this feat, it was unintentional, and they did it in quite different ways.

Modern historiography has frequently been traced back to the humanist scholars of the so-called Renaissance but not because of any new conception of history, since in this respect they did not wish to differ from their adored masters, the ancients. First, they revived interest in these historians, in Livy and Polybius and Cicero. Secondly, they had a "historical" way of looking at things, if we mean by that a personal and descriptive way as contrasted with the logical abstractions of Scholasticism. This sort of "realism" is a familiar feature of the Italian humanists. "To move from the *Golden Legend* to the *Discourses* of Machiavelli is to move from a gloomy Gothic-revival

landscape to a brightly lighted Renaissance interior," Professor Harbison wrote. Machiavelli was not a very good historian; in fact, he was
an extremely poor one. (Let anyone who doubts this be condemned
to read all through that endless and formless chronicle of political
intrigues, his *History of Florence*.)[1] But he had a feeling for the texture of specific, concrete things and events, as he showed in his famous
political writings. He was really interested in a science of politics, and
he supposed that he could use the data of former political situations
to this end. Such situations are all similar, he held, since human nature
does not change and the way of a man with power is constant and
perennial. The evening hours which he spent in the courts of old were
to Machiavelli an exact substitute for the hours he used to spend in
the courts of Florence. Like Thucydides, Polybius, Josephus, Ibn
Khaldun, and how many other historians, Machiavelli had formerly
played a part in the world of affairs and wrote about politics partly
out of frustration. He was a *homus politicus* who eagerly explored
every political experience. But, like the ancients, he possessed little
or no sense of historical development. To him, "historical writing was
an instrument to disclose the laws of politics" (Felix Gilbert).

The Renaissance humanists also advanced historical scholarship in
their antiquarian interests and in their collection of materials. They
collected documents out of a veneration for antiquity, especially for
those great and noble writers of classical times whose phrases came
ringing down the centuries. Their interests were largely philological,
not historical; but their textual labors heaped up matter for future
historians and made their tasks easier. But these humanists were
inhibited by their classical tastes. They adored and slavishly imitated
the ancient historians. Who should presume to supersede Titus Livy?[2]
If their concern to reestablish contact with classical antiquity kindled
a certain sense of history for this epoch—a feeling for at least one
past period—the humanists were not really very interested in history
as such. Of Erasmus this could be said almost as much as of Thomas
Aquinas, as far apart as these two great figures were on other matters:

1. Felix Gilbert has pointed out that Machiavelli did not especially want to
write this but received a commission from the city fathers.
2. The humanists awarded Livy the palm. They thought the Romans in general
somewhat superior to the Greeks, who reminded them of Scholastic philosophy;
and Tacitus' style, too far past the golden age, was not pure enough. They admired
Sallust beyond his merit because he lived at the right time, but Livy was the
greatest.

neither had a historical dimension. If Aristotle spoke to Saint Thomas as a present voice, Socrates did so no less to Erasmus, and Paul to Colet. The humanists accepted Aristotle's verdict that poetry out-ranked history and tended to look upon history as only a branch of literature. They did not value it highly.

Those who have studied the critical methods of the Renaissance scholars carefully point out that they were by no means always incap-able of gullibility and sloppiness. But they have also excited admira-tion. Lorenzo Valla's analysis of the forged Donation of Constantine became a classic of critical methodology. Based as it was on the detection of anachronisms and thus on a feeling for the period, this critique had a distinct historical dimension. (Could a man have written like this in the eighth century? Was this phrase in use then, or was this knowledge then available? Such were the tests Valla applied.) Leonardo Bruni's demolition of the myth of Florence's founding by Caesar has been highly praised. Archives were used. In writing the histories of their cities, the humanists followed the classical model as well as gratifying their local pride. Such histories were popular; indeed they treated virtually the only permissible subject other than war. But the critical method was scarcely new; humanists followed in the footsteps of the ancients here, of course, and medieval monks showed as much ingenuity in forging documents for the Church as Valla did in exposing them. What counted here was a change of loyalties, since some of the humanists were anticlerical if not anti-Christian. They were above all more *secular* in their interests, shifting the focus from cloister or curia to the civic life of the Italian cities, an intensely political arena.

Yet humanists were imbued with their cherished classics: they chose the same subjects, regarded history in the same light, and wrote in the same way. History was still confined to (mostly contemporary) politi-cal subjects, was considered to be "philosophy teaching by example," was written with rhetorical flourish, and was seen in no context of progression, just as before. But a new periodization came into being as a result of the humanist position. Humanists, looking back to an idealized antiquity, inescapably saw the in-between period as a "Dark Age" and themselves as the age of revival or renaissance. Thus a golden age–dark age–renaissance scheme of periodization, which was new, emerged naturally. The ancient view in the main saw, as we know, no general goal in history, but rather an ebb and flow in which the basic situation stayed much the same. The Christian view might contain radically apocalyptic notions of a final destiny, but Renaissance humanists were too moderate, too worldly to have such an outlook. They were seldom really anti-Christian, but their Erasmian Christian humanism played down drastic elements in favor of an ethical code for everyday living. They did inadvertently father a new time scheme, containing elements of the primordial golden age in the past and adding to it a fall from grace (psychologically familiar through the Christian doctrine of the Fall) extending over the long period from about A.D. 400 until the revival of culture in the Italian cities in the fourteenth and fifteenth centuries. False as it was in many respects in the light of our knowledge today, the idea of a long "Dark Age," an utterly sterile thousand years between Rome and Florence, strongly shaped modern conceptions of the past. In general, a "heightened consciousness of time" characterized the humanists. They were keenly aware of living in a certain age, at a certain moment in time.

When all is said, the humanists produced little in the way of historical writing of any merit. Their genius and greatness lay elsewhere, though the by-products could affect history. Professor Gilbert has indeed argued that, if not Machiavelli, his Florentine colleague Guicciardini was a great historian, his *History of Italy* "the last great work of history in the classical pattern, but . . . also the first great work of modern historiography."[3] If so, it is an exceptional case (though Bruno Aretino's *History of Florence* has also received praise). And though Guicciardini did undeniably have a stronger awareness of history than Machiavelli, the latter's influence and reputation far exceeded his.

THE REFORMATION

Of the Reformation, too, it may be said even more strongly that the by-products powerfully affected the emergence of modern historical-mindedness. The most significant of these by-products was the appeal to the past for support in this mighty battle of contending opinions. An important, indeed perhaps the central, part of the Protestant case involved such an appeal to history. From the Roman Church the

3. Felix Gilbert, *Machiavelli and Guicciardini: Politics and History in Sixteenth Century Florence* (Princeton, N. J.: Princeton University Press, 1965), p. 301.

Protestants appealed to the primitive Church, endeavoring to show that Rome had wrongly usurped authority and that doctrine was sounder and life purer before the Papacy assumed control of the Church. Between 1559 and 1574 the famous Magdeburg Centuries came forth to cannonade the papists with their ammunition of ancient documents. The first chair of history in Europe was apparently established at Heidelberg University under Protestant auspices.[4] Subsequently, the Calvinist university of Leyden in the Netherlands became the greatest center of historical studies. For their part, the Catholics, slow to respond, finally did so with a vengeance. Between 1588 and 1608 the *Ecclesiastical Annals* edited by Baronius (Cardinal Cesare Baronio, an Italian Oratorian, a new order of the Reformation period which became famous for its scholarship) sought to silence the Magdeburg guns, and behind this initial salvo whole batteries of Catholic guns rolled up. Catholic historians explored the early Church and particularly the patristic age in order to prove that papal authority and the Roman Church were legitimate.[5] The result of this competition was possibly the most fabulous flowering of scholarly virtuosity of all times. Nothing less than the zeal of religious fanaticism could have inspired such mighty labors. The early compilations were uncritical, crudely propagandistic, and utterly biased; yet out of this beginning grew notable scholarly work. The seventeenth-century *erudits* combined Renaissance technique with Reformatian motivation.

Clearly in some ways these efforts were most unhistorical: passionate partisanship dictated a course whose purpose was not to disclose the pattern of the past but to support a current ideological position. Still, such essentially propagandist motives can prove to be the most powerful of incentives to scan the past. What begins as narrow partisanship can turn into something less biased, and a closer look at some of these religious historians reveals that this often happened. They were not propagandists in any cynical sense even to begin with, for they sincerely believed that truth was on their side. They were not manufacturing it to order. Thus, they were the readier to follow where truth led. Quite often their materials and their quest took pos-

4. In 1557; but the title was Professor of History *and Poetry* still.
5. In England, where in the seventeenth century learning of this sort rivaled the continental schools, savants labored to defend on historic as well as theological grounds the peculiar position of the Church of England, based on episcopal but not papal legitimacy.

session of them, gradually and unconsciously, at the expense of their
parti pris. We can see this happening today, too. Young people, seized
by that lofty and narrow idealism to which intelligent youth seems
peculiarly susceptible, will embark upon their studies with the most
intense commitment to some cause or crusade. But it is a function of
historical study to tame such fanaticism; few can honestly find in the
data support for black-and-white positions. E. H. Carr has written
that every historian worth his salt begins with a bee in his bonnet, an
invigorating impulse to prove or disprove something. In the end, if he
reaches scholarly maturity, he will transcend the narrower sort of bias.
In any case, it is clear that Reformation historians frequently came
out a different door from the one by which they entered. The strictly
orthodox often were somewhat disquieted.[6]

The variety of positions of Reformation scholars was bound to
induce a skepticism from which historical objectivity could profit. The
ultimate product of all this controversy was the skeptical Pierre Bayle,
that lapsed French Calvinist who virtually began the Enlightenment
later in the seventeenth century. In demolishing each other the rival
religionists ended by casting doubt on all truth, which was not their
intention but which resulted from their attacks on each other's version
of the truth. It was a part of the larger story of the Reformation: in
the end, men wearied of the strife and turned away in disgust, to seek
other interests.

Meanwhile, some irenical trends appeared. Possibly one of the
functions of history is peacemaking. We can see that function at work
quite frequently. It appears, for example, in Robert Aron's post-1945
work on Vichy France, in Spanish accounts of the bitter civil war of
the 1930s, and in some accounts of the world wars. The historian
soothes the corrosive hatreds that have divided a community with
his habitual inclination to explain and not condemn, an ability to see
both sides, a relatively above-the-battle position: he exerts a healing
influence. The historian may or may not deliberately have in mind
such a social function. It may be that the issues raised in the fury of
controversy simply cry out for clarification and are so patently not

6. Bruno Neveu has recently studied *Un historien à l'école de Port-Royal:
Sebastien le Nain de Tillemont 1637–1698* (La Haye: M. Nijhoff, 1966). One
of the orthodox wrote to Tillemont that if he continued his history of the early
Church it would be necessary to reform the Breviary and forget most of the
saints! (p. 280).

simple victories for one side or the other that a lucid head is driven to explain how the question really lies. Propaganda is frequently the parent of "objective" history.

So it was, clearly, after the initial phase of Reformation controversy. A good example is the striking sixteenth-century French school that included Jean Bodin, François Baudouin, and La Popelinière. Baudouin tried to bring religious peace to divided France on the eve of the Huguenot wars. He gradually drifted back to Rome from Calvinism, but he always hoped for a reconciliation. The failure of his dream did not destroy Baudouin's irenic ideals, which contributed to the unusually high valuation his group put on history. Jean Bodin placed history at the top, "above all sciences." It appears to be significant that this French school arose during the long agony of civil and religious strife from 1561 to 1593 that nearly destroyed France. Students of this group also point out that it emerged not from the rhetorical or literary tradition but from the law. History had been held thrall for centuries by literature, a thralldom which humanists in some ways threatened to perpetuate. It now made its escape by way of law. Lawyers are perhaps not the most imaginative people, but they have many virtues, among which are the concern to establish facts by careful and judicious inquiry, a dislike for emotionalism, and a commitment to the peaceful solution of conflicts and quarrels. There is a strong case for their having fathered modern historiography.

Jean Bodin, the universal genius whose *Methodus ad Facilem Historiarum Cognitionem* (1st ed., 1566) was the leading tract of its time on historical methods, received a humanist education, studied theology, and then turned to the study of legal institutions. His arguments for religious toleration and his studies in the political theory of state sovereignty are classic, and he ranks also as one of the pioneers of modern economic theory. For talent and versatility he challenges Vico if not Leibniz; he exerted an influence on Vico, Montesquieu, and other better known pioneers of the social sciences. But his *Methodus* is marked by a baroque disorder; J. G. A. Pocock calls it a "strange semi-ruinous mass."

The Venetian friar Paoli Sarpi, author, early in the seventeenth century, of a multivolume *History of the Council of Trent,* is sometimes honored as the greatest historian to come out of the Reformation. His was polemical history, for Sarpi was a product and indeed a hireling of a Venice which was, though not anti-Catholic, quite antipapal, and his purpose was to combat the power of the Papacy through discrediting the Council of Trent which had provided for a strengthening of that power. But for learning and acuteness his work belongs with that of the fabulously learned Protestant champion, Isaac Casaubon, who undertook virtually a page-by-page refutation of Baronius. Milton, Johnson, and Macaulay—Protestants all—regarded Sarpi's as the best historical opus of its age. Lord Acton, a Catholic, was far less pleased. The most recent and careful student of the great council, Herbert Jedin, calls Sarpi's *History* one-sided, as obviously it was. Yet it was a brilliant job of research and writing and seems to mark a kind of coming-of-age after the cruder propaganda of just a few decades before. This furious and sustained battle of books, the product of ideological hatred, distilled some wisdom and maturity in the course of its long life. Sarpi's work has endured.

The Reformation carried on in a most intense way that popular revolutionary tradition of Christian millenarianism which we mentioned in connection with the medieval Joachimites. On every hand, we meet poor men excited by the ideas found in the biblical books of Daniel and the Apocalypse. There had never really been a lapse in this tradition. For example, the radical wing of the Czech Hussites, who arose early in the fifteenth century and thus anticipated Martin Luther and the high Reformation by a century, were extremely chiliastic, believing in an earthly Kingdom of God following the Day of Wrath, in which all sin and pain would be purged from the world, the poor would enter into their own, and everybody would live in perfect bliss. Toward this end they were quite prepared to do violence to the rich. They inevitably failed, not merely because they drew onto themselves the fearful wrath of outraged authority, but because they had absolutely no concrete ideas for organizing the new order, since they expected an automatic utopia. The German and English Reformation bore a similar fruit of radical millenarianists, usually embodying the hopes of unlettered poor people whose imagination distilled visions of an earthly paradise out of their misery and the intoxicating prose of biblical apocalyptic passages. This colorful chapter of social and intellectual history concerns the history of history because it kept alive, with a secular interpretation, the time sense of Western civilization—the idea of progress. We have here a crude but recognizable version of what Hegel and Marx would proffer in the nineteenth century. Drenched in biblical imagery, Reformation millenarianism nonetheless saw what was in effect a secular utopia lying at the end of the historic road and inspired revolutionary action to reach that destination.

THE SEVENTEENTH CENTURY

It is clear that the Reformation had set in motion all kinds of powerful new forces which would break through the old structures to produce new ones not dreamed of by Martin Luther when he innocently queried a dubious ecclesiastical practice. Of the many revolutions which belong to this period—the New World discoveries and explorations, the invention of the printing press, the whole scientific revolution from Copernicus to Newton, and the rise of consolidated territorial states under monarchical leadership—none was without its influence on historical writing. Intellectually speaking, probably it was science and nationalism that had the greatest impact on it. But science worked against history. In the aftermath of the sensational discoveries of Kepler and Galileo about the laws of physical motion and the dimensions of the universe, almost all thinking men began to be occupied on this frontier of knowledge. A mighty inquiry had been set in motion which would not rest until Sir Isaac Newton unveiled the laws of motion and of gravitational attraction in the 1680s. The historical school of Bodin and Baudouin which had looked so promising about 1590 was overtaken by this other, more exciting, realm of thought and faded into obscurity. We may think that there should have been room enough in the world for both. But at a time when men still naturally took for granted a kind of speculative monism in which one key conception guided the whole culture, as had been the case in the Middle Ages, there was hardly the capacity for more than one intellectual revolution at a time. Scientific rationalism, as purveyed by René Descartes and his followers, took over the intellectual dominion of the seventeenth century and did not surrender it until well into the eighteenth century. This was quite incompatible with the kind of skeptical and empirical study that history is, and in fact the Cartesians openly disparaged history on grounds Plato would have found familiar: it does not attain certain truth; it is an inexact and confused study; it cannot be reduced to mathematics. Moreover, the Cartesians, intoxicated by the success of science, boldly claimed control over areas of thought now considered scarcely fit for it. Hobbes

sought an exact science of politics, Spinoza of ethics, the French neo-
classicists of art. The chief contribution of the great Frenchman himself was a scientific method of universal applicability, which he hoped
would unify the realm of knowledge. Leibniz, at the end of the century,
despite more sympathy for history, still thought such a method
possible.

In some incidental ways, history surely profited from the great
scientific revolution. What we rather vaguely call the scientific method
embraces rigorously exact and critical standards of thought, both in
framing hypotheses and in testing them experimentally. Such an attitude is applicable to historical studies, and some of it rubbed off on
scholars whose prime interest was not in the physical sciences. In the
seventeenth century, humanistic studies of this sort tended to concen-
trate on the exact establishment of literary texts (philology). Such
savants were not historians, but they performed tasks historians found
valuable and used methods historians could adopt. Contacts between
the two cultures of science and the humanities were at this time somewhat closer, perhaps, than they later became. The Hellenistic scientist
Eratosthenes, for example, had been a founder of critical chronology;
the seventeenth-century master of philological erudition, J.-J. Scalinger,
was led to similar interests through the scientists' rediscovery of
Eratosthenes. In such ways the scientific movement spilled over in the
direction of historical studies. Isaac Newton pursued biblical textual
studies and enjoyed friendship with the great philologist Richard
Bentley. Other seventeenth-century thinkers whom we associate with
the Cartesian spirit exhibit the passion for deciphering the correct
text, authorship, and date of the Bible, Spinoza being the outstanding
example. That this sort of inquiry was of potentially great significance
for history is obvious. It involved the dating of documents and led
ultimately to the higher criticism of the Bible. Such caveats must be
entered against any sweeping dismissal of the scientific movement as
wholly irrelevant to history. Nevertheless, its basic orientation *was* in
an entirely different direction.

There is more truth in a single principle of metaphysics than in all
the books of history, declared the seventeenth-century philosopher
Malebranche. The historicity of the "social contract" did not concern
Thomas Hobbes and John Locke, who argued that such a contract
was a logical necessity and need not have actually happened at all.
The shining names of the Century of Genius were virtually all scien-

tists or rationalist metaphysicians. Other types did in fact exist, but their names are far less known; they were completely overshadowed. Nevertheless, even science could not quite monopolize the teeming seventeenth century. It has been described under other rubrics by historians—as an age of power, for example. The great states of modern Europe began to take shape, creating bureaucracies and fighting wars. The Puritan Revolution in England combined religious issues with a struggle to determine the shape and substance of the new national state.

Elizabethan England had produced what has been called a historical revolution. The spirit that produced it may be seen in Shakespeare's proud cycle of history plays, intensely interested in every moment of royal drama:

> A kingdom for a stage, princes to act
> And monarchs to behold the swelling scene!

and intensely in love with England, "This land of such dear souls, this dear dear land." William Camden's celebrated *Annals of the Reign of Queen Elizabeth,* written in a florid and grandiloquent Latin, and not very critical, was of a quite traditional type in formal aspects, but it does radiate this love of England and participated in what A. L. Rowse has called "the Elizabethan discovery of England." Needless to say, there was much to boast about in this glorious age, when Drake singed the king of Spain's beard, Ralegh planted New World colonies, Shakespeare molded the English language, and Queen Bess dazzlingly presided over it all.

We recognize here history's well-known function as the natural propaganda of the social order. It has frequently associated with patriotism, nationalism, with group integration of all sorts. There is something very human about this, and we need not disparage this sort of history unduly even if it is far removed from the critical or philosophical domains. When people feel deeply about an institution, a cause, or a community, they naturally wish to preserve the records of its life and dwell on them lovingly. Shakespeare's love of England, in the dawn of national consciousness, was spontaneous, and he was in no cynical sense writing propaganda. In the United States, there has recently been a rise of black studies in which Americans of African ancestry are trying, in what to some people seems to be a naïve as well as illiberal way, to glorify their race by exalting its traditions; but we know that this is an essential part of a discovery of identity and thus of dignity. A nation, as Ernest Renan once observed in a famous definition, is shaped from the common memory of deeds done in the past. Who can imagine the modern nations without their Shakespeares and Macaulays, their Bancrofts, their Treitschkes, and their Guizots? This sort of history steals into the schoolboy's reader and may fill him with tales that are both untrue and pernicious. He learns that George Washington never told a lie, that Charlemagne was a Frenchman, and that King Alfred was the soul of unselfish generosity. So we may resent this sort of history and correct it by going to the opposite extreme of debunking. Nevertheless, it is likely that this folk use of stories about the past will continue as long as new and vital institutions arise. We see it every day, working at the level of family or neighborhood life (fondly preserving stories and mementos of the past, frequently embellished). In the Age of Elizabeth it emerged at the national level, in written works, and helped to shape a national consciousness.

Of greater importance, however, in molding historiography was the new battle of historical propaganda touched off by the English revolutions of the next century. In the seventeenth century, England fell into its period of civil strife, as Parliament and king, Puritan and Cavalier contended for the state. As in the clash of Protestant and Catholic, both sides in the great dispute appealed to history. History became a handmaiden of propaganda, and yet historical work of enduring value emerged. Each side commissioned historians, who were charged with making the past disgorge proof that either the Crown or Parliament had precedent on its side and, subsequently, to write partisan accounts of the revolution itself.[7]

Thomas Macaulay once said that some of the greatest issues of English politics had turned on the researches of antiquarians, and he had in mind primarily the Puritan Revolution. Out of all this apologetic writing came an occasional masterpiece, such as Clarendon's *History of the Rebellion*. Clarendon, writing after the event, was with

7. John Rushworth's *Historical Collections* (1659) was a parliamentary and Cromwellian account of the events of the revolution; the Royalists commissioned John Nelson to reply. Neale's *History of the Puritans* was a subsequent defense of the Puritans against the Restoration reaction. In *The Ancient Constitution and the Feudal Law* (New York: Norton, 1957) J. G. A. Pocock has subjected the historical debates of Royalists and Parliament–common-law partisans to a close examination.

good reason disillusioned with both sides and wrote from a position that might be compared with Sarpi's or Tillemont's in the Reformation. Someone has said that the best history is written by renegades— by those who have been part of a movement but have left it after becoming disenchanted. Notably, some of the most perceptive writing about Communism in our time has come from ex-Communists. They have understood it from within and yet have become sufficiently distanced to see it objectively. If they are not excessively embittered, they are in the best position to write about it. Historical controversy of this sort is bound to produce some who would mediate or some who are disgusted with both sides or some who see that the evidence really does not wholly support either side and who therefore can write their history with some degree of impartiality.

The peculiarly precedent-minded nature of her political and legal system made this appeal to the past more urgent in the case of England. A good example of these seventeenth-century legal-historical inquiries dictated by political controversy is John Selden's *History of Tithes*. Selden, a gifted and fabulously learned man much admired by his contemporaries, undertook this bit of antiquarianism because of an important issue raised in the revolutionary period. Had the payment of tithes to the clergy existed before the common law, a divine-right prerogative of kings, or were tithes a creation of the common law, which might legitimately be regulated by that law? Selden wanted to find evidence to use in the debate which would not only decide a rather crucial issue but was related to the larger issue in this great conflict between Crown and common-law Parliament. It was important to discover precedents, which could then be used as ammunition; the precedents were not necessarily decisive but were one significant sort of evidence, felt in England to carry much weight. Here in England also, lawyers were important in the development of history.

Of such interesting exercises in political controversy it could of course again be said that they were not fully historical. It was not merely that they had a propagandistic motivation, for we are never likely wholly to escape that, and it is in many ways good that history should be relevant to some current situation. But this was not an interest in the past in order to see how it shaped the present. It was directed to the much narrower goal of finding out what practices had existed in the past in order to guide and justify present practices, the assumption being that usage and custom bestowed a kind of right.

This was the doctrine that Edmund Burke, a century later, called prescription. The Englishman's inclination to root his political constitution in historical continuity was much older than Burke and was clearly marked in the seventeenth century's memorable debates and conflicts. Inquiry into the past became, then, for Englishmen evidently more so than any other people, not merely an academic matter, but one of immediate and urgent importance, a matter of their very life. The English almost became a people who had to find out what their ancestors did yesterday in order to know what they should do today. Nothing could do more to encourage antiquarian research, and we immediately see why history and the law have so often gone hand in hand in England; why one of England's greatest modern historians, F. W. Maitland, dedicated himself to a history of the common law. (During the Puritan Revolution the Levellers rejected the appeal to history in favor of an appeal to "reason, equity, and the Law of God," but the Natural Rights school was with difficulty naturalized in England.) Nevertheless, the lawyer's search for precedents is at least a very narrow concern about the past. He does not wonder why the social order changes or why men once lived and thought differently; indeed, he may be committed to the view that they lived and thought much the same then as now, since the rules that governed them should govern us. But we must add that this sort of research did contribute to the birth both of critically trained historians and, indirectly, to a feeling for history and a love of the past.

At least one student of this period of historiography, F. S. Fussner, has described it as a "historical revolution" which carries us to the eve of the modern age of historical consciousness, with its relativistic and time-conditioned outlook, its tendency to see everything as development and evolution. But he may have exaggerated slightly, for the Cartesian influence was in the ascendant, and the great eighteenth-century Enlightenment exhibited, all in all, a decidedly ambivalent attitude toward history.

Chapter 4

THE ENLIGHTENMENT CONTRIBUTION
TO HISTORICAL THOUGHT AND METHOD

WAS THE ENLIGHTENMENT HISTORICAL?

We have reached the eve of the modern epoch. It is obvious that some exciting things happened to history during the Enlightenment, that seed bed of the modern mind. This great era had an apparent historical dimension. Pierre Bayle, who almost began it, wrote a *Historical and Critical Dictionary.* The eighteenth century began with a quarrel between ancients and moderns which raised the whole question of progress, and never stopped arguing about it. Montesquieu's great *Spirit of the Laws* combined history with sociology to begin the quest for a true science of man. Voltaire, this century's giant, wrote much history, and has been ranked as one of the founders of modern historical methods. David Hume, too, was a historian, marking a significant break with that tradition by which philosophers would have nothing to do with anything so imprecise as history. And the Neapolitan philosopher and savant Giambattista Vico also appears as a pioneer of modern historical thought. The Enlightenment under Newtonian and Lockean influence reacted against the abstract rationalism of the Cartesians in the direction of an empirical, experimental approach to reality much more suited to historical work. Edward Gibbon is only the most illustrious of many eighteenth-century historians; to name them all would fill a large catalog. The wars of religion well behind them, the *philosophes* were thoroughly secular-minded, thoroughly critical, thoroughly "modern." Still interested in physical and natural science, they were much more interested in man, and they brought into existence all the social sciences. At the same

45

time, they had a delightful gift of style and organization, which makes
them far more readable than the ponderous polymaths of the previous
century, those *erudits* who made a heap of all they found. In the time
of Voltaire, Hume, and Gibbon, history became genuinely popular
as well as scholarly and "philosophical."

Yet it must be said that the Enlightenment has persistently been
found wanting in true historical-mindedness. Collingwood declared
that during the Enlightenment "no attempt was made to lift history
above the level of propaganda." Notoriously unfair to the Middle
Ages and to the era of the Reformation, Voltaire and his friends
really had no conception of continuity. They can even be construed
as wishing to abolish the past; more than once they said as much.
And they wished, adds Ortega y Gasset, referring to the ideals of the
French Revolution, to abolish the future as well. For the ideal society
was a static one, related to that tempting idea of a "natural order"
which so permeated the eighteenth century. Despite a few atypical
specimens such as Vico, mechanism and not process remained the
guiding concept of the Enlightenment until nearly the end of the
century, by which time we have reached another epoch. When Lafayette suggested in 1788 that one might well begin the study of French
history with the year 1787, he was only slightly exaggerating a tendency shown by most of the eighteenth-century historians. The past
was useful only for exhibiting dreadful examples of how badly man
had behaved in the past and for demonstrating how he might get to
utopia. It was a record of "crimes, follies, and misfortunes," of superstition, ignorance, and error, illuminated by only an occasional example of reason and common sense. Can historians be biased against
the past? Eager to pursue its vision of a new moral world, the Enlightenment could almost be accused of such bias.

The Enlightenment remained determinedly neoclassical in its
tastes. It held to unchanging standards of excellence and idealized
the ancients, dismissing the Gothic style as barbarous.[1] Of Montesquieu, Oliver Wendell Holmes, Jr., once wrote that "He was not
able to see history as an evolution, he looked at all events as if they

1. The neoclassical artists were fond of using "historical" themes, meaning
classical ones; plays about Cato, Caesar, and others proliferated, and "history
painting" carried the most prestige in its field. There was thus a strong feeling for
at least one phase of the past, but not for others.

were contemporaneous."[2] In this respect, the *Spirit of the Laws* did not differ from Machiavelli's *Discourses* except in its richer empirical content. "Exemplarism," the familiar use of the past as a storehouse of lessons or examples—"philosophy teaching by example"—remained strong. Lord Bolingbroke's widely read treatise on history (*Letter on the Study of History,* 1735) was notable for this attitude. To Bolingbroke the only conceivable purpose of studying the past was to "inculcate the moral and practical lessons of statecraft" (Pocock). He saw it as an aid to the statesman but regarded historical inquiry for any other reason as absurd antiquarianism, unsuitable for a gentleman of cultivated mind. For anyone to study the Middle Ages with the goal of finding out what it was like to live in those times would have seemed the height of absurdity to almost any man of the Enlightenment.

Despite a certain fascination with the idea of whether or not there had been progress (and the Enlightenment philosophers did not agree that there had been progress in all fields, certainly not in the arts, religion, or morality), the outlook on the past remained, until near the end of the century, mainly cyclical like that of the ancients. The Renaissance had seen a golden age, a dark age, a recovery. Voltaire saw after this another relapse, during the Reformation era with its ghastly wars of religion, then a recovery in the time of Louis XIV— followed perhaps by another decline? Voltaire rather disparaged his own century in comparison with the great era of Racine and Molière, and he certainly thought Locke and Newton had spoken the ultimate words in science and philosophy. Thus, little continuity was seen in the past; instead, it was seen as a record of rather inexplicable alternations of light and darkness. Many eighteenth-century thinkers permitted themselves the hope that, now that Newton and Locke had enlightened the world, a permanent turn for the better had set in. Yet their optimism should not be exaggerated. "We preach wisdom to the deaf, and we are still far indeed from the Age of Reason," Diderot confessed to David Hume. That the vast majority of men were plunged into superstition and fanaticism and probably always would be was an idea congenial to the *philosophes.* Any consistent idea of progress or of development as the theme of history must await

2. Introduction to the 1900 edition of *Esprit des lois,* reprinted in Max Lerner, ed., *The Mind and Faith of Justice Holmes* (Boston: Little, Brown & Co., 1943), p. 381.

the very end of the century. Arthur O. Lovejoy, that keen student of
ideas, even asserted that the Enlightenment basically held a "negative
philosophy of history," that it believed that if there had been change,
the change was, on the whole, for the worse, a deterioration since the
golden age of antiquity.[3]

It is a complex and a contradictory age, and that is part of its
fascination. Yet we must come back to the invigoration which it provided for all fields of inquiry, and not least for history. Even if it was
not genuinely historical-minded, the Enlightenment's stimulus to
inquiry meets us at every point, and we must acknowledge our giant
debt to it.

Probably most challenging and exciting to historians is the typical
Enlightenment conviction that we may find, beneath the accidents of
events, the larger trends and processes. The great *philosophes* had a
commanding boldness in asserting this. "There are general causes,
moral or physical, at work in every monarchy," Montesquieu wrote
in *Grandeur and Decay of the Romans,* "which elevate it and maintain it or work its downfall; all accidents are the result of causes; and
if the chance of a battle—that is, a special cause—has ruined a state,
there was a general cause at work which made that state ready to
perish by a single battle. In a word, the main current carries with it
all the special accidents." We often find the same magnificent assurance that inquiry will disclose a fundamental and somewhat simple
order of things. This was the "faith of reason" that the Enlightenment
inherited from Newton and did not doubt could be applied to human
studies. Men of the eighteenth century were much better at proclaim-
ing this faith than at carrying it out—better at conjectural or speculative history than at actual detailed empirical investigation. (The latter
might have interfered with this clarity!) They almost seem ready to
say, with Rousseau, that the facts are irrelevant; if they do not fit the
framework, they ought to. But this confidence in reason was bracing.
One embarked upon the quest with an assurance that significant generalizations would be found.

The Enlightenment cherished the practical and the useful. History
had always been considered primarily a practical subject, and without
challenging this classical view the Enlightenment upgraded it. The

3. See his well-known essay "The Parallel of Deism and Classicism," in his
Essays in the History of Ideas (Baltimore: Johns Hopkins Press, 1948; reprinted
in paperback by Harper & Row).

mechanical arts and the practical sciences, once despised, experienced a renaissance at the hands of the Encyclopedists, who delighted in magnifying the down-to-earth useful things at the expense of vain metaphysics and idle imagination. "The only scope of History is *Utility*," wrote Peter Whalley, in *An Essay on the Manner of Writing History* (1746), adding that history is "the noblest, and most deserving of our serious attention, of all studies."

Finally, of course, the eighteenth-century writers wove wit and literary skill into all they wrote. This was a part of their basic *esprit:* it was in part a rebellion against seventeenth-century metaphysics and seventeenth-century erudition, against the baroque with its complexities and sinuosities, against incomprehensible philosophies and indigestible learning. They demanded that things be made clear and be a delight to the reader. In pursuit of this goal they might outrageously oversimplify, but they were never dull. That is why they became the most influential writers of all time and why they are still read and always will be. The combination of seriousness with wit and style is, after all, the quintessence of Voltaireanism, shared by Rousseau and Diderot and Hume. The style was elegant neoclassical, and by the time we reach Gibbon, near the end of the century, it has almost lost its savor, becoming too pat and in need of the drastic revitalization that romanticism was to provide. Yet it is always clear and comprehensible. An age of prose, the Enlightenment created a style admirably suited to exposition, which all historians can read to their profit and should read again and again.

VOLTAIRE

The eighteenth-century historians brought some specific innovations to the art of history. Biased against Judaic-Christian religion, Voltaire called for a widening of the scope of history to include other peoples and religions: "It is time to stop insulting all other sects and nations as if they are mere appendages to the history of the Chosen People." In practice, the great deist did not carry out his appeal to learn more about the Chinese, the Hindus, and the Muslims. In fact, Voltaire was so much a victim of the eighteenth century's inability to conceive of men as different—of, as Lovejoy put it, its "uniformitarian" view of human nature—that he made deists out of the Chinese and natural philosophers out of the American Indians. He refused to believe that

ritual prostitution could have been practiced in Babylon, that private
property could ever have not existed (as against his enemy Rousseau,
in his entirely speculative ideas about the *Origins of Inequality*), or
that the Crusades were motivated by anything but plunder. This
"rationalist fallacy," as it has been called by Michael Polanyi—the
belief that men and cultures were everywhere much the same—was
a drastic obstacle to any appreciation of other ages and civilizations.
Yet at the same time Voltaire is credited with being the first to
demand a widening of horizons to include world history.

Even more important was Voltaire's demand for an extension of
history to include subjects other than politics. His most eloquent
passages are on this theme. Instead of battles and intrigue, why do
we not hear about "a canal which joins two oceans, a painting of
Poussin, a fine play," or about population, how people made their
living, what the laws are and how they got that way, why some prov-
inces are rich and others poor—and a hundred other inquiries! "These
are a thousand times more precious than all the annals of courts or
accounts of campaigns in the field." Yet all past historians have
neglected these really interesting questions. This is an astonishing
and a memorable call for a revolution in historiography. Again, Voltaire did not carry it out, though he tried. His foremost historical
work, *The Age of Louis XIV,* includes topical chapters on government, economics, literature, science, the church, but without inte-
grating these successfully into the political narrative; the chapters on
writers, artists, and scientists tend to become mere catalogs. His
Essai sur les moêurs is, by general agreement, a very unsatisfactory
book. This is only to say that Voltaire did not have the needed materials and had not worked out the methodology of his new idea of
history. We may still be working on such a methodology. But he
broke through the confines of tradition to announce that history
knows no boundaries and that its interests extend to every phase of
human activity. This is a proposition that all contemporary historians
accept. Voltaire can well claim to have originated the idea of economic history, social history, intellectual history, cultural history.

How critical were the eighteenth-century historians? It is not necessary to say that Voltaire and his fellows boldly subjected all manner
of orthodoxy and authority to critical examination. But a really adequate historical methodology would seem to require more than a
skeptical spirit. It requires many tools and a consistent body of prin-

ciples. Beginning late in the eighteenth century at the University of Göttingen, German scholars began to develop such a systematic science of criticism. (The great *erudits* of the previous century, such as Mabillon and Duchesne, had forged some tools in the areas of paleography and diplomatics, the sciences of deciphering and testing handwriting and official documents.) They made Voltaire and even Gibbon look like amateurs. Voltaire's criticism of sources is rather hit-and-miss, sometimes inspired and sometimes wholly wrong. For example, he insisted erroneously that Cardinal Richelieu's *Testament* was a forgery, a case of being hypercritical.[4] His use of sources, too, was somewhat old-fashioned in its reliance on oral testimony, though he did make use of some archival material. According to Momigliano, Gibbon, who learned well from both the *erudits* and the *philosophes,* did not anticipate the German criticism and systematic use of primary sources.

Biased, incomplete, victims of the rationalist fallacy, lacking a sense of historical development—yet eager inquirers into human affairs, able to see the larger patterns, anxious to broaden the scope of history, brilliant writers who valued history highly: such were the *philosophes.* They may be credited with being the fathers of modern history, as so many others have been, or they may be seen as still enslaved to that substantialist view of things which had not yet suffered any significant change since the time of Plato and Aristotle. M. Eliade might choose to say that the "terror of history" had never sufficiently abated. To Voltaire, the past was still "a disordered collection of crimes, follies, and misfortunes amid which we can find some virtues, a few happy moments as one discovers settlements strewn here and there through wild deserts." Another French *philosophe,* the economist Mercier de la Rivière, called it "the shame of humanity, each page a tissue of crimes and madness." Perhaps this is indeed what it is. If so, it should be ignored for the most part; why should we remember such a chamber of horrors? We need to recall only the rare moments of happiness and virtue. Nevertheless, it is important to remember these and try to imitate them. Such, in the main, was the Enlightenment philosophy of history.

There were of course other motives in Enlightenment historiography. David Hume's important and influential *History of England*

---

4. See the introduction to Henry Bertram Hill's edition of *The Political Testament of Cardinal Richelieu* (Madison: University of Wisconsin Press, 1961).

was written to correct the "misrepresentations of faction" during the seventeenth-century revolutions. It was thus in the tradition of irenic history, designed to correct the crudities of partisanship and in so doing bind up wounds and secure a consensus. The great philosopher did not entirely succeed, since the Whigs charged him with a Tory bias. Hume also turned to history because of his mistrust of reason— not a typical Enlightenment trait. But his highly rational inquiries had led him to a profound skepticism, as a result of which he tended to value custom as reflected in existent institution and practices—in fact, in history. Hume, however, shared the lack of any historical dimension in his conception of human nature: "Mankind are so much the same, in all times and places, that history informs us of nothing new or strange in this particular. Its chief use is only to discover the constant and universal principles of human nature."

VICO

Vico, writing in remote Naples and not well known outside his own region for some time, was the great exception to eighteenth-century present-mindedness. Vico's chief contribution to history was his philosophical refutation of the old view that we cannot have exact knowledge of the past. The Cartesians had insisted that whereas we can have exact knowledge of physical nature, by measuring its quantitative properties and framing precise mathematically expressed laws, we can never do this in the study of history. Vico held that, on the contrary, we cannot fully understand physical nature because God made it and we are alien to it; but we *can* understand human history because it was made by men like ourselves whose minds we can grasp. Moreover, the study of the past enables us to know human nature more fully, which is the greatest goal of knowledge. And in general we understand things only when we know their origin, growth, and experience. This was a truly genetic approach and appears as a profound break with all previous thought. Vico today is usually presented as *the* founder of modern historical thought. In Patrick Gardiner's anthology on the *Theory of History,* he comes first. Benedetto Croce and R. G. Collingwood, those influential twentieth-century historians of historical thought, accorded him this honor. If it remained for Herder, Kant, and Hegel fully to develop this strain of thought later, the seed was in Vico.

It must be conceded that Vico's *New Science* (1st ed., 1725; final ed., 1744) was written in so curious and difficult a manner that it is hard to read, a fact which helped impede its ready acceptance. It was exactly this sort of wearisome jargon that the *philosophes* most despised. No one today is likely to turn to the book with pleasure; it joins that long list of writings which profoundly influenced mankind though detestably, grotesquely, or gracelessly written (a list that might include such varied names as Copernicus, Jeremy Bentham, Karl Marx, and John Dewey). Nevertheless, the Italian rises to eloquence in expounding his central insight:

In the night of thick darkness enveloping the earliest antiquity, so remote from ourselves, there shines the eternal and never-failing light of a truth beyond all question: that the world of civil society has certainly been made by man, and that its principles are therefore to be found within the modifications of our own human mind. Whoever reflects on this cannot but marvel that the philosophers should have bent all their energies to the study of the world of nature . . . and that they should have neglected the study of the world of the nations or civil world, which, since men have made it, men could hope to know.

For the rest, Vico's skirmishes with history contained a cyclical theory with stages within it, including an age of gods, an age of heroes, and an age of men, which bear some resemblance to August Comte's famous nineteenth-century stages, the theological, the metaphysical, and the positivist or scientific (perhaps they could be called, in Saint-Simon's categories, the theocratic, aristocratic-feudal, and democratic stages). The last stage ends in refinement, dissolution, and finally breakdown, whereupon we revert back to barbarism and begin again—a sequence not far from that of Ibn Khaldun or Arnold J. Toynbee. Vico sees interesting analogies between the European Middle Ages and the Homeric period of ancient Greece. Some have interpreted Vico's *corso, ricorso* (flux and reflux) to mean not a mere repetition but perhaps a spiral ascent, a progression through cycles as in Toynbee's *Study of History*. This is not entirely clear; yet the stimulation and excitement of such ideas is apparent.[5] This was merely speculative history for the most part, in which, it must be

---

5. It may be worth noting that one of the greatest of twentieth-century novelists, James Joyce, fell under Vico's spell: *Finnegans Wake* is based on the eternal *corso, ricorso*.

confessed, the later Enlightenment abounded. Such speculations preceded and stimulated the more pedestrian labors of testing them against the evidence.

Vico also provided some rules for historians to go by or, more exactly, some prejudices to avoid. They might be compared with Francis Bacon's famous "idols" or false standards which mislead us in reasoning (Idols of the Tribe, the Marketplace, the Theater, the Cave, in Bacon's picturesque metaphors). Some of these hit against the old habit of seeing all men as being alike. We should *not* assume that other peoples are like ourselves; we should *not* suppose that other ages were in the same state of development, and hence intellectual condition, as ourselves. Vico worked his way (after long travail, as he tells us) out of the "rationalist fallacy." Another of his perfectly valid points is that we should not suppose that the ancients knew more about themselves than we can know. They may have been deceived about their own times, and we can learn more about them than they knew, since we have the ability to correct errors, accumulate data, and see matters in perspective. (We *do* know more about the Greeks and Romans today than they did, that is, a modern trained historian has much greater knowledge about those times than anyone then alive had.)

This amazing thinker was also keenly interested in language and in myth as keys to understanding the past; he knew that myth may contain valuable clues to reality. He was aware that prerationalistic, primitive men thought metaphorically or poetically and that we must view them in this light. In all this and more, Vico sounds very up to date, and we recognize him as a true creator of our ways of thinking. His contributions to legal thought and philosophy were equally great; he has been seen as a precursor of Hegel and Marx and even Nietzsche; perhaps he founded anthropology. Far less famous in his own time than Montesquieu or Voltaire, he was much more profound, if much less readable than either, and has come into his own in this century. It is difficult to quarrel with the enthusiastic Vichians who raise the cry, "All hail to mighty Vico, John the Baptist of modern social science!" In the teeth of such adulation it may be comforting to learn that Vico was so inaccurate in mere factual detail that he got his own birth date wrong. Unhappily, such inadequacy in small things ("Confound details!" said Voltaire) often accompanies profound speculative brilliance such as Vico had.

TOWARD A PHILOSOPHY OF DEVELOPMENT

Vico mentioned Providence or the divine will as guiding or underlying the course of history. If there is a plan, where does it come from and why should it exist? The meaningfulness of history implies some sort of larger purpose, which must be part of a cosmic order. If so, is it a necessity, thus denying human freedom? Is man the puppet of forces imposed on him from without? This would seem to cause difficulties for Vico's "man makes himself" doctrine. The Neapolitan professor worried such questions without reaching a conclusion, as is understandable. His tendency to see God's will as *immanent* in the historic process, expressing itself in and through the development of human society, which, however, has its own laws, with man appearing as a free agent *unwittingly* serving the higher purposes of the divine Plan—this is what ties Vico to the German philosophers, to Hegel and Marx. Something similar may be seen in the eighteenth-century German *philosophe* Lessing, whose *Education of the Human Race* postulated a progressive revelation, God choosing to reveal Himself gradually through the course of history rather than through one message in ancient times, as traditional Christianity would have it.[6]

And indeed more than one late eighteenth-century thinker wrote what the Scotchman Dugald Stewart called ".Theoretical or Conjectural History." There was a whole Scottish school of this sort; in France, Turgot and Condorcet provide the most famous examples. Written in the aftermath of the French Revolution, Condorcet's progressive scheme of ten stages, presented in his *Sketch . . . of the Progress of the Human Mind,* was an exceedingly simplified view of an onward-and-upward direction, now in its next-to-last phase and soon to arrive at the nearest thing possible to perfection. But it was also significant for seeing civilization as a whole: it is not just one kind of progress but the movement of entire cultures that is in question, and it is in knowledge and general welfare that progress manifests itself. Condorcet's pamphlet became famous.

---

6. It would seem that through their universal genius, Leibniz, the Germans received more of a feeling for history than did the French through Descartes. "What philosophy, more nearly than his, has prepared the way for Hegel?" a recent student of Leibniz (Y. Belaval) asks. Friedrich Meinecke began his classic account of the growth of modern historical consciousness *(Die Entstehung des Historismus)* with Leibniz.

Of these schemes of historical development, the most significant
were those of Kant, Herder, and finally Hegel. With these figures we
are close to the boundary that divides the Enlightenment from the
romantic period, or that begins the nineteenth century. But with Kant
and Herder we are still in the eighteenth century, and the giant figure
of Kant belongs as much to the Enlightenment as to the next era; he
was virtually the transition in himself. Though dedicated primarily to
issues of epistemology and metaphysics in general, with a special
reference to scientific and religious knowledge, and the boundary
between them, Kant wrote one notable essay on history. This interest
he passed on to Herder and to the German idealist philosophers.
Kant's essay, "The Idea of a Universal History from a Cosmopolitan
Point of View," argued that there must be some cosmic teleology or
providential plan if history is to make sense. Individuals work toward
realization of ends of which they are unconscious. The full development of reason, of the human capacity for understanding, requires
the whole species: it is not possible for a single individual; it must
develop through time. All that has happened will be found to have
existed for some purpose. Thus, even wars are the means of driving
men toward a world government. Everything that happens has its
purpose, though this may not be evident to us. This "opens up to us
a consoling view of the future, in which the human species is represented in the far distance as having at last worked itself up to a condition in which all the germs implanted in it by nature may be fully
developed, and its destination here on earth fulfilled."

Herder immediately took up this idea. It would take a good part of
the next century to work out the details of this edifying prospect. The
Enlightenment, which began in the rather bitterly pessimistic skepticism of Pierre Bayle and had seen Voltaire sadly disenchanted by such
events as the Lisbon earthquake, ended in an optimism which came
to it from its ruminations on history. It had discovered the exciting
idea of a providence in history which differed from the old Judaic-
Christian providence in *evolving* in a sustained and logical way
through the natural workings of the social and historical process. God,
or, if you choose, Reason, revealed Himself or Itself in history, as
mankind marched toward perfection. "The total mass of the human
race, through alternating periods of calm and excitement, good and
evil, marches steadily, if with slow steps, toward a greater perfection."[7]

7. Turgot, *Discourse on the Progress of the Human Spirit,* 1750.

C hapter 5

THE NINETEENTH CENTURY: GOLDEN AGE OF HISTORY

VARIETIES OF HISTORICISM

At the end of the eighteenth century, history had become more philosophical, and philosophy had almost become history. Condorcet declared that philosophy had outlived its usefulness and that all the important truths are to be found in the study of the past. If, as the German philosophers suggested, the record of the human race's experience in time was the same thing as the revelation of Reason or Divine Will, then this transformation of philosophy into history was obvious. From another position, Edmund Burke, in his attack on the French Revolution which was so widely read in the years after 1790, found in the past, in the continuity of a people as expressed in their rooted institutions, a safer foundation for political and social life than the abstract formulations of political theory. Like Hume, Burke's mistrust of "the fallible and feeble contrivances" of individual human reason led him to lean on the collective wisdom of the people as summed up in those practices and structures which have sprung from their long experience.

During the first half of the nineteenth century, the tendency of Left and Right alike was to make of history not merely a source of examples and a road to wisdom but a purposive force pregnant with the determinate destiny of man. If conservatives were Burkean, and if Hegel's vast scheme perhaps belonged in the Center, men like the Socialist Louis Blanc also believed (before Karl Marx took it up) that "history follows a path traced for it by the hand of God" or of Nature—the same being true of Saint-Simon, from whom Comte borrowed much of his positivist historicism. "The supreme law of

progress . . . carries along and dominates everything; men are its
instruments." Today we are inclined to be most suspicious of such
schemes, which represent (in Karl Popper's unique use of the term)
"historicism" or "metahistory" or, in the phrase of the revisionist
Polish Marxist Kolakowski, "historiosophy." The fact remains that
such schemes were very widely taken for granted in the romantic era
and go far to account for the enormous prestige and popularity that
serious history attained at this time. If, as has recently been said,
"History acquired in the nineteenth century an importance which it
had never achieved before and does not hold today," historicism was
the principal reason.

The major German philosophers in this age of philosophy nour-
ished Kant's suggestion of providence into a powerful statement of
the case for metahistory. To make truth a matter of development,
of movement, was their central insight. The error of all previous
philosophy lay in viewing the world statically, for nothing stands still.
All is involved in the continual flux, the *Werden,* or "becoming," of
life. The dialectic, which works by a thing engendering its opposite
and then embracing it to form something new, which again engenders
an opposite and so on, made its appearance in German philosophy
before Hegel, in Johann Fichte, Friedrich Schelling, and Adam
Mueller. Fichte, working on the problem left by Kant's philosophy—
a popular and flamboyant person, capable of reaching a larger audience than Kant as in his famous *Addresses to the German Nation* of
1807—came to believe that basic reality is Idea or Spirit, all of which
is contained in a cosmic Ego of which our minds are a part. Those who
followed Fichte meditated on the relationship between the subjective
and objective aspects of reality and on how they engaged in a creative
interaction. Hegel's ponderous genius put all these heady conceptions
together in a vast *Philosophy of History.* History is a universal cosmic
process which works toward the full realization of the Absolute
Spirit. It reveals a dialectical pattern; behind the somewhat chaotic
record of external events (which Hegel was not so naïve as to deny),
we can perceive in each epoch a grand Idea, which is its contribution
to the stupendous whole and which constitutes nothing less than the
logic by which God realizes in time the purposes of the world. History
is logic, and logic is history; the real is rational, and the rational is
real. Hegel's view of history was not entirely a priori and theoretical:
there is a place for the empirical investigator, for we must study the

past to find the pattern. But when we think through the facts, we discover a theme or Idea behind them. And when we contemplate the whole sequence of ages and ideas, we find a logical order.

The tendency to trace all such ideas to Hegel is a mistaken one. In the early nineteenth century, the concept of historical destiny was widely abroad in Europe; it was one of those ideas whose time had come and was simply in the air. François Guizot, the French historian and statesman, whose lectures in Paris in the 1820s were so popular that they gained him admittance not only to the historical guild but to the political leadership of France as Louis-Philippe's first minister, had probably never read Hegel, who had scarcely yet been Gallicized. Yet Guizot taught that history has a goal, a direction, a plan. Each age is destined to make its contribution to the evolution of European civilization: "For fifteen centuries Europe and France have been moving along the same road towards freedom and progress." To Guizot, the goal toward which humanity had been advancing steadily for so long included representative, constitutional government and national unification in a free society. He was a Liberal (or Whig), who saw in this slow and stately march cause for extreme satisfaction, views which the Revolution of 1848 did something to disturb. None of these liberals doubted that, having come last, his own times had to be best—"the heir of all the ages, in the foremost files of time."

Guizot's 1500 years is significant. The French nation and representative government both evolved primarily from the Germanic tribes of early medieval Europe, so that Guizot put more stress on the Middle Ages than on classical antiquity. He saw a steady development reaching from the first "long-haired" Frankish kings down to the present. The romantics' interest in the Middle Ages helped rescue this period, of course. We find even a socialist like Saint-Simon urging that "If historians had analyzed and examined the Middle Ages more deeply, they . . . would have recorded the gradual preparation of all the great events which developed later and would not have presented the explosions of the 16th and following centuries as sudden and unforeseen." This resurrection of the Middle Ages played a crucial role in the general renaissance of history, for it made possible perspective on the past stressing continuity rather than cyclical movement.

In this age of nationalism, a force unleashed by both the French Revolution and romanticism and made possible by modern communications, the nation provided one obvious *telos* of history. Ranke said historical studies grew out of opposition to the Napoleonic ideas. It is hard to deny that national growth *was* a slow development and thus a good historical subject. If this theme of the gradual emergence of the nation, of the shaping of a people, were taken away from nineteenth-century historiography, its most popular classics would be destroyed. Macaulay was the Guizot of England, Treitschke of Germany, and many other historians used this as their theme. Liberty, parliamentary government, and, for the somewhat bolder, democracy provided another popular theme. Hegel himself thought that the whole grand march of God through the world, which his system posited, had culminated in the modern European nation under a constitutional monarchy, with ordered freedom under law. Socialists saw the reign of equality and social justice as the end product, that one far-off divine event toward which all creation moved.

"The sense of history has everywhere awakened," Friedrich Savigny declared. In tracing the history of this rise of "historicism," the German historian Friedrich Meinecke *(Die Entstehung der Historismus)* called it "one of the greatest spiritual revolutions which Western thought has experienced." It was nothing less than the discovery of change. In addition to the philosophical currents we have been discussing, many other things contributed to this discovery. Indeed, if we confined our explanation of the rise of nineteenth-century historical-mindedness to such forces, we might properly be accused of a one-sided idealistic interpretation of history. There was, first of all, the simple fact of change, which made men conscious of the role of change. It can be argued that the French Revolution and the Napoleonic period, coinciding with the crucial impact of the so-called Industrial Revolution, brought sweeping and drastic change to Europe for the first time in its history—change that affected basic social structures and ways of life, not just political leadership. It was change that did not stop but swept on with an irresistible momentum. "The age of historical preoccupation was made possible by the age of revolution," as Douglas Johnson, the biographer of Guizot, remarks. After 1789 and 1815, men had the sense of being adrift on a stormy sea and of being badly in need of a compass; accustomed to basic stability or very gradual change, they felt themselves swept with fearful rapidity toward an unknown future. The old order was gone, and it was not clear whether a specific new order would come and what it would be like, or whether there would be continual change and what this would mean for human nature, for society, and for culture. Men looked anxiously for landmarks.[1] But they were in a position to compare an old order with a new order, for the French Revolution and the Industrial Revolution opened up whole new historical perspectives.

At the same time, the relatively mundane matter of an improvement in access to the sources of history also helped the growth of historical research. The extensive use of archival sources was an outstanding feature of the history boom of the early nineteenth-century. Scholars explored these sources with a sense of high adventure and of imminent discovery. Now at last, one could, in Leopold von Ranke's famous phrase, find out exactly what happened. Governments had begun to collect their documents in public archives to which scholars were given access. The great public libraries and public museums were for the most part opened in the eighteenth century. The trend toward nationalism and the centralized state caused materials formerly contained in private houses or local registries to be deposited at the national libraries, such as the British Museum or the Bibliothèque Nationale, where they were accessible and usable.

THE GERMAN SCHOOL

The University of Göttingen in Germany, where since the latter part of the eighteenth century an important school of critical researchers was centered, took the lead in exploiting these resources. They trusted nothing but the documents, the primary sources, and they were determined to plunge into the archives and to appraise them systematically. Out of the German universities came the seminar method of conducting graduate-school research. Why Germany took the lead would be itself a matter for historical inquiry; it is a fact that

1. "When . . . the French Revolution took away the naïve acceptance of things, and at the same time failed to inaugurate the reign of Reason, many of those whose horror of meaningless drift could not be stilled by reliance on Divine Providence turned . . . to History as the guarantor of meaningful purpose and promise of inevitable dénouement." J. L. Talmon, *Political Messianism: The Romantic Phase* (New York: Praeger, 1960), p. 229. This trenchant statement packs in all the necessary ingredients.

(according to Herbert Butterfield, who has written an excellent essay on the subject),[2] as early as 1770, Germany was producing a far higher proportion of writings on history than any other European country. Göttingen seems to have been the center of a kind of reaction against the feathery and superficial sort of historical writing identified with Voltaire and the French. The *philosophes* had once reacted against stuffy pedantry by becoming witty and popular; now there was a reverse reaction, for the *philosophes* were felt to be mere dilettantes, who covered their laziness with cleverness. Germany experienced an intellectual renaissance in the age of Kant, Herder, Goethe, Fichte, and Hegel; she experienced a nationalistic reaction against defeat by Napoleon. She was also the leading center of romanticism, that new spirit which, among other things, exalted folklore, national tradition, and medieval subjects, and reacted against the abstract universalism of neoclassical taste by stressing the concrete and the particular. There can be no doubt about the association between romanticism and nationalism and between both and history. Nevertheless, the scholars at Göttingen were not in any obvious way romantic; they wanted to be solid, scientific, and exact. Yet their German pride in having their feet on the ground, as contrasted with the "windbag-history" of Voltaire, is evident. They were interested in the Middle Ages, and of course, as they went back to the roots of the modern state in medieval times, the theme of national development was a leading one in their studies. The stimulus to the quest for the roots of the modern state was provided by the absence, until 1871, of a unified national state in the German world. It was a source of much anguish to cultured Germans, who hated their petty states and yearned for national unity and strength.

It would be a mistake to see all historians, even German historians, as disciples of Hegel. The German historians came from a different

2. "The Rise of the German Historical School"; in *Man on His Past: The Study of the History of Historical Scholarship* (New York: Cambridge University Press, 1955).

One explanation of the German flair for history was given by Lord Acton's friend Döllinger: "The Germans . . . are the most adaptable of all nations," the most cosmopolitan. See John Ignatius von Döllinger, *Addresses on Historical and Literary Subjects,* translated by Margaret Warre (London, John Murray: 1894), pp. 31 ff. His argument was essentially that the Germans, people of the Holy Roman Empire, with less definite national characteristics than the French and English but a wider range of sympathies for all cultures, had for this reason a strong historical sense. It was a popular argument; Moses Hess, a Jew, wrote that "We Germans are the most universalist, the most European people in Europe."

background, that of the very precise and technical-minded school of archival research and systematic criticism; they did not much admire highly speculative schemes of history written by philosophers. They agreed with Herder's protest against Kant that "History is the science of what is, not of what possibly may be according to the hidden design of fate." They were content to begin in humble ways and shied away from theory. Yet they broadly shared the fashionable historicism of the day, of which Hegel was the main philosophical spokesman. Leopold von Ranke and his friends among the great German historians of the earlier nineteenth century accepted the notion of a cosmic plan into which all ages and peoples somehow fit. Hence, they felt justified in studying each phase of the past for its own sake. In Ranke's phrase, each is "equidistant from eternity"; each has its part to play in the great pattern and hence deserves to be understood as it is. This amounted to a relativism which refused to impose any yardsticks of valuation, any "presentism" or propaganda on the past. Every part of it had a right of its own to exist. Guizot had said that each age makes its own exact contribution, it does just what it has to do, no more and no less, to help along the grand design. Ranke's equidistance from eternity expressed the same idea, which was Hegel's also. This "Whatever is, is right" doctrine tended to silence all moralistic criticism of the past; whatever it had done, it could not have done otherwise and it had done rightly. It remained only to describe it accurately. Ranke believed in the grand pattern to the extent that at the age of 85 he embarked on his *World History,* for which he assumed his life's labors had been preparing him. The German scholars, then, saw a potential great unity. As its chief constituent parts, they tended to take nationalities and states, implicitly accepting Hegel's view that these were the principal vehicles of historical destiny.

It bears repeating that the philosophical view of history of the German historians and of other European historians who shared this vision actually strengthened their empirical investigation. Often today it is said that the Hegelian system, being abstract and speculative, was opposed to true historical inquiry. But in fact it paved the way for the careful and neutral description of the past by instilling in historians a belief that every part of that past was worthy of being described—not condemned or praised, not judged, not yoked to some present cause, but described. Ranke, who said "equidistant from eternity," also said "describe what actually happened." The two go together. True, a commitment to a priori theories about the past can

warp a historian's judgment, so that he finds what he has set out to
find. This has been so notoriously true of some of the less intelligent
but very enthusiastic followers of that great disciple of Hegel, Karl
Marx, that we tend to think of Hegelian-Marxian thought as the
necessary enemy of honest historical investigation. It need not be so.
Its strong faith that there *is* a pattern in events may operate as a
powerful inducement to study those events with scrupulous care and
try to tell them as they were. Of course, as we realize today, no one
can help bringing to his study of events a mental framework. But in
the era of Ranke and Barthold Niebuhr, philosophy worked to make
historians think they were looking at the past "as it really was," and
this was no bad thing. They had been cured of the vice of seeing the
past entirely through the eyes of the present.

Belief in historical destiny, whatever its dangers, also produced a
keen sense of the dramatic. The most romantic historians, like
Carlyle and Jules Michelet, felt the presence of great forces surging
through history and communicated a tremendous excitement. To
Michelet it was the people as well as the nation who were mighty,
awe-inspiring, sometimes terrible, carrying out the historical mission
to sweep away the old order in the French Revolution. Like all great
events, that one, of course, set in motion whole seas of historical
writing. To Michelet, it was the focal point of human history. The
masses and mobs who made it were in the possession of forces greater
than themselves, forces which they hardly understood. History has a
will of its own; by its "cunning," to use Hegel's word, it uses men as
tools. Such was the creed of the first half of the nineteenth century.

The great thing about the German historians was supposed to be
their methodology. "The Germans have taken the lead in historical
inquiries," Will Ladislaw tells Dorothea in *Middlemarch,* "and they
laugh at results which are got by groping about in woods with a
pocket-compass while they have made good roads." In what consisted
this vaunted German superiority? Was there some secret, or was it
just the infinite capacity for taking pains? The Germans themselves
would have said the latter. They tended to deny that there was any
magic formula, any way of applying standardized tests to the evidence
to determine its value. "That hearsay evidence possesses only as much
validity as the authority from which it derives is just about the only
precept which the critical method can boast of," said the crusty
Theodor Mommsen. Handbooks on historical methods and on the

critical method appeared, but the real gain was simply in getting at the sources and in organizing them so that they could be used. These sources were not only the official and private papers of governments and statesmen, they were also the nonliterary sources. Mommsen organized the Roman inscriptions; and there was the beginning of that great archaeological revolution which dredged up new materials in the ancient Near East. Napoleon's invasion of Egypt began the study of the monuments, inscriptions, and artifacts of that ancient civilization (two hundred scholars accompanied the French troops and brought back numerous objects). A retired German businessman, Heinrich Schliemann, realized his life's dream of digging up ancient Troy. Persian, Assyrian, Babylonian, then Cretan, Hittite discoveries; the deciphering of ancient languages; the finding of relics of pre-historic man—all this was part of the unfolding story of historical craftsmanship. To assemble all the evidence, written and unwritten, and to order it so that it could be made use of was the essence of the new "scientific" methodology. It was not much different from the method Charles Darwin used to establish his theory of the evolution of life. The theory was far from new; Darwin simply brought to it a mass of evidence which attacked the question at every point with over-whelming weight.

HISTORY AS SCIENCE

Perhaps the concern for accuracy, based on bureaucratic organiza-tion and leading to dry monographs, was suitable to a bourgeois and industrial age. We may need to be reminded how surprisingly little men had once valued factual accuracy. In discussing Sir Walter Ralegh's *History of the World,* which the aging Renaissance and Elizabethan adventurer had undertaken in his idle moments of imprisonment in the Tower, Philip Edwards remarks that "the notion of History as a faithful presentation of the events of the past for the reader to find what interpretation and derive what profit he can from them was quite foreign to Renaissance ideas. No historian considered an accumulation of accurate facts as his objective."[3] History was

3. Philip Edward, *Sir Walter Ralegh* (London: Longmans, Green, 1953), pp. 150–51. The notorious carelessness with which premodern historians not only failed to cite their authorities in footnotes but even cribbed whole passages without acknowledgment was not the result of dishonesty but simply of a lack of concern about the exact establishment of fact as such.

rhetoric plundering the past for instigations to present virtue or to action. It had not disturbed Herodotus' great reputation that he was considered to be the father of lies. Even Voltaire, much more careful about his facts—as he cheerfully commented, in an increasingly critical age one just could not get by with making them up—did not imagine that one ought to begin by a systematic effort to uncover all of them. The German scholars with their archives and their seminars and their systematic critical methods represented the trend which August Comte was just then identifying as the basic intellectual revolution of modern times, and to him *the* basic revolution: it was the transition to an age of positivism, to the cult of the fact. Or, otherwise put, the age of Science.

Like Mesopotamia, science was a blessed word in the nineteenth century, and all manner of causes were eager to secure some of its mana. Socialists, campaigning for their essentially religious vision of a better society, claimed that they were scientific. (The Owenites called their meetinghouses Halls of Science before Karl Marx decided that his was the only scientific socialism.) Virtually everybody wanted to be scientific, and it is not surprising that historians did too. They suffered from their failure to mount the sacred pinnacle. Thomas Buckle said flatly that historians were inferior to scientists because no Kepler or Newton had arisen to give them the dignity of all-embracing law. When we examine the innumerable nineteenth- and twentieth-century assertions by historians that they were being or trying to be scientific, we find that in actuality they meant rather different things. Quite often they meant merely being critical or systematic. Frequently they meant no more than that they were getting at the original sources, which, as we know, was an intoxicating discovery of the earlier nineteenth century. But sometimes they claimed to be finding general laws like those of the physical sciences or that they were in some other way uncovering the real pattern of the past. Comte and Marx and Herbert Spencer all thought they had found a plan running through history, a succession of stages or a progression which, having been decoded, revealed not only where mankind had been but where it was headed. Others, more modestly, permitted themselves to hope or believe that solid research done by trained professionals would gradually provide the materials for an eventual science of history, generalization becoming possible when enough indubitable particulars had been accumulated, or, somehow, that the whole house of history would be completed some day when all the bricks were made.

This is not the place to discuss what science is and whether history can ever be scientific. (See the discussion later in this book, pp. 151–166.) We may observe only that when we call a body of thought scientific, we normally mean more than that it is orderly, critical, and systematic; otherwise, both cooking and the compiling of telephone books would be sciences. Moreover, in this sense there is small doubt but that Thucydides, Tacitus, Bede, Machiavelli, Sarpi, and Voltaire were scientific (perhaps without knowing it, like Molière's bourgeois gentleman who found he had been talking prose all his life). We mean by science that knowledge leads to general principles or laws, which can be verified in experiment and enable us to predict, and which are permanent, unchanging, and universal truths. In the nineteenth century a few did so argue for a science of history. They were mostly amateurs and speculative theorists, but not altogether. They tended to derive from August Comte's positivism or to be post-Hegelians like Karl Marx.

Thomas Buckle, an Englishman writing in the 1850s and 1860s, which was very much the positivist generation, argued that whereas history had not yet produced its Kepler and Newton, it could be expected to in the age of science. Intellectual progress does take place, Comteans thought, and in the scale of ascending difficulty sociology (the science of society) comes last, but crowns all. The problem of such a science is more complex but not in principle insuperable. Positivists believed in firmly excluding all except the "hard facts" (we learn not to speculate about God, ultimate reality, first causes, final purposes, because questions about such things are unanswerable); after establishing these facts we detect regularities and relationships. Obviously, they argued, "laws" of predictive value do exist in human affairs. The rate of murder or suicide or divorce or unaddressed letters stays statistically rather constant, enabling forecasts to be made, despite the fact that we can never predict which particular person will kill himself or fail to address a letter.

But most positivists preferred sociology to history (in Comte's terminology, social statics to social dynamics), and few historians could ever really believe that the past repeats itself. Positivism in some ways was quite unhistorical, since it appeared to rely on an unchanging situation rather like the old classical type of history.

Buckle wrote history, but it is hard to see that he carried out the program he announced. The same might be said of Hippolyte Taine, the French historian and critic. Nevertheless, at the end of the century we find Henry Adams, the American historian, disturbed at the failure of history to get anywhere, going back to the hope of discovering great historical laws comparable to those of physics.[4] (He suggested a historical second law of thermodynamics, according to which since the thirteenth century Western civilization had been dispersing its energy.) Positivists were generally stimulating, often proposed interesting but dubious theories, and helped broaden the scope of history by being interested in broad social and economic trends or in intellectual patterns rather than in narrative political history.

It might be possible to classify Herbert Spencer as a positivist. He takes us into the realm of that other exciting nineteenth-century school of thought, the evolutionary or Darwinian school; but Spencer's larger system of social evolution is positivist in that it boldly asserted certain laws of social development to apply to all societies. There were a number of evolutionists who postulated laws of development or principles of change (adaptation) as constant and predictable. This applied more to anthropology than to history, but they linked primitive and civilized man in a single ascending ladder of evolution. Their schemes failed to stand up to the facts, and by the end of the century they had largely perished.[5] The "science" of anthropology remained, as a careful and systematic investigation of various primitive peoples, but it did not find any one ladder of ascent or even any invariable principles of development. It tended to discover that each people is different and can be placed in no scheme of evolutionary ascent.

Darwin's memorable establishment beyond reasonable doubt of the truth of biological evolution—the derivation, by comprehensible processes, of all living species from one or a few simple original species—gave a boost to certain kinds of historical studies. Although Darwin had not discussed the evolution of human societies, others were quick to apply his ideas to that realm. Not only Herbert Spencer

4. "Since Gibbon the spectacle was a scandal. History had lost the sense of shame. It was a hundred years behind the experimental sciences. For all serious purposes it was less instructive than Walter Scott and Alexander Dumas." *The Education of Henry Adams.*
5. It was in connection with a Spencer theory that T. H. Huxley made his memorable remark about "a beautiful theory slain by an ugly fact."

but, in another way, Marx and Engels claimed that they were doing for human social evolution what the great Cambridge biologist had done for the evolution of animal life: showing its exact laws of change, through struggle and adaptation. Apart from such sweeping claims, Darwinism encouraged a genetic approach to all subjects, not least those connected with man's ideas and institutions. In some areas this proved revolutionary. Consider, for example, what Nietzsche called "the genealogy of morals," embodied in a more pedestrian form in such works as E. A. Westermarck's huge *Origin and Development of Moral Ideas* (1906–8). Histories of morality were a frequent late Victorian phenomenon, in which historians such as W. E. H. Lecky joined anthropologists and philosophers. This reflected a naturalistic outlook on matters heretofore thought hardly appropriate for this sort of handling and may fairly be put down to the Darwinian influence. Instead of asserting rational proofs of some moral creed or presenting a new one, thinkers tended to describe and compare existing moral creeds, often on the assumption that this would reveal a scientific ethic, resting on the firm authority of fact. All of human thought, including religion and philosophy, became subject to a genetic, historical approach rather than to a logical, analytical one; thus the consequences of Darwinism greatly extended the range of historical studies. In particular, Darwinists and Marxists raised the question of dealing with ideas and ideals—the intellectual "superstructure"—in a thoroughly naturalistic way.

MARXISM

Historical "laws," comparable to those found by physicists, could conceivably be either (a) common *patterns* of development found in separate peoples, considered as isolated units, such as in Spencer's claim that *all* societies progress from the simple and undifferentiated to the complex and specialized; (b) common *processes* which explain all change, such as the Darwinian and Spencerian adaptation to environmental challenges, which kill off those who do not adapt— the "survival of the fittest" or "natural selection"; or (c) a discernible law of change which runs through the human race considered as one mighty stream or as a single tree. If we consider all history as one process, there obviously cannot be any "laws" in the first sense, or in the physicists' sense, for "If a unique plant lived forever and suffered changes throughout its career we should not be able to formulate any law in regard to its life cycle as a whole" (Morris R. Cohen, *The Meaning of History*). If we attempt to compare a number of different civilizations or societies and find common patterns of growth and decline, as Arnold Toynbee has more recently done (1934–54), we permit the criticism that in fact human civilizations have *not* been isolated from each other like so many different specimens. If we claim that such a principle as "adaptation to the challenge of the physical environment" explains all, we find that different peoples have reacted differently to the same environmental challenge. Obviously, the search for a science of society or history is incredibly complex, if not altogether impossible. In the nineteenth century, Marxism boldly claimed to have found the answer, in a relatively simple form. All societies pass through the same series of stages; the motive force is technological change giving rise to changed economic systems and hence to changed social relationships.

Marx was profoundly influenced by Hegel, under whose influence he studied philosophy (shortly after Hegel's death in 1831) at the University of Berlin. Hegel did not claim to be scientific; he was frankly metaphysical and argued cogently that empiricism always depends on a preliminary framework of thought, which is metaphysical—beyond science. But Marx and others of the "young Hegelians" changed the master's thought without much difficulty into a scientific materialism which kept the providential plan but considered it to be simply what emerges from an empirical, scientific investigation. It has frequently been alleged that Marx illegitimately retained Hegel's speculative system. He kept this nonscientific framework while claiming, purely as an article of faith, that scientific investigation of the facts *does* prove it right. Whatever the legitimacy of it, Marx did maintain that there is a dialectical evolutionary pattern in history and that history is a logical and purposive process. Beginning in primitive communism, it passes through several kinds of class society, from ancient slavery to medieval feudalism to modern capitalism, each marked by the domination of one class and by a typical mode of production, until it ends in the classless society of modern communism, which completes the historical process in a quite ideal society. (It is not altogether clear whether Marx thought this was one great stream or whether there are many human communities, all of which reveal the same pattern. The scheme seems obviously based on the Greek-Roman-Western model, but Marxists later tried to apply it to non-Western civilizations such as China. It appears to fit these much less well.) The motive force is, basically, Hegel's dialectic, transferred from ideas to matter: the eternal motion of things as they oppose and contradict each other. The stress on technological and economic forces reflected the preoccupations of this age of great industrial changes, of the problem of labor and capital—the "Mechanical Age," as Carlyle called it. As socialist or communist, Marx demanded revolutionary alterations in the economic order, and he welded this into the fabric of his historical philosophy.

Only a small minority of practicing historians (which Marx was not, though he wrote about some current episodes of his day) has ever found that the Marxist scheme stands the test of investigation. A recent historian, J. H. Hexter, has remarked that one can make it stand up only by resolutely ignoring three-fourths of the evidence and asking no very bright questions about the rest. But Marx did combine a most dramatic (essentially Romantic) picture of the inexorable destiny of history with a claim to being scientific. Not only that, he seemed to make history relevant by relating it closely to plans for revolutionary action; it provided a guide to that goal of changing the world by which the revolutionary socialist movement was inspired. At its roots lay something as simple as Joachim's medieval vision of the millennium. The science part was a verbal concession to the fashions of Marx's day. It was a thin disguise for an essentially religious vision. As a prophet, Marx may have succeeded; as a scientist, he failed. Yet until very recently, his loyal followers have continued to accept at face value his claim to have deciphered the riddle of history and to have become the Newton of the social sciences.[6]

HISTORY: POPULAR AND PROFESSIONAL

The earlier nineteenth century strewed new ideas and isms in its frantic wake, creating that "generous confusion" of thought which has

6. Recently, in the West, the tendency has been for even Marxists to see Marx as a moral critic of society and to dismiss the scientific façade. Georges Sorel, near the end of the nineteenth century, was among the first to assert that Marx should be seen as the creator of a modern religion. Henry de Man, in the 1920s, related modern socialism to earlier millennial archetypes. Jean-Paul Sartre's existentialized Marxism ignores the main body of Marx's writings entirely in favor of some long unknown earlier writings marked by moral criticism of industrial society, of a sort rather commonplace in romantic writings.

existed ever since. Conservatives, liberals, socialists, romantics, utilitarians, positivists, anarchists, Hegelians, Darwinists, Marxists, and many others competed in the marketplace of ideas. There was no longer any one orthodoxy. Christianity itself was fragmented: Protestants into an ever proliferating number of sects (the Great Revival of the first half of the century created a host of new ones); Roman Catholics into ultramontanists and nationalists, liberals and conservatives, and later modernists and traditionalists. This breakdown of intellectual authority into something like anarchy tended for a time at least to elevate history. Skepticism about all merely intellectual formations may encourage men to lean on history, which embraces them all, and is a sort of hard and indisputable underlying reality. In the eighteenth century, David Hume had reached such a position: we retreat from our vain disputations, all of which end in uncertainty, to take refuge in that solid certainty, the world of men and events which, rooted in custom and nature, goes on with a sort of animal instinct. There was a strong tendency for the Victorians to look to the past as a source of values, not, in the classical way, to find examples of values one already knew, but to discover values which one did not find anywhere else. "By what Man has done, we learn what Man can do, and gauge the power and prospects of our race"—so said Benjamin Disraeli, the statesman, disciple of Burke, and author of romantic novels. Walter Houghton, in his *The Victorian Frame of Mind,* notes how many other Victorian histories supplied heroic deeds and inspiration. Thomas Carlyle and Ralph Waldo Emerson shared this belief that the chief value of writing about the past is to show how great man can be. As critics of a society increasingly commercial and business-minded and devoid of heroism, they felt this the more acutely. Carlyle's "great man" theory of history has often been condemned as a baleful influence on history. It is best seen as a response to the conditions of his own day rather than as an effort to find the right way to interpret the past. Carlyle was a moral critic who found modern man wanting in ideals.

In our stress on the philosophers and the technicians of history, we should not overlook the great *popularity* of historical writing in the nineteenth century, especially in the first two-thirds of the century. Macaulay made the famous boast that he would write a history of England which should "supersede the last fashionable novel on the tables of young ladies," and he succeeded. Carlyle's *French Revolu-*

tion was an equal hit. Others, such as George Grote, Thomas Buckle, W. E. H. Lecky, J. R. Green, and John Morley, carried on this tradition of history which was by no means meretricious or *merely* popular, being written by men who had first-rate minds, excellent pens, and some pretensions to real scholarship, but which was sometimes as eagerly read as a novel by Dickens or Hugo. Perhaps George M. Trevelyan, along with that sometime historian Winston Churchill, have best preserved this style into the twentieth century, although it has decidedly waned. Its authors are better termed men of letters than professional historians. In the United States the most nearly corresponding writers were the classic New Englanders Francis Parkman, William Prescott, John L. Motley, and George Bancroft. France had its Michelets and Guizots and Lamartines, the latter two combining active political careers with their literary work as did Macaulay, Motley, Bancroft, and Morley.

In this connection we cannot overlook the popularity of historical themes with the greater poets and novelists. Robert Browning, Alfred Tennyson, and Matthew Arnold all spent a good part of their inspiration on long narrative poems, which no respectable poet today would dream of doing, Tennyson favoring the Middle Ages and Browning the Renaissance. After the immensely successful Walter Scott, Charles Kingsley and many others satisfied the public appetite for historical novels.[7] John Ruskin made his great literary reputation, which was extended into other fields, in art history: *The Stones of Venice, The Seven Lamps of Architecture.* These last examples are all from England, but the counterparts can be found in other European countries and to some extent in the United States.

The professionals in the British universities—Bishop William Stubbs, Edward Augustus Freeman, Samuel Rawson Gardiner—carried on a sometimes bitter rivalry with these powerful amateurs. James Anthony Froude, mid-Victorian historian of the English

7. Even when they did not choose specifically historical subjects, as in Kingsley's *Hereford the Wake* or *Westward Ho!,* the greater Victorian novelists tried to examine the actual texture of events and of people in society in a basically historical or sociological way. Compare George Eliot's *Middlemarch,* with its effort to plumb the lives of "the number who lived faithfully a hidden life, and rest in unvisited tombs."

The counterpart of medieval hagiography existed in such works as Samuel Smiles's *Self-Help* and *Lives of the Engineers,* and the former was more popular than any novel.

Reformation and the Age of Elizabeth (4 vols., 1856–58), became the center of a violent historians' vendetta, as much for his alleged outrages against the facts as for his unconcealed Protestant bias (Mary Queen of Scots was simply "a bad woman," and Elizabeth herself was guilty of the sin of being insufficiently firm in the Protestant cause). Froude was a vigorous and versatile Victorian with a lively style, a real gift for narrative, and a considerable talent for misreading his sources, though he certainly did consult many. We are inclined to forgive him when we think of him as a man of the world, with many other interests, to whom history was important but was not the only thing. How well it was integrated into the very fabric of nineteenth-century life! Lord Acton, the great liberal Catholic who became Regius Professor of Modern History at Cambridge toward the end of the century, is another example: he was active in the affairs of the Church, editor of magazines, leader of the liberal faction at the great Ecumenical Council of 1870, friend and correspondent of Prime Minister Gladstone, and withal a truly outstanding man of history even if he never quite got around to finishing his major works. Gladstone dabbled in history. German historians also, and even more so, played a large part in political affairs, as leaders of movements or as advisers of statesmen. Thiers followed Guizot in the lineage of French scholar-statesmen, which included Tocqueville. There were innumerable amateurs, men who wrote the classic nineteenth-century works in their spare time. George Grote was a banker; Heinrich Schliemann, the pioneer archaeologist, was a retired businessman; James Ford Rhodes, the American historian, was a retired iron manufacturer.

The professionals, more narrowly academic but also more accurate and painstaking in their work (and usually less biased), increasingly made life difficult for the amateurs. Freeman took careful aim at poor Froude and almost ruined his reputation. The great nineteenth-century amateurs were often so passionately committed that they could not be fair. Froude's extreme Protestant bias was also that of John L. Motley, the American historian of the Dutch revolt, whose massive account votes for the Dutch rebels on every page, as Bancroft's was said to vote for Jackson. (Motley has been corrected by the recent Dutch historian, Pieter Geyl.) Froude and Motley were part of that "Whig interpretation" which saw modern history as the rise of liberty and made liberals out of the early Protestants, a manifest error.

In 1894, when the Regius Professorship of Modern History at Oxford was to be filled, some reacted with horror at the mention of the name of Frederic Harrison. Positivist, political radical, brilliant essayist, man of letters, Harrison admired Carlyle and deplored the trend toward a narrow specialization, in which a major scholar would spend his life mastering "ten years in the fourteenth century." It has since become a familiar complaint. But Harrison was insufficiently expert to meet the requirements. Froude had received the post, despite his professional failings; Harrison did not. (It went to York Powell, whose name few would recognize today.) Professionalism had taken over.

The professionalization of history spread to other nations from Germany in the 1870s and 1880s. In England it is often dated from the appointment of Stubbs at Oxford in 1866; it arrived in France by 1881. The first graduate schools offering specialized training on the German model appeared in the United States in the 1870s.[8] In a memorable passage in the introduction to his *Study of History,* Arnold Toynbee recalled how as a child he watched the books change on the shelves of a distinguished professor whose home he often visited (in the 1890s) from general works to "the relentless advance of half a dozen specialized periodicals" and how he disliked this; how Theodor Mommsen, the great German scholar, wrote *The History of the Roman Republic* (1854–56) in his younger days, but then turned his talent to the editing of inscriptions and the writing of monograph articles published in learned journals. To Toynbee this was the Industrial Revolution advancing on the humanities—a depressing spectacle. He was not alone in greeting this trend with a lack of enthusiasm. A notable holdout, George M. Trevelyan, a nephew of the great Macaulay, wrote in the 1900s with some bitterness that "The public has ceased to watch with any interest the appearance of historical works, good or bad. The *Cambridge Modern History* is indeed bought by the yard to decorate bookshelves, but it is regarded like the *Encyclopaedia Britannica* as a work of reference."[9] The market for public reading was being supplied, he thought, by "prurient journal-

---

8. In Justin Winsor's cooperative *Narrative and Critical History of America,* (1884–1889), only ten of thirty-four of the authors were professors, and only two were professors of history. In the American Nation series, 1904–7, twenty-one of twenty-four were university professors.

9. *Clio: A Muse and Other Essays* (London and New York: Longmans and Green, 1913).

ism," since "serious history is a sacred thing pinnacled afar on frozen heights of science, not to be approached save after a long novitiate." The complaint that historians no longer wrote for the general public, as had Carlyle and Macaulay, but for each other, is a familiar one and has largely continued unabated ever since.

But professionalism was taking over in all walks of life in the nineteenth century. It was the time of the rise of most of the professional classes, representing the increasing division of labor in a growingly complex society. The general education that had so long served Europe, based on close reading of a comparatively small body of classics, which included the great Greek and Roman writings as well as the Bible, was under fire and gradually gave way, though it still constituted the core of an English gentleman's education down to 1914. Specialization meant expertise and gains in competence. It also meant less membership in the general culture and hence loss of contact with the popular mind. Or, to be exact, there had once existed a reading and thinking public, a culture, which was made up of a fairly restricted number of those who had received a liberal education (quite a small number in Victorian England, compared to the total population), but which had unity and cohesiveness. They had not only learned the same things but had even gone to the same schools. (Oxford and Cambridge remained the only two universities of social distinction, though new ones such as the Benthamite University of London were rising. By and large, the English utilitarians, followers of Jeremy Bentham, showed much more interest in economics and sociology than in history.)[10] This general culture was now threatened both by the coming of professionalism and educational specialization and by the rise to prominence of a genuinely popular culture, a mass culture, which lacked roots in any traditions and was fed by the gutter journalism of the yellow press. This was a cultural crisis which affected all of intellectual life.

But the gains from expertness should not be minimized. Toynbee

10. Bentham was too much an absolutist rationalist to be guided by history, though he used it, exemplar-fashion, as a storehouse of edifying examples of reform. John Stuart Mill, the leading Bentham disciple, rejected Hegel but adopted Comte, and could praise "that series of great writers and thinkers from Herder to Michelet, by whom history, which was till then 'a tale told by an idiot, full of sound and fury, signifying nothing,' has been made a science of cause and effect." But Mill embraced sociology at the expense of history in the long run, like most positivists.

expressed dismay at Mommsen's turning from a broad interpretation of Roman history to the editing of inscriptions. Today these collections of inscriptions are a vital part of the equipment of every historian of the Roman era, and it is hardly too much to say that they revolutionized the field by adding a large and well-organized body of information to the meager literary sources surviving from ancient times. Most historians regard this solid addition to knowledge as a finer achievement of Mommsen's than his somewhat subjective and perhaps dubious interpretation of the Roman Republic (which included a strong admiration for Caesar as dictator and imperialist). One can go on forever spinning interpretations of the past out of one's prejudices and imagination, and there is really nothing to choose between interpretations on any rational grounds. But to add some real knowledge, where none existed before, which will last forever afterward and be used by all future historians: is this not a worthier thing?

FIN DE SIÈCLE

We have tried to set forth some of the leading themes in nineteenth-century history. But there was so much of it that this is almost impossible. It is also difficult because the nineteenth century was such a diffuse and many-sided era. It produced a bewildering variety of ideologies. There is a socialist tradition in historiography, which includes notable works on the French Revolution by such great French socialist intellectuals as Louis Blanc and Jean Jaurès (a tradition carried on into the twentieth century by Albert Mathiez), as well as works by the Germans of the Marxist school: for example, Karl Kautsky wrote some interesting history. The English Fabian Socialists fell back on history after having rejected the a priori economic theories of Ricardo and Marx; when they found these rationalistic "proofs" of human exploitation faulty, they appealed to the simple facts of the case. Sidney and Beatrice Webb wrote histories of the trade unions, local government, and social welfare; Charles Booth wrote his monumental history of life and labor in the city of London from the position of an earnest social reformer. In Germany the "socialists of the chair" led by Gustav Schmoller similarly converted theoretical economics into institutional or historical economics.

There is also what Herbert Butterfield has called the Whig Tradition (see his *The Whig Interpretation of History,* a popular essay in the ideological presuppositions of history), which was an interpretation of modern history as the story of the winning of liberty from tyrants. From Macaulay to Charles Trevelyan to George Trevelyan there was carried on an outlook which the Puritans and Whigs had begun in the seventeenth century. John Bright read Hallam aloud to his wife. John Vincent, historian of the Liberal party, observes that "The real compass of thought uniting the middle class, or the Liberal section of it, was . . . a view or recollection of English History." This powerful political tradition, that of nineteenth-century middle-class liberalism, thus rested at bottom on a certain set of ideas about history, pointing toward the destined triumph of civil liberty and constitutional government through long courses of evolution.

Those who reacted against modern liberalism and socialism also entered the lists. The French Revolution was a battleground between republicans and monarchists all through the century in France. In England the Whig interpretation never had the field to itself, though its works were the more brilliant. A now forgotten *History of Europe,* written in the 1830s by Archibald Alison, a Scottish lawyer and sheriff, sought voluminously to prove, as Disraeli said, that God was on the side of the Tories. It may be said in summation that everybody tried to show by writing history that God, as revealed in the historical process, was on the side of his party or cause.

Lord Acton and Professor Döllinger of Munich tried to establish Roman Catholic theology on the basis of historical development. Research in biblical history stirred up that tremendous row over what was called the higher criticism, which shook all churches in the last decades of the century, raising fundamental questions about the literal truth of events related in the sacred books of Jews and Christians.

The fact that no movement or creed or intellectual position was without its historical writings suggests the enormous authority men felt to be invested in history in the nineteenth century. It also suggests that an inevitable weakening of that authority was bound to take place in time. Could history really support so many different causes and positions? There is a gradual growth throughout the century of the skeptical view, already expressed by Napoleon: history is a set of lies agreed upon *(une fable convenue).* In 1864, Froude expressed it as follows:

It often seems to me as if History was like a child's box of letters, with which we can spell any word we please. We have only to pick out such letters as we want, arrange them as we like, and say nothing about those which do not suit our purpose.[11]

It is true that Voltaire had said something similar a century earlier. Yet we know how potent the conviction had been that history is one thing and can be found out scientifically, that it is orderly, logical, and purposive, and hence will reveal to us not only exactly where we have been but even where we are going. "It is not I to whom you are listening, it is history itself that speaks," Fustel de Coulanges told his enraptured audience. Writing in 1887 in the *North American Review,* Gladstone declared that "complex and diversified as it is, history is not a mere congeries of disjointed occurrences, but is the evolution of a purpose steadfastly maintained, and advancing towards some consummation." The faith in historic order, purpose, and knowability filled the nineteenth century. At least it filled the first half of that century, which has often seemed to be very different from the latter half: the first half was optimistic, enthusiastic, a bit naïve, somewhat confused but brimming over with vast projects for wholesale reform, full of messianic hopes and dreams; the second half (with the revolutions of 1848 forming a major boundary line) was growing disenchanted, weary, realistic, skeptical, and even decadent—a time of alienated artists and cynical politicians. Like all sweeping historical judgments, this one does not entirely hold up, but there is much truth in it, especially so far as concerns continental Europe.

The element of bias in "scientific" history was rather sorrowfully revealed in 1870 at the time of the Franco-Prussian War, when the big guns of both countries—Fustel de Coulanges leading the French, Mommsen the Germans—lined up to a man on the side of their own country. The French made history prove irrefutably that Alsace was French; the Germans, that it was German. Such episodes doubtless made it increasingly difficult to believe that history itself spoke through even the well-trained historian. Whose history? At this time, of course, currents of thought coursed through Western civilization which induced a greater skepticism in general. Marxists were saying that all thought is class conditioned (except of course Marxist, which was excepted from the rule): bourgeois historians, they held, give us only cleverly disguised propaganda for capitalism, whatever their advertised pretensions to scientific objectivity. Darwinism led to the

11. "The Science of History," in *Short Studies on Great Subjects,* reprinted 1967 by Cornell University Press.

view that all knowledge serves the purpose of adaptation in order to survive, a profoundly naturalistic vision which, in the hands of a Nietzsche, undercut the claims of any thought to be outside the power struggle of life. Furious historical controversy was going on not only between nations and between classes but in the religious debate about the higher criticism which broke out in the last two decades of the century. It cannot be said, of course, that historiography had ever been without controversy. Yet, in an age when science was performing so many other miracles, the claims of scientific and professional historiography to be at last attaining the goal of ending such controversy and finding the Truth had been given credence. Now these claims were seen to be dubious. The scientific professionals were themselves bitterly at odds when it came to anything that mattered!

A glimpse of one *fin de siècle* historian would not then be amiss in concluding this chapter. Jacob Burckhardt, the Swiss historian of the Italian Renaissance and of ancient times *(The Age of Constantine)* published his *The Civilization of the Renaissance in Italy* as early as 1860, but it did not receive recognition as a classic until the 1890s. It coincided with the vogue for other Renaissance studies, such as the work of Walter Pater, which became virtually a manifesto of the esthetic movement of the 1880s and 1890s, in what was manifestly a desire to escape from the modern age. The rejection of an ugly and materialistic society was extremely apparent in this fastidious stylist, who withdrew to the quiet backwater of the old city of Basel to teach and write—a city rich in humanistic traditions (Erasmus had worked there) and somehow apart from the modern world of industry and democracy and nationalism. Burckhardt was disillusioned with these modern ideals, which represented to him a debasement of culture. In imagination he would return to the aristocratic Italian Renaissance, which was saturated in art and made an art of life itself. Burckhardt was a student of Ranke and a thorough professional in his research methods. He differed from most of the Rankean school in caring less for politics than for culture and in seeing far less progress in human affairs. Politics, in an age of ugly Bismarckian nationalism and, to Burckhardt, an equally ugly plebeian democracy, had turned sour, and he could not believe that this Europe of belching smokestacks, yellow-press-fed masses, and tasteless bourgeois society was an improvement on the past. He conceived of the historian's task in a new age of barbarism to be that of keeping alive the vivid image of other, more civilized times. Development plays relatively little part in Burckhardt's historical work. He strove to depict a civilization or culture at its one ideal moment of completion. A mature civilization such as that of the Italian cities in the age of the Renaissance had to be a whole, a unity, as was Athenian culture in its golden age of antiquity. To paint the portrait of such a high civilization is to create a work of art as well as scholarship. It involves careful selection of materials, and one must first steep oneself laboriously in the best sources, as Burckhardt told his students, in order to get a feeling for the period and an awareness of what is typical. But the writing of the book demands above all a gift of style and an artistic imagination.

Burckhardt came close to carrying out Voltaire's program for a *Kulturgeschichte,* and he inspired others to do the same after him (Karl Lamprecht and J. H. Huizinga among others). Another aspect of Burckhardt's modernity is his awareness of how subjective such portraits are. He was aware that someone else would see it differently:

To each eye the outlines of a given civilization probably present a different picture. . . . On the vast ocean upon which we venture, the possible ways and directions are many; and the same studies that have served for this work might easily, in other hands, not only receive a wholly different treatment and interpretation, but might also lead to essentially different conclusions.

Reaching this level of sophistication about the process of historical creation—that it is an art, not a science, highly subjective, its truths relative—we have reached the end of one age of history and the beginning of another.

Ernest Renan, the post-Comtean French positivist and higher critic who was a major literary figure of the later nineteenth century and who shared to the fullest his century's interest in history, tried to use the past as a bulwark against skepticism and declining faith. He looked to it to provide values. Like Matthew Arnold, he would go forth into the past to find and cull from it the best that men have thought and said and done. He would cure modern skepticism by a recourse to history. But this quest was bound to fail, for we cannot make the events of history yield values any more than any other events. We may place a valuation on them; they themselves are simply there. History itself does not really vote for either Brutus or Caesar, Protestants or Catholics, Whigs or Tories. Realization of this great fact was bound to come, and when it did come our conception of history was bound to change. Twentieth-century historical writing has largely fallen under the influence of this relativism.

*C*hapter 6

HISTORY IN OUR OWN TIME: THE TWENTIETH CENTURY

THE NEW VIEWS OF HISTORY

Our discussion of the more recent trends in historiography might begin by reflecting that historical writing has always been susceptible to the influence of general ideas in the surrounding atmosphere of the age. Historians require a structure of ideas which they use to select and group their empirically discovered facts. They readily take on the coloration of their times. In a romantic epoch they wrote romantic history; in a nationalistic one, nationalistic history. They were often stimulated by the theories of a Marx or a Comte, but when disenchantment set in history could, with Burckhardt, point to the ivory tower.

The realization of the flexibility of history—of its tendency to reflect the climate of opinion of an age—has undoubtedly been one of the leading discoveries of modern historical thought. It gives rise to a tendency to talk, not about history, but about historians, and to be aware of the influences coming from outside the historical profession itself. It is a theme to which we will return. By way of entry into the rich profusion of this century, so violent, so disturbed, and so brilliant, we may observe that at the turn of the century historians found themselves stimulated by a striking group of social theorists and sociologists, including Emile Durkheim, Max Weber, Vilfredo Pareto, and Thorstein Veblen. It was the great age of sociology. This group considerably refined the crude generalizations of Marx, Comte, and Spencer while retaining large powers of generalization. They were learned as well as analytical. To the sociologists were added the new psychologists, Sigmund Freud and Carl Jung, who have so deeply influenced modern man's vision of himself and society. A new kind of political science, influenced by psychology and sociology, appeared in such works as Graham Wallas' *Human Nature in Politics,* in Weber's writings on the modes of political domination, in M. Ostrogorski's and Robert Michels' realistic studies of political parties, and in Veblen's analysis of class social psychology. These were exciting years for social theory. It offered the historian conceptual tools and significant insights into human motivations. Sometimes suspicious of sociology because some sociologists tried to dismiss the historical dimension as unimportant, most historians became aware of how much they might benefit from sociological concepts. At any rate, the influence of such concepts, coming from other social or "behavioristic" sciences, is beyond question. Historians such as R. H. Tawney in his *Religion and the Rise of Capitalism* directly followed up suggestions from Max Weber about the "sociology of knowledge." In the United States a "cultural approach to history" emerged in the 1930s as a self-conscious "school." Charles A. Beard was influenced by Loria, the Italian social theorist. The important French school, grouped around Lucien Febvre and Marc Bloch, in the journal *Annales d'histoire économique et sociale,*[1] dedicated itself to a new kind of social history influenced by the other social sciences. These are only examples.

Sociology and Freudian psychology were not the only new dimensions in thought. Friedrich Nietzsche, William James, and Henri Bergson brilliantly ushered in a new era of philosophy, post-Hegelian and post-Darwinist. Then came World War I, which overturned the whole physical and moral universe of the modern world. We still live in the aftermath of the two world wars, the totalitarian revolutions, the political convulsions resulting from the wars. Some historians turned pessimist and inquired into the decline of the West; most ideas of progress seemed dead beyond recall. This was especially true in Europe; it was less so in the United States, perhaps, until quite recently.

Historical writing would, then, bear the marks of all these revolutions, in thought and in deed. It will be as difficult to give a coherent account of it as it is to give an account of the twentieth century itself: the sheer quantity of writing and the incredible accumulation of

1. Founded 1929; now titled simply *Annales,* with subtitle *Economies, Sociétés, Civilisations.* It has continued to exert a strong influence on French history.

knowledge were far greater in terms of number, than that of any earlier period—beyond all comparison. Writing at the end of the nineteenth century, the American historian Henry Adams, addicted to the view that Western civilization was exploding in fragments at an ever accelerating rate, calculated that by 1921 it would have ceased to exist. Perhaps he was right. Perhaps it is no longer possible to give an account of an age, a century. Perhaps we have only the particles of a shattered culture. But history has preserved its vitality and its popularity, if not its unity, in this frightening but fascinating contemporary world. Like the age itself, it has shown a constant effort to try to revolutionize itself.

American historiography in the first two decades of this century went through a revolt aimed primarily at the older Germanic, Rankean school of history, which had powerfully influenced American historiography in its initial stages of professional development (for example at Johns Hopkins University and Columbia University, important centers of graduate study). The revolt was against the subject matter of this school, which was chiefly political and constitutional; against its hostility to present-mindedness, made into a reproach for being, as we might say, not relevant enough; and against its colorless or just-as-it-happened ideals of perfect objectivity. Perhaps the revolt was rather more marked in the United States than in Europe because of the depths of sheer tedium reached when somewhat uninspired American minds turned their attention to writing without emotional commitment about subjects remote from American interests. The revolt was mingled with a cry from the West that this historical work looked too much to Europe and was too much a product of an Atlantic Coast culture which no longer represented the center of gravity in the expanding nation. Indeed, Frederick Jackson Turner was, by all accounts, its originator, when he raised the cry in the 1890s that the western frontier was a more significant place to look for American political institutions than the European Middle Ages and that American culture owed little to Europe but was an indigenous product of a unique American experience. At the same time, in a rather positivist manner, Turner sought to direct attention to broader social and economic factors and also to local or regional history. The frontier was at times more interesting to Turner as sociological process than as historical narrative. John B. McMaster, and in England John Richard Green, had somewhat earlier sought to protest against the Rankean dictum of E. A. Freeman that "History is past politics." Green announced rhetorically that he intended to spend more time on Chaucer than on Crècy, on Queen Elizabeth's poor laws than on her battles, on the Methodist revival than on the escape of the Young Pretender. But he, like McMaster, was something of an amateur—interesting, but writing, as Carl L. Becker once wickedly said of someone, "without fear and without research"— relatively. Turner was a thorough professional, trained in the methods of the Hopkins seminar, but asking that this skill be directed to American themes.

The Turner revolt, which caused a considerable stir in American historical circles, was followed by the Beard revolt and the Robinson revolt. James Harvey Robinson became identified with what was called in the United States in the 1910s the New History, which was marked by a stronger reaction against political history in favor of social history and for more relevance or present-mindedness, conceived rather vaguely as helping to bring about progressive social and political goals. This did not prove very productive, and Robinson could be accused of a good deal of superficiality. But the instinct to escape from the clutches of a historiographical tradition considered to be both narrow and arid was strong. Charles A. Beard's wide-ranging mind received influences from European economists and socialists. His much-discussed *Economic Interpretation of the Constitution* (1913) called attention to economic and class aspects of the political process in a way Americans found quite exciting, and his many other writings revealed a gifted pen and a restless, curious intellect. Beard subsequently wrote some essays—"That Noble Dream" and "Written History as an Act of Faith," essays often reprinted—in colorful and persuasive style if with somewhat loose logic, attacking the idea of Rankean objectivity as he conceived it. These writings probably acquainted most Americans for the first time with that growing feeling of the subjectivity and relativity of historical writing which we have already mentioned. Faced with an inadequacy of evidence (we can never know anything like *all* of the past) and the inability to deal with this evidence in anything like a scientific way (it cannot be manipulated or experimented with), and aware also of his own position as a relative observer stationed at a certain time and place, the historian must know that he is biased and that tomorrow another work will replace his. Each generation must rewrite history, making its own terms with the past. "The pallor of waning time, if not of death," Beard wrote in his picturesque style, "rests upon the latest volume of history, fresh from the roaring press." History, one may say, is a tool we use each generation or each year to help get along in the world, discarding the old tool for a new one whenever necessary.

The similarity of such ideas to those of the great American philosophers of this generation, William James and John Dewey, has caused them to be labeled "the pragmatic revolt in American History," with which very imprecise string one may in some ways tie Turner, Beard, and the new history together. The influential American historian Carl L. Becker, who wrote a good deal on the nature of history itself, also was fond of pointing to climates of opinion, to the relativity of all historical thought, to the need for frank acceptance of the point that "Every generation . . . must inevitably play on the dead whatever tricks it finds necessary for its own peace of mind." Perhaps this doctrine enabled men like Beard and Robinson, who belonged frankly to the progressive side in the political controversies of the day, to indulge their bias with less sense of professional guilt. In Britain, there were Socialist historians, not only the Webbs but also such distinguished professionals as Tawney and the husband-and-wife team of J. L. and Barbara Hammond, who managed to combine academic respectability with a frank commitment to a left-wing political cause. (Not that the Hammonds' account of the Industrial Revolution escaped severe criticism from other economic historians.) Since then, American historians in particular have shown a tendency to present themselves unblushingly as political partisans. (We have a current group calling themselves "radical historians," meaning, it seems, more than that they propose to adopt unusual methods.)

These somewhat novel approaches to history commanded widespread acceptance, yet also aroused considerable opposition and a certain uncomfortable feeling. It has come to seem too obvious to require much debate that the historian *does* bring to his work a mental framework which in part determines the structure of his books. As the French historian H. I. Marrou has put it, "the past cannot be isolated in a pure state and grasped in any isolated manner; it is fused into an insoluble mixture into which enters the reality of the past, its 'objective' reality, but also the present reality of the active thought of the historian who is seeking to re-create the past."

Not only in legend but also in veritable history as well there is unmistakably something personal or subjective which is woven into the events described and is recognized by the intelligent reader as a prejudice or a point of view or a supporting mental substructure. Even when history is composed with the most wholehearted submission to the evidence, aspiring, according to the demands of some of its most recent hierophants, to a coldly scientific attitude towards its material, the ideal is never realized. For, when the mastery of the evidence has been effected, it must, in order to be converted into a history, be shaped in the mind of the investigator; and in that process it will inevitably acquire something of the form and color of the vessel in which it was prepared. Moreover, this personal contribution is not personal in the sense of being wholly original with the chronicler or historian under consideration. As an ephemeral and, let us add, an eminently social creature, he is the child of his environment and exhibits innumerable earmarks indicative of his particular time and place. It is for this reason we are obliged to inquire with regard to every history that comes into our hands: Who wrote it? When and where did the writer live? With what particular outlook or religion or philosophy did he face the problems of history and of life? And we shall invariably find that the answers to these questions defining the historian's individuality enter, though not regularly in the same degree, into works passing as histories. They may have been composed with the most devoted attention to the facts, but the facts on getting themselves ordered in a logical or a chronological series have had something extraneous imposed on them, something that is not native to them as mere facts. Call this addition form, mind, interpretation—there it is! He who lacks the skill or penetration to detect this often hidden agent with its quiet manipulation and directive comment, he who reads history, any history, as if it were something impersonal communicating an absolute and final truth has never reflected on the necessary limitations of this department of literature and is likely in the end to take from it more injury than profit.[2]

The point so beautifully expressed above by Professor Schevill has become a truism among historians; it is still likely to come as a surprise or a revelation to the neophyte approaching history for the first time. He does, naïvely but naturally, suppose that what he reads in an imposing book, replete with footnotes, written by a learned professor, is truth; or he may even suppose that what he reads in a not so imposing book written by a man without a Ph.D., if it seems intelligent and plausible, is truth. A fuller development of these issues will be postponed to Chapter 11, on objectivity and value.

2. Ferdinand Schevill, *History of Florence* (New York: Harcourt, Brace, 1936), pp. xiv–xv. Reprinted by permission of James Schevill.

Objections to the pragmatist-relativist-subjectivist outlook as conveyed by Beard and Becker took several forms. Some historians, like the neophytes, shied off from it instinctively. There were survivals of older views. In his 1923 presidential address to the American Historical Association, Edward P. Cheyney reaffirmed his belief that historians were scientists engaged like other scientists in finding laws. So important a figure as Arnold Toynbee has supported this position. Absolutist positions such as Marxism held to a faith which could not be shaken by such "bourgeois" waverings. Others felt that relativism reduces the historian to a propagandist pretentiously crusading for whatever cause is momentarily popular and that present-mindedness is, after all, a danger to the proper understanding of the past.

Such substantive issues are not dealt with in this section of this book. Here we record the presence of such debates as a significant part of twentieth-century historiography. Meanwhile, from another direction came a viewpoint which proved to be more than a little helpful to historians in finding a way out of the dilemma. This viewpoint had probably originated in Germany in the later nineteenth century chiefly with Wilhelm Dilthey and in Italy with the outstanding philosopher Benedetto Croce; it was represented in the English world by the brilliant philosopher-historian R. G. Collingwood (*The Idea of History,* 1946).

In many ways this Dilthey-Croce-Collingwood school, as we might call it (ignoring certain minor differences among its chief exponents), agreed with the relativists. It declared that history is present knowledge, which must and does spring from current interests; it is "contemporary thought about the past." Also, we do not find just one truth about the past; there are innumerable truths—as many as there are perspectives. We do not, as Ranke thought, apprehend *the* past "exactly as it was"; we see different pasts at different times, and what we see depends on our present situation. For positivist history, which he held to be the sort that seeks "facts" about the past and then tries to arrange these facts in order to reach generalizations, Collingwood entertained much scorn. Leaning on Vico, whom Croce as a fellow Neapolitan was particularly in a position to expound, and whom indeed he recovered from obscurity for most non-Italians, this school stressed the knowability of the past by means of intuition and historical imagination: because those who lived in the past were people like ourselves, with minds basically similar to our own, we can feel our way into their situation and rethink their thoughts. This must be done with the aid of careful research; the Croceans would agree with Burckhardt that only after long, careful study of, and much critical reflection on, the sources, can one's historical imagination be brought into play. But essentially the goal is to enable ourselves as historians to get inside past minds so that we can virtually experience again their thoughts. The tag of idealist or neo-idealist has been placed on this school because of its stress on historical knowledge as knowledge of past mental states.

Some might object to this idealism, though it means no more than historians normally take for granted when they try to answer questions about motives, as they often do (what was in Hitler's mind when he threatened Czechoslovakia?) or seek to give a feeling for some former age (what was it like to be a medieval monk?).[3] But the Croce-Collingwood influence has been helpful to historians because of its stress on the autonomy and worth of historical studies and because of its clarification of the scientist versus nonscientist issue. History is a science, since it relies on the systematic collection of evidence and on rigorous criticism of that evidence. It is not at all a science like the physical sciences. It is the science of the particular, seeking to understand some one thing in all its inwardness and uniqueness. The natural scientist usually seeks to draw general laws or principles from the external observation of many particulars. The historical scientist seeks knowledge of the particular by getting *inside* it. (If a zoologist did this, he would try to learn what it is like to be an animal, that is, how it feels to be that animal.) History is a special kind of science. As such, it has dignity and importance. It is not a failed attempt at a science on the model of physical science; neither is it a branch of literature. It is the science which understands the past, by its own special methods, in order to illuminate the present.

Croce's school tied this conception of history to a general philosophy which was a new kind of historicism. (Sometimes this is *the* definition given to the word, which has caused some confusion.[4]) There is no "final philosophy"; all thought is relative to its time and

3. It is undoubtedly true that historians had in fact aimed at such goals long before Dilthey and Collingwood told them they should. For example, a letter of Hippolyte Taine to Alexandre Dumas, May 23, 1878, speaks of the "applied psychology" with which he sought in his history of the French Revolution to get at the *mental state* of a Jacobin. And Taine is often thought of as a positivist.

4. See Dwight E. Lee and R. N. Beck, "The Meaning of Historicism," *American Historical Review* (April, 1954), and Calvin G. Rand, "Two Meanings of Historicism," *Journal of the History of Ideas* (October–December, 1964).

place. Every intellectual construction, Croce wrote, is "sufficient for the day . . . but not sufficient for tomorrow, when it must be refreshed or reformed." All thought takes place in a historical context. The ultimate reality is only history, then; in the last analysis, we can say of any idea only that it was an idea which came to light at such-and-such a time under such-and-such conditions. If history must be rewritten by each generation, so must all other branches of thought, it appears. There is no ultimate standard of validity, at least for political and social and esthetic judgments. A thought "escaping history" would be like a man climbing out of his own skin. Thought, like skin, is the matrix in which mankind lives. If a movement arose to denounce history as dangerous and false and to attempt to banish it from intellectual life, this movement too would be a historical fact which historians would record and it would be explained as a characteristic of the period. The reaction against history is a part of history! God, or some absolute intelligence, seeing the whole stupendous unity of things, may be able to render final judgment, but men never can. So the study of thought becomes the study of the history of thought. Croce's historicism differed from Hegel's in finding more freedom and less determinism in history and in being far less dogmatic; but it agreed that philosophy is history, if not that history is philosophy in Hegel's sense.

HISTORY AND TWENTIETH-CENTURY EVENTS

Collingwood was virtually the only British philosopher to take a serious and sustained interest in the theory of history until about 1950; since then, interest in it, which largely stems from his work, has considerably expanded. Left to their own devices, historians are seldom very theoretical or philosophical. As a group, they are inclined to be robust and active-minded, not very subtle; as Marc Bloch commented in his book on *The Historian's Craft,* they love life and like to be involved in it. More sensitive, introspective, and intellectual types are likely to be attracted by literature; intensely analytical minds will gravitate toward philosophy or the more theoretical sciences. Historians are not usually comfortable when theorizing about their work; they prefer to *do* it, plunging in with energy, determination, and a rough-and-ready empiricism. Unquestionably, they *should* reflect more on the nature of their task, and they have been doing more of it lately. Most of them agree that they ought to know more about the other social and human sciences, but in fact the huge expansion of specialized knowledge in all fields, with the accompanying tendency for each discipline to become a separate world, has probably lessened rather than increased contact between scholars working on different subjects. Probably, historical work has been influenced more by the events of this century than by philosophical ideas or other intellectual formulations. The latter come through rather slowly. One sometimes has the impression that Freud, whom nearly everyone has known about for at least forty years and who is now rather old-fashioned and discredited in advanced circles, has just recently dawned on the awareness of historians. Many examples exist of historians making use of the leading ideas of this century (Toynbee was influenced by some of Jung and of Bergson, the French *Annalists* by Bergson), but hardly in any consistent way.

The events of the century obviously influenced historians in choice of subject matter; how many thousands of volumes have been written on the two world wars, on the development of the Soviet Union, on the rise and fall of Hitler's state! Vast, dramatic, and tragic action has marked this century and has stimulated historical research, which has tended to increase. The number of volumes on World War II is many times greater than that on World War I, though the latter was probably the more interesting and dramatic war. In World War II, governments subsidized huge official historical projects; the published United States Army History of World War II, written by trained scholars, alone runs to more than ninety volumes. We live in an age of bigness; one result has been institutionalized research. One of the greatest twentieth-century historians, Sir Lewis Namier, came to believe that only a team effort could meet the needs of the modern historian, who is confronted with staggering and ever increasing amounts of material. Modern technology enables a great deal more in the way of documentary evidence to be preserved. Microfilming techniques can store and transmit it. The technological revolution confronts the individual historian with *too much* material.

It can be no part of the task of a short outline of the development of historical studies to itemize particular controversies, but the long inquest into the origins or causes or "responsibility" for the 1914 tragedy may be singled out. It exhibited a pattern not unlike that of the Reformation or Puritan Revolution or other passionate debates of history. In 1914 the German historians to a man defended the rightness of their country and placed the blame for the war on the

Allied powers; the reverse was true in the Allied countries. Along
with practically everyone else, historians eagerly rallied to support
the war with their pens, issuing manifestos, creating documentary
evidence of the enemy's war guilt and war atrocities, and doing other
propaganda work. There were very few exceptions (one thinks of
the English scholar G. Lowes Dickinson among others). Historical
"objectivity" completely broke down in the face of this massive con-
test of nations. Later, however, an irenic trend set in. A huge post-
mortem conducted after the war with the aid of a good deal more
documentation (though in fact the additional documentation does not
seem to have been the decisive factor)[5] tended to acquit each side of
deliberate aggression in 1914. It also exposed war propaganda and
accused historians of betrayal of the canons of the profession. To
some extent, historical research played the role of peacemaker in the
1920s and early 1930s; but when World War II again ranged an
aggressive Germany against the Western democracies, some historians
reversed themselves again and decided that Germany, since she was
guilty in 1939, must have also been guilty in 1914. It cannot be said
that history came out of all this with much credit. Immense historical
labors were performed; many interesting and learned books were
written; an absorbing debate went on. Was anything really proved,
except that historians are more elaborately prejudiced than other
people? One must hope so, but there are doubts. For in this debate
it became evident that no amount of factual evidence could decide
an issue which depended at bottom on value judgments brought in
from outside and applied to the evidence.

Those Marxist historians who worked for the cause of the USSR
after 1918 and those historians who stayed in Nazi Germany after
1933 (to the honor of the profession, many did not—a vast exodus
which enriched and often much changed Anglo-American intellectual
life)[6] freely accepted the guidance of history by political ideology.
History was frankly to be considered propaganda; it was to serve
Soviet communism or the Nazi state, respectively. Needless to say,

5. Dickinson's "revisionist" arguments, presented during the war, did not differ
much from those brought forward in the 1920s and 1930s. The important factor
was a sharp change in attitude because of extreme postwar disenchantment with
the war in the Allied countries.
    6. The extent of this debt may be judged from a sampling of these names, all
refugees from Nazi Germany or Austria: Karl Popper, Karl Mannheim, Werner
Jaeger, Hans Baron, Paul Kristeller, Leo Strauss, Erwin Panofsky, Rudolf Carnap,
Eric Auerbach.

historians were not alone in this state of subservience. German scientists, such as the Nobel Prize winner Johannes Stark, declared that "even for the scientist, the duty to the nation stands above any and all other obligations. . . . In his work he must serve the nation first and foremost." He approved a National Socialist science to be distinguished from Jewish and international science,[7] and it was on this basis that German scientists rejected Einstein's theories. On this basis, too, the Russians revised their history textbooks from year to year depending on the tactical needs of the moment, whether it meant removing Trotsky from the Russian Revolution or speaking more favorably of the Nazis (1939–41) or playing up patriotism during the war. They did this quite candidly, believing that, in Lenin's formula, whatever serves the cause of the revolution (Communist party; Soviet Union) is justified, a principle derived from Marx's view that all knowledge serves either one side or the other in the class struggle.

Amid these depressing twentieth-century developments—frightful wars, totalitarian dictatorships, mass murder—the idea of general progress expired. In John T. Marcus' phrase, one witnessed "the collapse of redemptive historicity." It was no longer possible for thinking persons to believe that mankind was fulfilled in history. The postwar years after 1919 produced a chorus of formal renunciation of such beliefs, which had been so firmly held before 1914. The poet Ezra Pound put it in a line: Western civilization was "an old bitch gone in the teeth." The Russian philosopher-theologian N. Berdyaev wrote in 1923 *(The Meaning of History)* that "Man's historical experience has been one of steady failure, and there are no grounds for supposing that it will ever be anything else." According to the new versions of Judaism and Christianity, the old "liberal" theology, which had almost fully accepted Hegel's view of redemption through history, was an illusion and an abomination. It is an illusion, Reinhold Niebuhr wrote, that "growth fulfilled the meaning of life, and redeemed it of its ills and errors."[8] The new "crisis" or "dialectical" theology, dominant in Germany and found widely throughout the West from 1920 until very recently, was headed by Karl Barth, closely followed by such philosophers as Rudolf Bultmann, Emil

7. See George L. Mosse, *Nazi Culture* (New York: Grosset and Dunlap, 1966), pp. 205 ff.
8. *Faith and History: A Comparison of Christian and Modern Views of History* (New York: Scribner's, 1949), p. 69.

Brunner, Reinhold Niebuhr, and Paul Tillich. They all were concerned to make the point that there is no clear meaning discernible in history, for men cannot read God's purposes, which may require evil and destruction at any time on earth, and so history must often appear broken and terrible to men. A significant number of historians professed to see no sense or order whatever in the past—a return to Voltaire's view, and parallel to the blind, cruel chance displayed in the naturalist novels of Thomas Hardy and Emile Zola.

"Men wiser and more learned than I have discerned in history a plot, a rhythm, a predetermined pattern," wrote H. A. L. Fisher, in words Arnold Toynbee took as a challenge. "These harmonies are concealed from me. I can see only one emergency following upon another as wave follows upon wave . . . ; the play of the contingent and the unforeseen." Michael Oakeshott has declared that the historian loves Clio precisely because she is so capricious, "a mistress of whom he never tires, and whom he never expects to talk sense."[9] The brightly colored past, as Apollinaire called it, more real than the dull present, can be a source of amusement and amazement, a refuge from the present, an astounding spectacle—it can fascinate, even if one gives up the idea that it has meaning and purpose. But can such a justification for history really promote it to the top rank in the realm of knowledge? Can the golden age of history survive the destruction of the idea of progress?

Perhaps the most ambitious answer to this challenge to the worth of history was provided by those historians who accepted the fact of the decline of civilization and sought to account for it. They thus hoped perhaps to learn how to check it, by an examination of history and especially of other great declines compared to this one. It may be significant that this ambitious project came less from the academic professionals than from some semiamateurs on the fringe of the profession. Two historians who emerged temporarily into great popularity right after the war—"Two Wrestlers with an Angel," as Huizinga has called them[10]—were H. G. Wells and Oswald Spengler. Spengler was an obscure German high school (Gymnasium) teacher before his book *The Decline of the West (Das Untergang des Abendlandes)*

9. "The Activity of Being an Historian," in *Historical Studies: Papers Read before the Second Irish Conference of Historians* (London: Bowes and Bowes, 1958).

10. See the able essay by this title in J. H. Huizinga, *Dutch Civilisation in the Seventeenth Century and Other Essays* (London: Collins, 1968).

launched him into fame immediately after World War I. He had an amateur's cavalier disregard for facts which did not fit his thesis; he was opinionated, conceited, even without intellectual integrity; yet he presented a dazzling thesis with dramatic power as he sought to explain the life cycle of civilizations. The twilight of the gods broods over Spengler's great book; all civilizations are born in barbarism and must return to it. All was pessimism among the intellectuals in the 1920s; Spengler's book suited the mood. His view of civilizations as having life cycles rather like an individual was open to all kinds of criticisms, but it afforded some explanation, perhaps even some consolation, for what seemed to be the collapse of Western civilization. Polybius long ago had noted the curious consoling power of history: "The memory of other people's calamities is the clearest and indeed the only source from which we learn to bear the vicissitudes of Fortune with courage." The Stoics and Epicureans knew that it helps us when we see the inevitability of things. In a long prose poem, Spengler told us that we are no different from the rest; we too are mortal. Spengler was not without learning, and his attempt to show that cultures are organic, having styles of life and art which represent their personalities, was often brilliant. Attached to his view, it may be noted, was a profound relativism of thought. He held that what determines the intellectual activity at any particular time is the state of life in which that civilization finds itself. The birth of Western science in the age of Galileo came because Western civilization had reached a certain stage of growth—just as boys' thoughts change when they reach puberty. No one can escape being a product of his times. Spengler, like Marx, did not explain how *he* alone could escape this all-pervading determinism to view matters objectively.

H. G. Wells was already world famous as novelist, essayist, and political reformer before he turned his attention to history after the war with his *Outline of History* (1920). The hardly endurable tragedy of the war brought down with a crash all those hopes for illimitable progress which Wells, a socialist, had entertained before 1914, and it drove him, as it drove Arnold Toynbee, to nothing less than a total reassessment of man's condition. (This cannot be said of Spengler, who viewed the war with some equanimity as a necessary step at this stage of history and only regretted that Germany had lost it!) Wells's scientific, positivist, progressivist mind was at opposite poles from Spengler. Wells was largely blind to art. He believed that man's salvation lay in a kind of world social-welfare state, and he was still optimistic enough to think that if all the intellectuals of the world united they might yet save the world. The *Outline of History* was mainly old-fashioned Enlightenment and Comtean history. It shows utterly no interest in, or capacity for, getting inside the minds of former ages or for appreciating them for their own beauty or brilliance. Like Voltaire, Wells poked fun at most of the past and foresaw the possibility of producing a materialist utopia through modern science. The *Outline of History* resembles Spengler only in the gross inadequacy of its research, in being called forth by the war, and in a broadness of scope and boldness of generalization which, whatever its errors, showed that when challenged by fate men still turned to the past for guidance. It had an incredible popularity that was indicative of the thirst for history with scope and sweep and style, which academic professionals seldom supplied. Wells agreed with Arnold Toynbee on at least one point: to him, the future held a world state to be based upon a common world religion; it was destined to organize science for human welfare on a vast scale and would be able to abolish war. Wells felt this as a messianic hope or as a possible achievement of human intelligence, but he also seemed to predict it as an almost inevitable historical trend. Thus, he sought to revive a redemptive historicity. The world state was also a lesson of history in the sense that, as Wells believed, the historic record warned man that unless he achieved such unity he would destroy himself. But though he succeeded in finding a huge audience for a serious work of history, one with scope, boldness, and style, Wells failed as a historian. Stuffed with factual errors and fanciful interpretations, the *Outline* was written with so much ignorance and arrogance that no trained historian could grant it respect. This revival of a glorious amateurism confronted all the antagonistic forces of a well-intrenched professionalism.

Arnold J. Toynbee wrestled with the angel far longer than Wells and Spengler and was much more a professional. On the eve of the war, he was a brilliant, highly imaginative young classical scholar at Oxford. He could not serve in the war because of an illness, and he resolved to compensate for the slaughter of so many of his friends on the plains of France by dedicating his life to the search for an explanation and a cure. He conceived the idea of *A Study of History* as he read Thucydides and compared that tragedy with this of World War I; he outlined the plan soon after the war, but he did not begin writing it until 1929, having been occupied chiefly with his work as editor and, to a large degree, as writer of the *Surveys of International Affairs*—remarkable feats of annual condensation and commentary—published by the Royal Institute of International Affairs in London, of which he was director. The first three volumes of the *Study* were published in 1934; the next three, in 1939. He concluded with four more volumes in 1954 and a volume called *Reconsiderations* in 1961 in which he attempted to answer his numerous critics. In the initial classification, which Toynbee later altered, the *Study* constituted a comparative analysis of the origin, growth, breakdown, and disintegration of no less than twenty-one civilizations or societies. He was far more of a trained and careful historian than Wells or Spengler, and his mammoth work (each of the ten large volumes was richly packed with footnotes and appendices) represented a much greater quantity of research. Indeed, it was an achievement of erudition which seemed at first almost unbelievable. Though inspired by World War I, it was not widely known and discussed until during and after World War II. It was then equally, or even more, timely. Of this remarkable assault on world history no one could complain that it was written without research, though critics were to claim that its research was not adequate to its stupendous subject.

Toynbee was a positivist in that he saw his task as one of comparing the external patterns of the several civilizations in order to discover laws or regularities in their growth and decay. He claimed to have found such laws. Yet these laws were expressed so vaguely that most critics found them little more than striking metaphors of occasional utility in human affairs: Challenge and Response; Withdrawal and Return; the tendency to keep to well-tried patterns; the tendency for leadership to become less creative in declining eras (some of the laws seemed mere tautologies). Toynbee also thought he saw a rhythm in all civilizations. For example, he perceived a "universal state" phase which invariably marks the beginning of breakdown and produces a "universal religion" which survives the destruction of the state and provides a bridge to the next civilization. All these claims to have discovered exact regularities aroused skepticism, but no one doubted the tremendous imaginative power of the work. Claiming to be a scientist, Toynbee in fact far more impressed most readers as an artist-prophet.

Filled with striking metaphor and wide-ranging literary allusion,

A Study of History became quite popular for a work so serious and learned. It was abridged for more popular consumption, and Toynbee wrote and lectured all over the world, becoming a household name in the 1950s. No other contemporary historian has been so widely known or so much discussed. But critics increasingly accused him of playing fast and loose with the facts of history and of being more a seer than a historian. The *Study* approaches metahistory and intrudes a personal vision far too obviously to suit professional canons. Other very serious questions about the ability of comparative history on so vast a scale to disclose laws of the development of whole civilizations as well as difficulties about clearly identifying these civilizations drove Toynbee to withdraw or modify a considerable number of his conclusions in *Reconsiderations*. It is generally agreed that this remarkable work is a modern classic by one of the twentieth century's most extraordinary scholars. But because he had ranged so widely, Toynbee exposed himself to the criticisms of countless specialists and soon became the most attacked historian in history. Professional historians in the great majority remained unconvinced of his work's validity, and it had little influence in most of their areas of study. Toynbee, who declared that professional historiography had become too narrowly specialized as well as too "parochial" to satisfy a human need for bold and broad historical generalizing, evidently failed in his audacious effort to write such history convincingly.

The temporary success of Toynbee's work testified to a potentially large public interest in such broad-gauged history. Like Spengler and Wells, he had in fact offered a version of historicism, in that it is claimed that history has a plan and a goal. He saw in the rise and fall of civilizations a long-term progress. They die, to be sure, but in dying each gives birth to a higher religion, which is passed on to the next generation of civilizations. In Toynbee's metaphor, the wheel goes around, but the wagon goes forward. In the end, there will be unity in a single global civilization under a world state with a single world religion which represents the best qualities of all the religions. We find a little here of Wells's vision of a material paradise presided over by science, though most of the time Toynbee seemed scornful of modern Western man, in a Spenglerian way, for his "Faustian" or power-conscious culture. Toynbee was a kind of combination of Spengler and Wells, at times seeming to decree the almost inevitable death of every civilization, and at other times asserting that we can if we will prevent the death of our civilization. But on the whole, his message of salvation was different from the scientific utopia of H. G. Wells. Toynbee placed his hope in religion, which was for him "the serious business of the human race." His call was for a spiritual renewal based on a synthesis of the major world faiths.

In a curious way Toynbee seemed to recapitulate almost all the phases of Western historiography. A drowning man, it is said, sees his whole life flash before his eyes, and perhaps this is what Toynbee signifies. He was a positivist seeking scientific laws; he was a historicist finding a plan and pattern in the past, with an appointed destiny at the end of the road. He was also an exemplarist finding lessons in history which might be applied to the solution of current problems. His vast system of history contains every type of historical thought known. But none carried conviction. In a torrent of criticism, some of it devastating, critics refuted his laws and disparaged his providential view. Great as his book is, it seems unlikely that anyone will want to follow in Toynbee's footsteps.[11] It is as much a dead end as *Finnegans Wake*.

THE CRISIS OF HISTORIOGRAPHY

Spengler and Wells were amateurs. Toynbee, no amateur in his special field of ancient Greek and perhaps also Islamic studies, was forced to rely on fragmentary knowledge derived from secondary sources in large areas of his all-encompassing work; in general, he disparaged "technical history" and was treated with scorn by the professional technicians. They made history very relevant, indeed, by trying to use it to redeem a civilization fallen on evil days, making it yield answers to grave problems and point in a direction leading out of the troubled times. But their work would not hold water; it was neither factually nor conceptually sound. It became evident that they were, although unconsciously, arbitrarily *imposing* on reality an order much too grandiose. Pieter Geyl's basic criticism of Toynbee, that his conclusions "are not based on the facts of history . . . they are imposed upon it," is very widely accepted. The fact is that modern

11. O. F. Anderle, a Dutch historian, has tried to carry on a school of historical research under Toynbee's plan, correcting his errors but following his basic procedure. "Comparative History" has attracted some interest, usually on a more modest scale; and there have been other attempts to write "World History."

man does not really believe that he will find in history the answers to his problems and an indication of the direction mankind is to go. Herbert Butterfield, in his *Whig Interpretation of History,* said that Clio is a complaisant lady who will do whatever we ask of her—in effect, a prostitute: "History is all things to all men. She is at the services of good causes and bad. In other words she is a harlot and a hireling. . . . We must beware even of saying 'History says . . .' or 'History proves . . . ,' as though she herself were the oracle. . . ." In a celebrated outburst against history, the outstanding modern writer and thinker Paul Valéry declared that "History will justify anything. It teaches precisely nothing, for it contains everything and furnishes examples of everything." (He added the further reproach, identical with Karl Popper's, that history is also "the most dangerous product distilled by the chemistry of the intellect," for its myths delude whole peoples, teaching them to hate other peoples.)[12]

In the 1950s and 1960s, much was written about a crisis in historiography, and many ways out of it were suggested. It may be useful to review the difficulties which confronted history. It seemed to have failed in several of its main hopes. It failed as science. The total science of man dreamed of by eighteenth-century philosophers such as Montesquieu and Condorcet and then by Comte, Buckle, Marx, Spencer, and Toynbee had evidently failed, for the empirical data stubbornly refused to conform to any of the schemes suggested. By selective use of evidence, the data could be forced to conform to any number of theories; but Clio thus violated exacted her revenge by revealing data which the theorist had concealed or overlooked. None of these theories withstood criticism, and it began to seem that none ever would, if put forward as an exclusive statement. Whether these were generalizations about the life pattern of societies or about the motive force of history or about anything else, they all failed. Exceptions could always be found, and other patterns, other moving forces, could always be exhibited. It cannot be said that this quest has entirely been given up, for there are some who still insist that history will yet find its Newton; but there is decreasing ground for optimism. Pragmatically, one could regard such theories as occasionally true for a particular purpose or situation—as a set of keys the

12. See "On History," in vol. 10 of Valéry's *Collected Works,* ed. D. Folliot and J. Mathews (London: Routledge & Paul, 1963). This essay was written in 1931.

historian could draw upon as he found them useful in unlocking particular doors. But this use was far from that of a simple basic law, such as Newton's gravitational theory, which had so long been awaited. One faced an infinitely pluralistic historical universe which would always escape man's complete understanding.[13]

As progress or development or destiny, history had also failed. If certain aspects of culture such as technology could be said to show steady improvement in efficiency, there was no reason at all to suppose that all aspects did, or that societies as a whole move toward greater fulfillment or ability to satisfy human cravings or whatever rational definition of progress was adopted. There seems in fact to be no plan or order to the past; men struggled and created, sometimes succeeding and sometimes failing, in ways that can be described and analyzed but reveal no one rhythm or direction any more than they reveal invariable laws. If any final goal exists, it is hidden and must remain hidden from human vision. It may be worth stressing that almost all modern historians are sure that the future is unpredictable. The more we know about the human situation, the more we see the infinite number of variables and the utter impossibility of prediction in any meaningful or major way. "The historian who tries to forecast the future," Collingwood wrote, "is like a tracker anxiously peering at a muddy road in order to descry the footsteps of the next person who is going to pass that way."

Historians rejected schemes of progress and inevitable development for many reasons. Such schemes abuse the past in the interest of some dogma. Aware of the baffling complexities, virtually all experienced historians will repeat, with E. L. Woodward, that "Most philosophies of history . . . appear to me to be grounded on an arbitrary and oversimplified selection of facts." By cloaking dubious causes with the mantle of authority, they have caused great damage. In sorrow, Karl Popper dedicated his book *The Poverty of Historicism* to those

13. Neopositivists such as Karl Popper and Carl Hempel have tried to save "scientific" history by arguing that though history does not find laws, it *applies* them: whereas most other sciences use particulars to arrive at generalizations, history uses generalizations to explain particulars. If true, this position is perhaps trivial. In any case, these neopositivists agree that history has no predictive functions, and Popper has been most severe with those who claim to have discovered inexorable laws of historical destiny—a delusion, he thinks, that has done more harm to mankind than any other sort of thinking. See his *The Poverty of Historicism* (Boston: Beacon Press, 1957); also discussion later in this book, pp. 149–150.

millions who had been led to slaughter by these nonexistent laws of historical destiny—to those who had believed that their nation or their movement or their race had a divine mission or destiny when it had nothing of the sort. Moreover, this notion is so deeply implanted in the modern mind that it becomes the leading modern superstition: it is the belief that what comes next must be better. This actually is a contempt for history. If today is automatically better than yesterday, why pay any attention to yesterday? T. S. Eliot caught this in some lines in *Dry Salvages,* where he says that evolution "becomes, in the popular mind, a means of disowning the past." The true historian looks sympathetically at the past. He is not convinced that it has nothing to teach the present and welcomes its differences. But the historicist ignores the past as he invents what he imagines to be something absolutely new and therefore better: the "new politics," for example, or the "new education," or whatever it may be. Popular thought is filled with historicist assumptions that everything new must be better. If in popular parlance we say of something that it "belongs to the nineteenth century," we have given it the supreme insult, even though most of our latest ideas come from the nineteenth century. If we can tie something to the wave of the future we have guaranteed its value. All this maddens the historian, and he now wishes to use history—true knowledge of the past—to attack and discredit such a vulgar progressivism.

To many, the practical manifestation of failure that historiography revealed was its loss of all cohesiveness and unity in a wilderness of specialized and ever smaller subjects. The nineteenth-century pioneers had been content to wait for the expected synthesis while calling for careful preliminary work on details. Only when each county had been surveyed would it be possible to draw the great map of the whole land with any accuracy. They were confident that when all the little questions had been answered the big ones could be. It seems, however, that little questions lead on to littler ones virtually ad infinitum and that we get further and further away from any synthesis. Historians increasingly fear to risk *any* historical generalizations, aware that some specialist somewhere might prove the generalization faulty. The dreadful fate of Toynbee was a warning. The inexhaustible nature of empirical reality appeared to be established: if we aim at something like total coverage, we can go on forever investigating the past and never complete the job. Total coverage is an illusion. Yet historians have gone on grinding out ever more microscopic pieces of research, impelled perhaps by the tradition of writing Ph.D. dissertations. It is difficult to deny that such research is potentially worthwhile. Can we have too much knowledge? Yet complaints multiplied about the triviality of much historical research, about the absence of any coherent over-all program of research (one dug wherever one happened to find a supply of evidence), about the absence of meaningful generalization and synthesis, and about the failure of contemporary specialist history to serve the public need for knowledge and guidance.[14] Ortega y Gasset thought that perhaps "God would not forgive" the historians for making so little of their matchless opportunities. "If history is falling into disrepute, if for many people it seems to be lost in unessentials instead of guiding us . . . ," Geoffrey Barraclough wrote, "the reason is not far to seek: what it needs is a larger vision, a breakthrough to new dimensions."[15]

"It is now generally agreed that there is a crisis in historical writing," a reviewer of a book on the subject recently wrote. A recent survey[16] found that only about 20 percent of professional historians, compared to more than 60 percent of physicists, thought that the state of their profession was eminently satisfactory—a fact which probably reflected much more than the amount of public subsidies coming in the two directions. "Future histories of English historical writing," a young historian wrote in a special issue of the London *Times Literary Supplement* dedicated to "New Ways in History" (April 7, 1966), "are likely to reveal the first half of the 20th century as a time when most historians temporarily lost their bearings." These young historians were inclined to blame this loss of direction on the habit of "grubbing away in the old empirical tradition" and believed that salvation lay in doses of sociology, of statistics, of computers, or of almost anything rather than what historians had been accustomed to do in the past. Perhaps they are as confused as their elders; but of their dissatisfaction there can be little doubt.

Of course such a crisis is not confined to history. A 1964 sym-

14. For an example of a very common type of article, see Theodore H. Von Laue, "Is There a Crisis in the Writing of History?" *Bucknell Review,* vol. 14 (1966), pp. 1–15.

15. In H. P. R. Finberg, ed., *Approaches to History* (Toronto: University of Toronto Press, 1962), p. 109.

16. Bernard Berelson, *Graduate Education in the United States* (New York: McGraw-Hill, 1960), p. 212.

posium addressed to *The Crisis in the Humanities* (edited by a historian, J. H. Plumb) included complaints from almost every discipline. The modern intellectual world suffers from indigestion brought on by too much knowledge, in a knowledge explosion related to the university explosion, which finds far more scholars writing far more books and articles, as governments and universities subsidize research as never before. In such cognate fields as anthropology and sociology and psychology, the old nineteenth-century syntheses have also broken down leaving, for example, microsociology rather than macrosociology, a miscellaneous array of small-scale studies with no adequate overarching structure of theory. Equally, the more exact sciences, such as organic chemistry, go on multiplying every few years. This anarchy in the world of knowledge is an aspect of modern culture's centrifugal tendencies, of the bigness of everything, of the immense accumulation of knowledge in constantly multiplying ratios. The result has been to reduce scholars to ever decreasing domains over which they can claim mastery: the bulk of material is so great that no one can hope to keep up with more than a small zone of knowledge. Specialization in history reaches the stage in which we have experts in just a few years in American history or in one period of one European country. "We are all confined to our own antheap, which is generally dusty, small, and low," an eminent British scholar recently sighed.[17] It is a familiar complaint, and it seems to get steadily worse.

17. H. R. Trevor-Roper, in *The Spectator*, October 25, 1968.

Chapter 7

RECENT TRENDS IN HISTORY

History as a subject of study has never regained the prestige that it held in the nineteenth century, when in a typical opinion Henry Sidgwick the philosopher could write that "a belief in the Historical Method is the most widely and strongly entertained philosophical conviction at the present day." But historical inquiry still maintains great vitality. In the decades following World War II, historians not only developed several new emphases but continued to argue about the nature of their discipline. One older hope faded. Few historians expect to find any vast system governing all historical change. Toynbee's vast outline already seems anachronistic. The newer strategies—new subjects, new frames of reference, new analytical tools, and new uses—have been much more limited.

The search for new and fitting subject matter has ranged in all directions. To Geoffrey Barraclough, the needed new dimension in history was simply global history, i.e. new peoples and places. This was in reality, as we know, a Voltairean position, but it took on new meaning for a generation which in an especially vivid way widened its horizons to embrace non-Western peoples. Expansion of the range of historical studies did happen, of course; the rapid growth of African and Asian studies brightened the historiography of the 1950s and 1960s, an inevitable by-product of the modern era. As the Indian historian S. K. M. Panikkar has put it, we can no longer hold to "the faith which was so firmly held in the past that everything of value developed on the shores of the Mediterranean." If one conceived the basic problem of history to be the need for some unification of knowledge, one might wonder whether this addition to the body of knowledge solved the problem or whether indeed it did not make it worse. Swelling the size of history departments, the arrival of addi-

105

tional specialists on exotic parts of the globe accentuated the condition of departments as a congeries of unrelated specialists. Increased knowledge about non-Western civilizations tended to shatter such generalizations as Western-oriented historical analysis had been able to suggest. To take but two examples: Toynbee turned out to be weakest on Chinese history, where it appeared he had sought to impose a Western model on the data of Sinic history of which he really knew almost nothing, with the result a total disaster. And, commenting on the applicability of the term "feudalism" to Chinese history, the eminent Sinologist Arthur F. Wright[1] pronounced this Western concept a source of confusion and distortion and recommended its discontinuation, along with other terms derived from European experience. On the whole, careful studies of non-Western societies destroyed illusions of a common course of human development, whether Christian-Judaic, Enlightenment, Marxian, or Toynbeean. This did not prevent them from being interesting and stimulating. The momentous consequences are probably still being worked out.

Those who saw salvation in world history were counterbalanced by some who recommended more attention to quite local history; they advised getting down to the real grass roots and encouraged what Carl Becker had once called making "everyman his own historian." "Since the war more and more French historians have been undertaking detailed regional studies of institutions and societies," the author of an article on French history noted in 1962,[2] adding that this was "the study of local societies and institutions for their own sake and in their own context, and not with a view to making general statements about France as a whole." The tendency of history to become more microscopic was due in part to a search for fresh subjects when the possibilities of finding anything new to say about the familiar national themes seemed remote. It also agreed with some general trends of recent thought, resting on a conception of history as having greater value when it draws closer to the actual lives of real people; it is related to the social historian's desire to dissect a living society, an actual village or city or province, rather than

1. "On the Uses of Generalization in the Study of Chinese History," in Louis Gottschalk, ed., *Generalization in the Writing of History* (Chicago: University of Chicago Press, 1963).
2. *Times Literary Supplement* (London), May 4, 1962.

a necessarily somewhat abstract nation. In a plea for this sort of history the British scholar Peter Laslett called it "The World We Have Lost," implying that somehow historians had overlooked, right under their noses, the way people lived. The author of the article cited above spoke of "abandoning the arid, dreary uplands of political history on the government level" (which had scarcely seemed so arid and dreary to our fathers) for "the minute dissection of a commune or the history of a provincial society." American urban historians announced a movement away from the viewing of the various cities in the light of national themes, preferring to look at them from a purely local angle. One of the major historical enterprises of British scholarship is the Victoria History of the Counties of England; another, similar in its microscopic approach to the study of the past, and bearing marks of the influence of one of the greatest of twentieth-century historians, the late Sir Lewis Namier, is the huge history of Parliament based on biographies of every member. All over the Western world, it would seem, local history has experienced a boom of almost revolutionary proportions; local repositories once considered too trivial for concern are no longer safe from the eager attentions of historians.

Historians were looking in still other directions in the 1960s. Perhaps even more striking than the extension of frontiers—outward or inward—was the interest in subjects formerly not treated or scarcely treated at all. The program demanded by Voltaire and adumbrated by pioneer social historians like J. R. Green and H. D. Traill was now carried out in full; indeed, with what some might think an excessive fullness. There were societies and journals dedicated to the history of education, and there were numerous scholarly books on the subject. There were histories of ladies' dresses, of diet, of family planning (many of these influenced from the direction of sociology), of crime and punishment, of clergymen and pornographers, of doctors and quacks, and quite literally of cabbages as well as of kings. There was a history of dogs on the American frontier. Economic history, having apparently exhausted the larger topics, descended on individual business firms, producing an impression that eventually every commercial or industrial enterprise of any consequence will have its full-length history. Anything bearing the title "Urban" and having remotely to do with any aspect of cities, from sewage disposal to park planning, experienced a boom. These are but random examples. The total impression is of an almost desperate search for open spaces, chiefly no doubt by apprentice historians in need of viable and publishable dissertations, and of a mighty out- pouring of books at which one hardly knows whether most to marvel, to laugh, or to be dismayed. A recent *Bibliography of Historical Works Issued in the United Kingdom* between 1961 and 1965 counted 4,883 items, or about a thousand a year. American produc- tion is of course even greater, and since 1965 one has the impression of a continuing increase. Thus in the English language alone there are several thousand strictly historical books each year, not to men- tion the tens of thousands of articles. No historian can keep up with history any more; he is doing well to stay abreast of his own small zone of specialization. We are back to a lament previously voiced. The energy of history, as it sought new avenues in order to escape from old cul-de-sacs, landed it in a new dilemma, that of an anarchic profusion.

From the viewpoint of the university curriculum, which he com- pared to "an historical supermarket, full of goodies in penny packets," one veteran historian has protested against this dilution of history with all sorts and varieties of history, including fads of the moment and some products sure to fade with the season.[3] The trend in the curriculum has been toward non-European and recent history and toward experimental and interdisciplinary subjects. Professor Elton argued that the real value of history as a study lies not in its subject matter as such but in building in the student "standards of judgment and of powers of reasoning" and that this is more likely to come from the intensive study of long-developed fields than from a sampling of a multiplicity of new and strange ones. Though hardly a majority view, this opinion strikes a ready response in quite a few professorial hearts. It is indicative of a wide divergence of opinion among his- torians about the values and purposes of history and of a need to clarify these values and purposes.

Among some of the youthful historians of the 1960s, the unques- tioned purpose of history was as a tool for a radical reconstruction of decadent Western societies. They have at least introduced a new verbal fad—radical history. To some, perhaps, the label refers to

3. Geoffrey Elton, "Second Thoughts on History at the Universities," *History*, vol. LIV (February, 1969).

subject areas, to either the history of radical movements or of exploited peoples ("history from the bottom up"). Others seem to imply, by the label, some ideological test for historians. But if the term has any precise and enduring meaning, it surely refers not to a particular subject area or to any qualifications for historians but to one possible use of almost any good history. Only the most honest and penetrating understanding of our past permits the type of thorough criticism that is a necessary preface to any lasting social reform. This seems to be the central message of the "New Left" historians. Their critical purposes have most often directed these radical historians, paradoxical as it may seem, to the more traditional subjects and methods. Few have embraced the newest techniques in comparative and statistical history. But today no historian can ignore these innovative techniques.

Today the label "comparative history" is much in vogue; there are journals devoted to comparative studies. Yet the label is not always precise. Too often any study that extends beyond national boundaries is called comparative, even though only one continuous subject is present. In the most narrow and precise sense, comparative history implies a special frame of reference that may be used by a historian. As such, it deserves careful attention.

In one sense, historians have always made comparative judgments. Our histories are well sprinkled with national and cultural comparisons. American historians freely note similarities and differences between America and Europe, for example. European historians often make national comparisons. But such comparative references may be quite loose. The image of Europe reflected in American historical studies, and particularly in those concerned to identify American uniqueness, is often a simplistic and false stereotype. National typologies usually are but rough caricatures. From this perspective, the concern of comparative history is simply for greater rigor. When a historian compares, he should do justice to both sides, either by doing extended research on both subjects or by making an attempt to master the best of existing literature about the nonfocal subject.

But comparative history implicates much more than this. It relates to the difficult problem of historical explanation and particularly to causation. Continuously historians try to suggest causes for significant changes in a society, such as a revolution, rapid industrialization, or shifts in basic beliefs. As best he can, the careful historian tries to identify an array of necessary conditions that preceded a significant change and at least in part account for it. He may even try to assess the relative significance of various conditions; in the most exact accounts, he may even assign a numerical weight to each causal factor. In order to select such causal factors the historian inevitably uses some theory about the ordinary or normal behavior of his subject, be it a person, a group, or a nation. Without some such theory, he would be hard put to distinguish necessary conditions from an often large number of attendant but coincidental circumstances. His theory may be about the behavior of all societies; all human societies; a certain class of societies; or, safest of all, one particular society. Further, his theory may be rough or *ad hoc,* largely a matter of seemingly plausible, common-sense inferences from a meager amount of empirical observation. It may be a commonly accepted theory, one shared by almost everyone in the society.

One way the historian can improve his frame of reference and thus bring more rigor to his causal analysis is to borrow from social scientists some well-developed and empirically vindicated theory about such social change or some purely analytical model that possesses proven empirical relevance. If the borrowed theory is only a brilliant imaginative construct untested against actual societies, the historian would be taking it on faith. If empirically vindicated, then the comparative work has already been done by social scientists. But it may not have been done properly. The historian is always free to reject it. And existing analytical models may not fit his particular case. Finally, there may be no theories or models to borrow. In either of these cases, the anxious historian, seeking more assurance for his causal judgments, has only one alternative. He has to compare his causal assertions about his focal subject (say Revolution A) with another like subject (Revolution B), provided there is such a like subject.

Such comparison is perilous and difficult. First, there must be some common phenomenon (another real revolution) and not two different events sharing a common name. Secondly, the two subjects must be fully discontinuous in either time or space. If these criteria can be met (and they rarely can be for major, transnational events, such as revolutions), then the overlapping circumstances that preceded the events have additional causal weight. The distinct circumstances in each case have less (or no) causal significance. If Revolution A followed a general decline in prices, and Revolution B, similar in every respect, occurred without such a drop in prices, then a historian might be inclined to drop price changes from his list of causes of Revolution A. Seemingly, then, as far as revolutions are concerned, price fluctuations are insignificant variables. Enough such comparisons (ten fully similar revolutions, let us say) might allow a quite reliable ranking of the various causes of revolutions.

But comparable subjects are rare, particularly at the level of such complex events as revolutions. Such words as "revolution" usually denote quite variant events reflecting some vague common quality (rapid and violent change). Attempts to compare unlike entities (two particular revolutions) may be suggestive to a historian and may lead him to look for heretofore unnoticed conditions. But such loose comparison cannot yield any rigorous causal discriminations and may not significantly improve our knowledge of either. But for events of lesser complexity, which are clearly similar in most respects (usually intranational and intracultural events), comparison can be a valuable research technique. It is not surprising, however, that such rigorous comparison has been most useful in very restricted topical areas, usually in conjunction with statistical analysis of some sort. One note is necessary: for the historian, such comparison is always in behalf of fuller and more accurate accounts. But aside from its purpose, such comparison is formally similar to the comparisons of a social scientist, who is bent not on telling a particular story but upon developing, improving, or verifying some general theory or analytical model.

Combining radicalism with comparative studies, recent historians (as Georg Iggers notes in the case of Germany, and as is true elsewhere as well) have shown interest in social, recent, and generalizing types of history, in reaction against the older idealist and historicizing tradition. This desire to be radical and relevant involves them in disputes with other historians who are quick to sense a drastic danger in excessive present-mindedness, which can falsify the past and refuses to let it speak with its own voice. This schism in the ranks of historians often extends to what is loosely called *quantitative* history, even more in vogue today than historical comparisons. The two are closely related, except that the misplaced adjective, quantitative, denotes not a frame of reference but certain techniques for analyzing and interpreting data. The auxiliary tools needed for interpreting massed data such as statistical techniques may be compared to older historical tools such as diplomatics and heraldry. When histories were (or are) primarily about individual thought or behavior or about political or intellectual elites, and when they were necessarily based on quite limited, testimonial evidence, the most valuable research tools were those that helped the historian authenticate documents or draw every possible inference from a few artifacts. Perhaps the most famous of all historical manuals, by Langlois and Seignobos,[4] focused almost entirely on the interpretations of documents of the traditional sort. But with more recent history, including an increased concern about the external and patterned behavior of groups or of large numbers of inarticulate common folk, the research problems have changed. Often, in a welter, even a flood, of records, reports, and statistical data, most of undoubted authenticity but of problematic significance, the historian has been forced to find ways of sampling, grouping, abstracting, and comparing data. He has to count more and calculate more exactly.

But, one can protest, historians have always counted and calculated. Indeed they have. If quantitative history only signifies this aspect of historical inquiry, then it is in no wise new. It would be hard to find any history without quantitative language; it is much easier to avoid comparative references than it is to avoid assertions of quantity. Judgments of ratio or proportion, for example, are inescapable (*"most* Americans vote in national elections"). Used in this simple way, the mandate of quantitative history is simply greater rigor. When possible, especially when it adds needed precision, a historian should count exactly, determine precise ratios, and even try to convert complex entities into discrete, comparable units.

Such rigor in itself does not and should not mean the end of all verbal judgments of quantity (such as "many," "most," "several," "a few"). Quite often the purpose of the historian (or of everyman) is well served by such terms. Exact quantification of an obvious condition, where such exactitude serves no useful purpose, can be mere pedantry. In other contexts, there may be insufficient evidence for more exact and numerical judgments. Also, rigor in counting can be quite pointless if it is not combined with conceptual rigor. It is, unfortunately, a great deal easier to count than to define. Numbers, charts, and tables can be merely ostentatious unless the various cate-

4. C. V. Langlois and C. Seignobos, *Introduction to the Study of History,* trans. by G. G. Berry (London: 1912).

gories used are exact. It is much harder to clarify the meaning of the words "liberalism" or "nationalism" or "imperialism" than it is to count the people who supported these forces. It means little to show how many Americans believe in God unless the word "God" is given a precise meaning. Most often what is countable (votes for a political party, shifts of population, changes in income) cannot provide answers for the really meaningful questions historians are likely to ask. It is indeed possible that the most countable is the most trivial or the most superficial. The deeper questions of explanation and interpretation defy statistical solution.

When used in a more narrow and precise sense, quantitative history involves using some truly new tools of historical research. Being abstract and precise tools, they have one great merit: they are easily learned. In fact, facility in their use often gives young historians an unwarranted sense of historical mastery. The first tool is statistical. Although some of the theoretical foundations of statistical analysis can be traced to the ancient Greeks, most contemporary use of this tool rests on probability theories that were perfected only by late nineteenth-century mathematicians and logicians. The first extensive use of such analysis by historians can scarcely be traced further back than the 1930s, and most of it stems from the post-World War II period. Fortunately for historians and social scientists who lack advanced training in symbolic logic or higher mathematics, they can acquire the needed statistical tools without having to have a thorough understanding of the underlying theoretical foundations. After only a few months of intensive training, any historian can find margins of error in samples, analyze data in behalf of various types of significance, and correlate various categories of data.

But despite the theoretical tools, much contemporary quantitative analysis would be humanly impossible without electronic assistance. Thus, there is a growing role in history of what, all too loosely at times, are called computers. The computer provides the historian with the means of storing and retrieving vast amounts of raw data; more importantly, it can with lightning speed carry out complex computations that would take a single person a lifetime. Just as with statistical tools, the historian does not need a complete understanding of a computer, either logically or electronically, in order to use it. The most complex intellectual work is already built into the master programs of contemporary computers. At a lower level, most computer centers employ trained programmers who are available to help researchers prepare their data for use. Moreover, simple programming skills are easily within the competence of any historian.

So far, at least, the more elaborate quantitative operations have proved most useful for political, social, and economic historians. In each case, the analytical techniques have often been borrowed directly from cognate social sciences. But in principle, any subject matter, including even intellectual history, may lend itself to statistical treatment. The critical determinant is not the subject area but the purpose of the historian and the evidence available to him. One could, for example, count the number of references to God among a selected population and correlate this word frequency with other determinable factors present. From these findings one could suggest some possible conditions necessary for religious belief. Obviously, as any trained quantifier would point out, the concepts "God" and "religion" are much too loose for such computations. Possibly, the analysis would lead to some formally interesting results, but it would yield nothing of cognitive importance. The finding (not the figures used) would be ambiguous in the extreme. But even such a poor example does reveal that, even as in sophisticated comparative techniques, quantification is related to causal analysis and thus to the overarching problem of explanation.

Given enough data, complex group behavior may yield interesting results to causal analysis. But even here the collection of data and its analysis have to be guided either by some well-accepted theories or by comparison with essentially similar but discontinuous phenomena. In a welter of possible conditions, the historian or social scientist must select some for detailed study. To use one example from historical literature: were lowered wheat prices in selected Kansas counties a prime cause of increased voting support for populism? If one accepted a theory that voting behavior is largely determined by economic interest, he would surely examine such variables as wheat prices. Unless guided by some such theory, he would scarcely know what conditions to investigate. In selecting what he assumes to be significant variables, the historian may be very impressionistic. He almost has to be if there are no prior validated theories for him to rely on.

The statistical data used by a historian may duplicate the same data used by a social scientist. The purpose alone varies. The historian may borrow a hypothesis or a general theory about human behavior (or about the behavior of Americans) in order to formulate his research problem and to guide his selection of significant variables and data. But his object in all this is the illumination of some particular historical problem (what caused a Populist upsurge in Kansas?) or the improvement of some narrative (a history of American third parties); it is not the perfection of some theory or hypothesis. His research may incidentally add support to some such theory and thus be of direct use to a generalizing scientist. But it is the use of data and not its content or location in time that distinguishes the two disciplines. And despite its abstract simplicity, quantitative data is in no sense better than other data; the nature of the problem determines what data is relevant. It is foolish and also naïve to claim that a history supported by massive, statistically analyzed data is more scientific than another history which rests on perceptive interpretations of the nuances of meaning present in a speech or in a diary. But the research skills required are quite different. Unfortunately, those skilled in the use of one type of evidence will, more often than not, choose only topics that fit the method; in myopic smugness they may even come to hold that only such topics are proper to the discipline.

With all this said, one still senses that the most bothersome issues raised by quantitative methods, and to a lesser extent by comparison, still need to be discussed. But these larger issues are obviously more than methodological. Some are metaphysical and involve basic questions about the limits of the generalizing sciences, the status of culture, and the distinctive attributes of man (all these issues will be treated extensively in succeeding chapters). To some historians, the newer quantitative techniques, or at least the exaggerated claims of some who use them, have seemed threatening not only to their research habits but even more to their conceptions of man and of history. In defensive overreaction they have rejoiced in the limited early returns from quantitative studies and have often refused to consider the possible, even if marginal, utility of statistical techniques for their own research. Some of the least mature and knowledgeable quantifiers have fallen in love with mere technique (the worst possible sin for a historian) and have either remained blind to the status and limits of any research tool or have so fallen under the mystique of a behavioral science that they have, often without realizing it, repudiated history. Whether justified or not, images of a warm, humanistic culture versus a cold, abstract scientific one lurk behind these growing conceptual gulfs and threaten a greater professional factionalism than ever before experienced by historians. It seems like one engagement in the larger battle of what C. P. Snow immortalized as the "two cultures." Urban historian Asa Briggs has noted that despite frequent statements to the effect that quantitative and qualitative procedures should be complementary and not mutually exclusive, in practice "there tends to be a gap between them."

Articles by the "quantifiers" frequently talk about technique more than about subject matter. Instead of discreetly concealing methodological apparatus in footnotes, they parade it ostentatiously, rolling up batteries of formidable statistical and mathematical artillery which are often then used to crack some quite small nut. Such methodological preoccupation, to many "humanists" essentially barbarous, is not confined to the quantifiers; it is indeed a kind of disease of professionalization and specialization. A recent new journal dedicated to interdisciplinary studies (the formalization of what one formerly took for granted, that, in the old saying, the historian ought to know something about everything as well as everything about something) announces that it will encourage "methodological contributions which will discuss techniques" of research and analysis. Trapped in microspecialization, historians create new specialties called "interdisciplinary studies," vainly seeking an answer to the problem. And they turn to technique and the computer expecting this *deus ex machina* to resolve the difficulties, as so often is done these days.

The problem of the larger framework for history, such as nineteenth-century ideas of progress had supplied, can hardly be solved by quantitative research and new fields. Some historians, it should be observed, said goodbye to such frameworks with a light heart. Carl E. Schorske has argued that "One need no longer bemoan the spread of 'specialization' in scholarship and teaching" because its "blighting qualities" can be overcome by "exploiting the microcosmic potentialities of the special study and by imaginatively conceiving its significance in the light of a comparative approach."[5] In this view, the microscopic research subject brings its own rewards in the form of

5. *Colloquium* (John Wiley), no. 2 (October, 1964), p. 5.

enriched understanding of humanity and of mastery of techniques of investigation. And comparison between these microcosms presumably illuminates their meaning "imaginatively."

Conceding that detailed studies can be rewarding and that comparison can be illuminating, one must still wonder whether this is an adequate defense of history. At any rate there have been some fairly desperate attempts to resurrect the idea of progress. In his essay on "The Historian's Dilemma" in the book *Crisis in the Humanities,* J. H. Plumb concluded that salvation lay in believing in Progress despite everything. E. H. Carr had given this same advice in his lectures on *What Is History?* (See Chapter 5, "History as Progress.") We are to have faith that we are progressing even if it seems as if we are not. Back to the idea of progress—back to Marx—back to Buckle—one fears it cannot be done. Historians of all people should know the irreversibility of history. And twentieth-century man, living amid threats of universal disaster and signs of immediate decay, can hardly be expected to embrace so dubious a faith for the benefit of historians.

The disappearance of the sense of order in history has been one of the leading themes of our day. Historians are not responsible for it; it is a part of our *Zeitgeist.* Existentialist philosophy reflects it, and it is found widely in modern literature. James Joyce's *Finnegans Wake,* which is a kind of history of all humanity,[6] does not have an ending but leads back to its beginning in an endless circle, a *corso, ricorso* like life itself. In John Barth's novel *The Sot-Weed Factor,* which is a *reductio ad absurdum* of the waywardness of historical causation, we read: "The Poet Wonders Whether the Source of Human History is a Progress, a Drama, a Retrogression, a Cycle, an Undulation, a Vortex, a Right- or Left-Handed Spiral, a Mere Continuum, or What Have You. Certain Evidence is Brought Forward, but of an Ambiguous and Inconclusive Nature." This loss of guidance from history is unquestionably a leading cause of that major philosophical descent into absurdity which goes by the name of existentialism, the most striking and important serious intellectual movement of recent times.

---

6. "What Joyce is doing, then is to make his hero re-live the whole of history in a night's sleep"—Anthony Burgess. It would be interesting to compare the vision of history in the nineteenth-century novel to that in the novel of the twentieth century.

Some existentialists have accepted the absurdity and irrationality of man's condition and have gone on from there to assert that man creates his own values by freely choosing and acting. In one sense, this is the ultimate skepticism and subjectivism. We have seen through all myths, not only the religious ones which hold that there is a God who presides over an orderly world, but the myths of reason which postulate an orderly nature or a transcendental reason. We see that these were all human inventions. We now must accept that whatever values there are, men have made up and bestowed upon reality, which in itself is chaotic, protean, senseless. This corresponds to the modern historian's discovery that the patterns are in him, not in the past.

In some ways certain existentialists are quite historical-minded. Man has no essence or nature; he creates himself by his choices and actions. He is, in brief, a product of history. Not that he is determined by it. To the notion that history itself has a will, which represents a universal order, and which uses Man as the tool of its providence— in brief, to Hegelian or deterministic-Marxian types of nineteenth-century historicism—existentialists are wholly opposed. Man is free to choose; the future is open; nothing is determined. But his options are presented to him by history. He may in principle be free to choose any values, but in reality he finds these limited by the existing social situation, which sets the problems and provides the ideas. This is what leads Ortega y Gasset to say that "History is the systematic science of that radical reality, my life. . . . The past is I."

Jean-Paul Sartre came to believe that existentialism is only a method and must have a more definite social doctrine. He chose a kind of existentialized Marxism—utterly unorthodox Marxism, it should be stressed, utterly unacceptable to the hierophants of Moscow or, for that matter, of Peking or Havana—based on some of the less familiar and long unpublished early writings of Marx and on Hegel's *Phenomenology,* an early writing long obscured by his philosophy of history. We need not go into all that; but these significant contemporary currents of thought relate closely to the historian's dilemma. Rather than pine nostalgically for a vanished historicism based on the discredited belief in an objective order of things—divine and/or rational—the historian may accept the death of God and of reason, which means accepting the essentially chaotic state of human affairs and human history but rising to the challenge of imposing upon that chaos an order which comes from his will.[7]

The climate of opinion recently, as reflected in existentialism, in phenomenology, in the literary movement of *chosisme* (presenting the object or thing itself without asking its meaning or interpretation), and in some ways in linguistic philosophy, has been moving toward the concrete particular and away from generalizing systems. In politics the trend has been away from ideologies. Weary of systems, which always prove false and which narrow the mind, contemporary thinking man seems content to bathe in the stream of actual existence, to explore each moment of it, and not to weaken this particularity by abstraction. The twentieth-century revolution in physics has accustomed him to a pluralistic universe rather than to a monistic one: each area seems to have different rules and to require different suppositions. Although it is dangerous to generalize about our incredibly complex intellectual world, filled as it is with a myriad of subworlds, the trend seems clearly marked. It is favorable toward history in many ways. In the humanities and in social studies, there is a continuing and relentless critique of scientism (cf., as an example, A. R. Louch, *Explanation and Human Action,* 1966) which leaves in ruins all efforts to generalize about human affairs and reduce them to "laws" on the misapplied model of the physical sciences. Insofar as historians have attempted to discover such laws or have adopted schemes of inevitable destiny, they are struck down too; but in a multistructured realm of innumerable *ad hoc* situations, each with its own explanation, the historian is better equipped to survive than other "social scientists." (Some existentialists, to be sure, have expressed a wish to abolish the historical dimension altogether and to live only in the personal—an extremist reaction which surely is altogether unrealistic.) He has committed himself to no theoretical systems and to no specialized pseudoscientific jargon. He uses the language of everyday humanity

---

7. An example of Sartrean historical writing has recently appeared, André Decouflé's *La Commune de Paris, 1871* (Paris: Editions des Cujas, 1969). It attempts to show that the celebrated Commune was unique and spontaneous, owing nothing to tradition or history and not ideological but just a "happening." In pursuit of this dubious thesis the book seems to use sources in a highly arbitrary manner; yet the existential interpretation does contribute to understanding this historical episode by casting it in a somewhat new light. See the perceptive review of the book by Louis Greenberg in *Journal of Modern History,* September, 1970.

and is accustomed to look at particular situations as they are, without elaborate preconceptions. If, then, man is really prepared to give up integrative system-making and to live in an intellectually pluralistic society, he will find a large place for history of a rather traditional sort.[8]

Historians are, in the main, not likely to be long detained by such philosophizing. But they cannot escape their times. Facing the challenge of modern society, with its massism, its threat to dehumanize man, its bewildered quest for values, its enormous quantities of knowledge which it cannot synthesize, its overspecialization, and all the other evils which plague it—along with all the inestimable advantages which it has, its communications and information facilities and comforts, its global horizons and broadened cultural opportunities— facing all this, historians see a large place for their subject. Despite all its problems, it is flourishing, as measured by the number of books produced and sold and the number of students interested in it. It continues to produce numbers of the leading intellectual personalities of our time. A complete list is impossible; but consider, in the United States, such advisers of the great and writers of widely read works as Arthur M. Schlesinger, Jr., John Kenneth Galbraith (economist but also historian), Henry A. Kissinger (historian and political scientist), George F. Kennan (diplomat and historian); or in Great Britain such distinguished public personalities as Toynbee, Trevor-Roper, Sir Isaiah Berlin, Sir Denis Brogan, A. J. P. Taylor, A. L. Rowse, Roy Jenkins (historian and statesman). Among the reasons for this the most notable, surely, is that history answers to an instinct for *wholeness* which is a special need of the modern fragmented and specialized world. It tries to deal with the total culture. A few years ago a philosopher raised the interesting question of why there should be a special subject called history at all.[9] Is it not just an aspect of other subjects and could not these subjects supply their own historians? Put in terms of university departments, could not political science, economics, art, physics, and literature each do its own historical work, the history of

8. As Ortéga y Gasset has pointed out, mankind vacillates between unity and pluralism, rationalism and relativism; it turns to unifying abstract structures of thought but finds these inadequate and turns back to plural experience. This too it is likely to find unsatisfying, and so we get cycles of dogma and rejection of dogma. On this analysis the present pluralistic phase may not last.

9. See John H. Randall, Jr., *Nature and Historical Experience: Essays in Naturalism and in the Theory of History* (New York: Columbia University Press, 1958), pp. 23–28.

each branch of knowledge so far as they feel the need for it? (Most of them in fact feel little need for it; past physics may hold no interest for the physicist.) For history evidently shares with philosophy the distinction of having no special subject matter of its own. (It shares its subject matter with the other disciplines; it is the one that can touch all the others.) If we ask why, indeed, we should not abolish history as a separate subject, the answer almost immediately arises. We need history precisely because it ties things together. In the categories of systematic knowledge it is about the last claim we have on the common culture (philosophy now having abdicated for the most part its function of taking the large view and tackling the "big questions"). It is, for one thing, something the general public can still understand. (Very likely it has given up trying to understand most of the physical sciences, economics, philosophy, much of political science, and even sociology, with their specialized jargon.) Sir Isaiah Berlin has noted with approval the historian's instinctive resistance to the development of a specialized jargon, his insistent clinging to the modes of general discourse. Taking in theory all of human life as his province —*humani nil alienum puto*—the historian in fact almost always tries to deal with it as a unity. He chooses the public themes, the social life, the general culture. And because of this, modern society has great need of him, a need that is likely to continue.

History can only flourish in a reasonably stable society, marked by continuity if not by progress. The "terror of history" about which M. Eliade writes, and which he thinks was the reason it was so typically rejected by archaic societies, inhibited the full development of history as a distinguished field of inquiry and literature as late as the eighteenth century; we recall Voltaire's aversion to so much of the past, with its crimes and follies, that he could not really find his way to a fully developed historical outlook. Only, perhaps, in relatively fortunate epochs can history come into its own. Then men look back on the past with some degree of pleasure and approval, for it led somewhere, it was creating something. Even in the nineteenth century, that minority which rejected modern civilization tended to reject history too. Baudelaire thought it was a "ferocious beast" clinging to man and dragging him down; Nietzsche called attention to the danger of the past crushing life. (See his *The Use and Abuse of History*.) We need not, perhaps, retain an immaculate notion of progress in all things, but to sustain history we must surely keep alive a belief in a minimal degree of continuity and process. It is likely that history would disappear if society should dissolve into a chaos of strife and confusion. But then, so probably would all higher knowledge and all civilization.

A further reflection on the future of history may be added. Its sheer quantity is already a problem, and this increases constantly. At present we have only about five thousand years of human civilization to deal with, in a few areas, and even Toynbee could spot only twenty or so historic societies to deal with. In comparison with the vast eons of time this is nothing. Assuming that man remains on earth as a civilized creature, what do we contemplate for ten thousand or a million years hence? (Our own solar system presumably has at least a billion years to go in its life cycle.) The provincial dimensions of our little "history of civilization" on the old model—Greece and Rome, the Middle Ages, modern Europe, the United States—become evident. Will the study of history not break down through the sheer weight of numbers? Could anyone possibly learn it all, even in capsulized form? Will it be possible to maintain even the idea of a history of civilization or a general civilized heritage to be absorbed through historical, literary, and other humanistic studies? Will history either cease to exist or become localized? We know how much importance is attached to history in the Soviet Union, where it is heavily subsidized, stressed in the educational program, and in general treated as highly important. But for what reason? As a means of inculcating respect for the established order, as an arm of propaganda of the Communist state. So, indeed, it is in many other places. But if it loses its universality to become only what it is often called, "the natural propaganda of the social order," it will sink in dignity and abandon all the finer hopes placed in it.

Such speculations about the future cannot be answered, as all historians know. About all we can say is that history has thus far shown tremendous vitality in our civilization. It looks back on a distinguished heritage. That heritage is as varied and complicated as life itself, which history records and of which it is a part. What a long and crooked way it has come since Thucydides! Its best excuse for existence is that it is life. As long as men live and try to make some sense of their living, they will try to take stock of their past experiences, the life already led, as one evident way of understanding. But in doing so they seem always to reflect their own times and its peculiar values, for they themselves cannot escape being a part of history.

History has revealed its universality by the fact that during its history it has at various times made an appeal to all the categories of human experience. Croce once said that there are four realms of human intellectual aspiration: the true, the useful, the beautiful, the good. It is a tribute to history's catholicity, and to its ambiguity, that it has been claimed for all these areas, but rejected by them all. The ancients tended to make it useful, and also good—an aid to the good, at any rate, supplying the concrete examples of virtue. But they denied it truth, since it is too imprecise and conjectural, and also denied it beauty, ranking it as inferior to poetry though it might aspire to some lesser esthetic qualities. Later, men decided that history was indeed truth: the revelation of Absolute Mind. But this view has not survived. We are not likely to think any more, either, that history is morality or practical social engineering. At least we are far more aware of its limitations in these areas than formerly. Burckhardt thought that history's real function was as a work of art, locating it thus in the realm of the beautiful. Perhaps this is closest to the modern view; and yet, in the last analysis, none of these categories is satisfactory for history. It falls partly in each, but eludes exact definition. In that respect it is like life itself, of which it is the mirror.

One notable trend recently among historians has been an increasing concern about theory and method. They have been challenged by philosophers to "amend their casual and often inconsistent thinking."[10] To some historians this trend is not altogether agreeable. There are grounds for believing that when a subject becomes overly self-conscious about its methods, it is decadent. "In the great ages of Art no one theorized about aesthetics," art historian Bernard Berenson once remarked, and perhaps this is true in other domains as well. Moreover, the historian instinctively clings to the realm of common discourse, as we know; he resists being drawn into esoteric realms of theory. He would rather be inconsistent and human than inhumanly consistent.

Yet historians cannot really escape theory, and the emergence of journals such as *History and Theory* in the past few years (since 1960, in this case), together with a spate of books about philosophy and theory of history, many by philosophers (reflecting a strong

10. Review of R. Stover, *The Nature of Historical Thinking* (Chapel Hill: North Carolina University Press, 1967), in *Philosophical Books,* vol. IX, no. 3 (October, 1968), p. 26.

recent development of interest in history from that quarter, a result in part of Collingwood's influence) but with some historians participating in the debate, testifies to this fact. Perhaps the wisest remarks on this question of theory and practice came from Baudelaire, who in his essay on Richard Wagner declared that while critics seldom make poets, "every great poet naturally and inevitably becomes a critic. I am sorry for the poets whom only instinct guides; I believe them to be incomplete. In the spiritual life of the best ones, a crisis inevitably arises wherein they wish to reason out their art, to discover the obscure laws in virtue of which they have created, and to draw from this study a series of precepts the purpose of which is to produce perfect poetry." Good historians usually become interested in their art, too, and wish to explore its theoretical foundations. One cannot write history from theory, but one cannot write the best history unconsciously, either. Historians do not ordinarily find their way to history via theory, they simply fall in love with it or find it interesting for reasons they would be hard put initially to define. But as they develop they do become concerned to "reason out their art" and thereby write better history.

The second part of this book is concerned with the theory of history, adopting an analytical approach whereas this first part has been historical. But we can record, as a logical introduction to that section, that at the present stage of its development history is marked by an increasing interest in its theory. (Likewise in its history, for similar reasons.) In this respect, it is in step with the modern spirit in other walks of intellectual life, for modern novelists likewise are more self-conscious about method, and in philosophy the linguistic school urges everyone to examine his vocabulary most carefully in order to escape intellectual confusion. To be acutely aware of how much of our thought relates to previously unexamined assumptions and archetypes of the mind or to linguistic confusions or to personified or reified abstractions seems a vital part of our contemporary intellectual spirit, with its subjectivism and skepticism, its awareness of myth. (In a book called *Mythologie de notre temps,* Alfred Sauvy has pointed out how myth-encrusted are the "social sciences.") The leading philosophical school, in addition to linguistic analysis and existentialism, is called phenomenology; it is dedicated to careful examination of such usually unexamined preconditions of thought, the unexplored topography of the mind as it exists prior to all thought and expression.

For history such exploration is relatively new in any thorough and systematic way. Not so many years ago Morris R. Cohen, a philosopher with a wayward interest in the philosophy of history, remarked that it was the most neglected of all fields. It is true that historians have shown an occasional desire to talk about their craft and its curious ways, its possible value, and its strange imperfections; a literature of this sort goes quite a way back, and it is valuable. Macaulay, Froude, Acton and many other great historians left interesting essays on such themes. But there was little system in such inquiries, nor were historians really very interested in them. They were much too busy doing the arduous work of historical inquiry, a work demanding, as has often been noted, both relentless energy and great intellectual concentration. The ruminations of historians on methodological themes were occasional pieces. The philosophers were scarcely interested. The term "philosophy of history" meant speculative and conjectural schemes of history such as Hegel's or Comte's, and these went out of fashion. Today it means theory not about the past itself but about how the human mind goes about creating a coherent and useful reconstruction of the past.

We may in conclusion review some of these questions about history which have come up in the course of its long history and have recently seemed more urgent than ever. Is there any coherent pattern or any meaning in the events of the past? Is it a predetermined pattern, excluding free will in some degree? Can one derive from past events valid generalizations about human social behavior or profit from the "lessons of history"? Is it possible for the historian to rise above his special position in time and space and see the past objectively, or is he condemned always to read his prejudices and peculiarities into it? If so, does this make history only a variety of propaganda? Can historians make profitable use of methods and ideas from such other disciplines as sociology, psychology, economics, or even mathematics? Is history an art, a science, an applied science, a branch of ethics or of politics—or is it something unique which partakes of all of these areas of human thought and action? Is it possible to enter imaginatively into the minds of past actors on the stage of history and thus re-create their motives? Should we study the past for its own sake or to shed light on the present and its problems? And what exactly does this study of the past supply that is valuable or useful to man? About these and other questions historians have disagreed and are disagreeing.

PART II

THE CHALLENGE
OF HISTORY

Chapter 8

INTRODUCTION AND DEFINITION

As the preceding chapters have demonstrated, self-conscious historians have long grappled with the numerous theoretical and methodological problems suggested by their own discipline. Most of these problems have never been solved to the complete satisfaction of either all historians or of all the increasing number of philosophers who think about history. Thus, the controversies still rage, and at an ever more subtle and rigorous level. Near ignorance of these perplexing issues scarcely becomes a historian. But historians must not become so morbidly involved in theoretical perplexities that they flounder in innervating anxiety. They still need to create histories. The best antidote for either extreme—ignorance or innervation—is a discriminating and wide understanding of these controverted issues or of a subject area now generally termed the critical philosophy of history. This and the following chapters should provide some of that understanding.

One must not make either too many, or the wrong, claims for the value of philosophical self-consciousness on the part of historians. Above all, one must not expect such self-consciousness automatically to make one a historian. A philosophic genius may develop a clear and precise definition of history, see its exact relationship to other disciplines, understand all its methodological intricacies, and appreciate its various personal and social uses, but yet be a poor historian. The exacting demands of historical inquiry have to be learned through practice and assimilated as working habits. There is no shortcut. An awareness of theoretical issues will, at best, only provide some important critical guidelines in the learning of such habits. But a critical understanding of history does contribute immensely to appreciation, to an awareness of both the intellectual dilemmas and the intellectual challenges of the discipline. Unless leavened by such an appreciative awareness, a historical apprenticeship can be an intellectually deadening pathway to mere technical proficiency.

No problem about history is so encompassing, and thus quite so perplexing, as definition. What is history? Any answer inevitably begs other theoretical issues, such as generalization, explanation, causation, objectivity, and use. Also, almost any simple definition forces one to become a partisan of some minority viewpoint. No definition, and certainly no brief definition, can encompass the many varied, often eccentric conceptions offered by historians or by philosophers. Thus, one may emphasize history's subject matter, its selective criteria, its verification techniques, the logical form of its explanations, or its conceived function or use. It is therefore no surprise that the very word "history" is a vast ambiguity.

The most crucial distinction in assessing varied definitions of history is the quite significant difference between a definition of a deposited or completed history, and particularly of its logical form, and a definition of historical inquiry, and particularly of the focal object of such inquiry. Since recent philosophers have been so concerned with formal and logical issues, they more often than not have taken histories (not historians) as the object requiring definition and have easily accepted either a simple narrative definition or at least some qualified narrative conception. Working historians, on the other hand, are most often inclined to define history by reference to the immediate goals of their own inquiry, and thus they often stress causal or structural analysis or interpretative judgments and either minimize or exclude narrative construction. From their definitional perspective, such exclusion is justified, for their immediate object in pursuing some line of inquiry and even in reporting on it is usually not the telling of a story.

The different perspectives are not exclusive or in conflict. Even though working historians, particularly in highly developed and elaborately specialized fields, rarely tell stories, they are nonetheless contributing to often well-known stories, either by refining or by extending them. In fact, today, most historians are engaged in just such an undertaking. Many stories, about nations, cultures, or individuals, have been often told. At least in their main outlines and dominant themes, they are already a part of general knowledge. But no story is perfect. Each invites new insight and additional elaboration. Thus, a historian may seek out new causes, more carefully describe some pattern of culture or personality, or introduce some new theory that makes sense out of heretofore mysterious events. If viewed in isolation, apart from the ever tentative story that originally suggested this area of inquiry, such products of the historian hardly seem historical at all. His assertions may be in the past tense, but collectively they may reveal no development in time and suggest nothing remotely resembling a coherent story. Thus, it is at least verbally confusing to describe an analysis of the causes of the French Revolution as a history, but it is quite plausible to cite it as a possibly important contribution to a history of the revolution.

As a unified story, any history may reflect the earlier research findings of many individuals, even though only one author has constructed it in its present form. Those who carry out the detailed research, even though some by inclination or ability never come to tell such stories, are surely deserving of the title of historian, perhaps as much as is the storyteller. They may even reflect more demanding skills; in any case, they possess quite different skills. But only because someone has, or eventually will, construct the stories can the nonstorytellers earn the title of historians. In this sense, their role, however critical, is contributory. This makes even more clear that the word "story," or its more pretentious twin, "narrative," stands for inescapable attributes of any history. For example, a history always relates time-separated events. Given such events, some must come before others; this makes it possible to locate beginnings and endings. And given some relationship between events, there is always the possibility of locating some pattern or theme. These characteristics—beginnings and endings, development in time, continuity or thematic unity—are all properties of stories.

These very elementary distinctions allow some working definitions. A *history* is, at the very least, a story. A *historian* either tells or somehow contributes to the telling of stories. But obviously a history is a special kind of story, for it is both a purportedly true story and also always a story about the past. And, at least by conventional disciplinary classification, and possibly because of intrinsic qualities in its subject matter, we usually reserve the word "history" for stories about the human past or about the humanly related past. Thus, we have the most complete provisional definition: *a history* (not a historical inquiry) *is a true story about the human past*. However arbitrary, this definition will serve us well as a point of departure. Almost every

word in the definition begs elaboration and qualification. Even if most
philosophers and historians were willing to accept such a provisional
and simple verbal definition, they would still mean quite different
things by the words used. Thus, such a definition implicates almost
all, and resolves almost none, of the subtle problems that haunt
history. But it can be a working tool for seeking out the exact sense
in which a history can be true or how it can be made true; how pastness, or time, enters into and conditions all historical judgments; and
how the historical subject matter—man—conditions the type of
explanations offered by historians.

History, as the telling of stories about the past, was undoubtedly an
ancient even though nonrigorous activity, although few early storytellers sought "truth" in the sense of severely factual accuracy. We
have none of the early product. Surely soon after man first developed
a language he began to recount memorable past events and to construct sagas and epics. But man's earliest conceptual products, as well
as many of his later ones, did not develop in pure form. He did not
distinguish true from purely imaginative stories or his stories from his
earliest theories about his universe. Early men, as average men today,
easily merged many forms of linguistic activity—purely imaginative
(fantasy, poetry, numbers); imaginative, cognitive, particularistic
(history, common-sense wisdom); and imaginative, cognitive, and
general (cosmology, early forms of empirical science). Such complex
human constructs as religion often made use of all human arts, including expressive forms in its ritual and linguistic forms in its epics and
its theories about gods and nature.

But whether isolated in fact or not, constructing stories about the
human past is a distinctive conceptual activity. Like all conceptual
arts, it requires imaginative construction. As a literary art, it involves
not only conventional rules of grammar but has to meet the formal
requirements of a story (theme, development). Since telling a story
requires many inferences, the historian as storyteller must observe
some conventional rules of logic. Since he tries to tell true stories, he
must adhere to accepted rules of evidence. And whenever history
attains the level of a demanding art, it requires contributory nonstorytellers who, in highly specialized inquiries, rigorously attend to problems of inference and evidence. These inferential and evidential
requirements decisively separate history from other forms of literature.
Almost incidentally, the final narrative form, and much more crucially,

the necessary incorporation of particular, nonrecurring, qualitatively unique, humanly significant aspects of events as well as the narrowly abstract and general features, separate it from the generalizing sciences. But this last distinction is so crucial and so at the center of contemporary historiographical controversy that it will receive detailed attention in the next chapter.

But one can still ask: Why restrict history to the human past; why exclude natural history? Before answering this question, one must respond to another question. What is the human past? Surely we now see many events, remote from and unknown to a person in the past, as vitally related to him and thus typically and correctly incorporate them into a history about him. Even though unknown by such a person, these events were very significant to him; if they had been known, he would have feared or acclaimed them. (Unknown to me, a rumor about my private life prevented me from obtaining a crucial position. My biographer may find this out.) Thus the historian of mankind often has to use a criterion of relativity that his historical subjects could not have shared. And because of vast chains of possible relationships, almost any nonhuman event, such as even an event in the solar system, can be shown to have some vital relationship to particular men—to their survival or their suffering or their fulfillment. Thus, the human past, so expanded, seems to have no clear limits. It can, by one perspective or another, include almost any conceivable past.

The distinction between human history and natural history has to be drawn another way, by attention to selective criteria rather than by any intrinsic quality in much of the common subject matter. The historian of mankind selects only events as they relate to human purposes, whether the subject so understood these relationships or not. The natural historian, on the other hand, may select from among some of the same events and may even on occasion combine them in a similar temporal order, but he selects events not because of their direct relationship to human purposes. That many of his recorded events did relate to human purposes is completely incidental to him, for it is outside of his frame of reference and has no role in what events he selects or in how he orders them. Moreover, an intrusion of human purposes and values as selective criteria would be distorting and confusing to him. Of course, he may well expect his natural history to be of some use to someone, to serve some human purpose.

Some conception of use must have guided him in selecting the natural history that he was to write and even in selecting how he would construct it. Without some such object in mind, no one would write natural histories. Thus, the compiling of natural histories, as an example of purposeful and significant human endeavor, becomes a prime subject for the future historian of mankind.

We can now begin an answer to the original question: why restrict history to the human past? The question is two-pronged. It may be considered largely semantical: why restrict the English word "history" to stories about the human past? The answer to this has to be that, at least in part, the restriction is arbitrary. Given a difference of selective criteria that allows one to distinguish between human and natural history, one may still broaden the meaning of the word "history" to encompass both, and indeed one has strong reasons to do so since they share a formal similarity (both are stories about the past). But one may want to narrow the meaning of the word so that it properly applies only to human history and demand a qualifying adjective for "natural" history as something other than the real product. This restriction of meaning seems arbitrary, but it may rest at least in part on an apprehension of a major difference in the subject (not the form) of the two types of history, a difference that justifies a different label for two distinct products.

Thus, the question may be seen as more substantive than semantical. Beyond the possibility of discriminating between them, what are the principal differences between human and natural history? If the difference is great, if in fact, as the more partisan proponents of human history have argued, the two are worlds apart, as qualitatively different as any two subjects could ever be, then the word "history," if our language is not to be terribly confusing, should be the exclusive property of only one of quite polar disciplines. When put this way, the question opens up a real can of worms and is an entrée into the most basic issues concerning history. What is at issue is nothing less than man himself and his assumed or asserted uniqueness. After all, man talks, conceptualizes, values, purposes, enlists in causes. Rocks and plants and dogs do not. Therefore, the argument can be put, the human past is qualitatively different from the past of inanimate objects or even of nonconceptualizing (or mindless, unspiritual, amoral) animals. This is so even if men are also animals and are in some sense constituted by chemical compounds and are thus, in some perspective, under certain descriptions, subject matter for natural histories or, to implicate another issue, for general types of explanation.

Unless a special status can be given to man, either as substantially different from animals or as so different in function as to mean a virtual difference of kind, then the special claims for human history evaporate. It becomes not only a mere, distinguishable subclass of natural history but, in the same sense as natural history, an early and more primitive form of science, a preface to more lawful, universal, timeless, and thus useful ways of dealing with phenomena. Often history may be the only realized way of dealing with phenomena, especially human phenomena, but in this perspective it always begs a better way and must yield when such can be produced.

If, by claiming some substantial uniqueness in man, one tries to validate some special status for human history, he has to enter the labyrinth of traditional metaphysics. He has to deal with ontological issues, or with conceptions of reality. This strategy is no longer in fashion, although it flourished among nineteenth-century idealists. It is also a strategy full of traps and confusing polarities. Yet the ghosts of traditional ontologies—of reductionist idealisms and materialisms and unbridgeable dualisms—still lurk in the wings. And however many times the old mind-body problem is laid to rest in its now well-marked philosophic grave, it still lurks all too often in the interstices and ambiguities of our language, ever ready to exact its due in confusion and perplexity. Most disquieting of all, so long as competing views of history retain their ties to mechanistic, mentalistic, or vitalistic ontologies, they involve unbridgeable gulfs open to no intellectual reconciliation.

The metaphysical traps suggest that, for the historian at least, the most fruitful way of seeking out or vindicating human uniqueness is not in ontological excursions but in the humble analysis of distinctive modes of behavior. Such an analysis avoids major speculative leaps and can be exempt from the censure of deeply felt private beliefs. Such an analysis cannot bypass all ontological issues; these cannot be so easily routed, although they can be ignored. But such an approach does provide the means for either bypassing or ignoring reductionist ontologies of all types. The following pages will involve such an analysis and offer at least a preliminary sketch of certain unique features present in human societies. These features will then serve, in subsequent chapters, to vindicate the possibility that historical thinking constitutes a distinctive discipline that deals in a distinctive way with distinctive phenomena, finally making a distinctive contribution to human aspirations.

Man talks, both aloud and to himself. This is his most distinctive behavior. It is quite enough. In all of our as yet experienced universe, only man has developed a symbolic language. Such a language both facilitates and conditions learning. Man has either entirely or in large part replaced instincts by elaborate but acquired patterns of behavior. In fact, such learned behavior includes learning to talk and to think, or to manipulate symbolic meanings. And almost all other human behavior is interactive with, and conditioned by, this linguistic behavior. The word "culture" can be used, if a bit too loosely for some scientists, to designate not only a body of shared, evolving meanings, encoded in and expressed by the conventional symbols of a human society, but also for all aspects of nonlinguistic behavior displaying the influence of such symbolic meanings. Used in such a general sense, culture is as broad as mankind, and has little relationship to endless attempts to discriminate between particular "cultures." Linguistic tools are surely as important a component of human behavior as either inheritance or the aspects of behavior learned without the direct or indirect aid of language. In fact, the most distinguishing human behavior—that for which we feel justified in using the term "man"—is culturally determined, for it is either the using of symbols or behavior closely related to symbols. Thus, the use of symbolic language radically separates man in function but not in structure from other organisms. By use of conventional symbols he is able not only to think and communicate but to project alternatives of action and to unite with other men in common projects made possible by shared meanings. He is able to be part of a communicative universe, or a community, that displays some organic unity of its own, which has, in its organization and reciprocal relationships, characteristics that are not a mere sum of its separable individual parts. In fact, if completely separated from a communicative universe, an individual never becomes a man, for he cannot learn to talk.

Historians, ever constructing and perfecting their stories about the human past, may, among other things, endlessly recount the developments of new meanings in a given human society. They may focus on the meanings themselves, or particularly on broader and more encompassing bodies or systems of meanings (ideologies, religions, and sciences), or on the behavior variously conditioned by culture, on habits, institutions, and stylistic forms. But no historian can grasp all facets of culture; a complete cultural history is impossible. Moreover, any historian is a participant in some human society, more than likely of the one he writes about, and thus he is always captive to some of its most basic assumptions. Yet, in a curious sense, he is also master of these assumptions. For any belief or cultural form, if it attains any degree of awareness in a historian, may become a subject in his narrative.

When emerging man learned to talk (it might be less confusing if the word "man" referred only to talking and thinking animals rather than to a certain biological species), he became a veritable god. He now had, at least potentially, a tremendous power to control events, and in his symbolic creations he now possessed new objects of great esthetic value. But as with all new tools, he had to pay a price. Even the earliest symbols (expressed either as words or gestures), loose and rich as they must have been, were still selective and abstract. No symbol could be as full as the perceptual image that it stood for. Man only encoded the more arresting and striking features of an experience (of a pure phenomenon, of sense imagery and feeling). Possibly the first symbols were like proper names and thus were least abstract. They stood for specific, individual things, not for classes of things. But symbols did not have great utility until they were even more narrowly selective, encoding only the more general features of an experience. Only then did they become class terms or concepts. Only then could a word or gesture warn of danger from bears rather than from "Bruin"; only then could a broad community of meanings develop, stretching far beyond the particular objects encountered by individuals. But greater generality, apart from adding to usefulness, forced symbols ever further away from the richness of perception and toward quite abstract and narrow regularity and similarity. The elusive, vague, rich, discontinuous nuances of experience remained largely uncoded and uncommunicable.

To reduce the content of any experience into a concept, to class-name it, is to narrow it to the elements or features also present in other unique but somewhat similar experiences. Some persons, remarking this aspect of language, glorying in existential experience, have berated symbols and concepts. But in all ages, overintellec-tualized men have loved regularity and order and have glorified the generalizable features of experienced objects. To them, that which was shared with others was the archetypal form, the real essence, of the object; all the particularizing features, those not subsumable under the essence, were accidental or scarcely real at all. It has been equally inviting to ontologize these essences (Platonism), to see reality as being composed of them or of a divine mind that thought them into being and sustained them. Here in the realm of essence there was an ideal order, existing prior to any experiencable object and possibly being the creative source of such objects. Much of Western history can be written around the infatuation with concepts or essences or pure meanings and the inverse disillusionment with the existential richness of immediate perception. Finally, in the twentieth century, the evaluation may be switching, with essences never less loved.

By use of precise concepts, man was able to make all types of distinctions and either discover or create all types of order. He came to believe that one basic distinction was that between himself as conceptualizer and the experienced world that, by concepts, he slowly transformed into a world of conventional and discrete objects. And indeed, self and world, ego and nonego, mind and matter were key concepts, and they still are. They were also sophisticated concepts, for they required inference as well as symbolic invention. Systematic concepts about man as in some sense a mind or spirit and about a world as in some sense material or physical are twice removed from experience, first by the selective generality of class concepts and, secondly, by inferences made from certain conceptualized experiences to the idea of a unified self and some cohering world. These basic conceptions not only abetted religious and scientific myth-making but supported such fundamental metaphysical positions as idealism and materialism. Soon man had his pet pictures of reality–his luxuriant conceptual ontologies—and he too easily ignored the selective and abstractive character of all concepts.

By such a genetic perspective on concepts, it is rather simple to distinguish at least the major forms that human conceptualization could, and eventually would, take. But such formal distinctions rarely fit ordinary discourse. Almost no one fits into one conceptual niche. We are all, at least at times, metaphysicians, theologians, historians, scientists, and dreamers. We rarely consider how these roles interact. In any clear, self-conscious way, it was the classic Greeks who first distinguished professional scientists, philosophers, and historians.

And with this first professionalization of thinking there was both a boon in intellectual rigor and an exaggerated affliction with types of intellectual myopia. Before long the most prestigious conceptual systems, in whatever specialty, became coercive world views, and during their ascendency successfully camouflaged the selective bias that must characterize all such views. Today, we are still legatees of a world view, of a peculiar way of conceiving reality, that has only been one important bequest of the very successful post-Renaissance physical sciences.

The historian must ever emphasize what becomes so evident to him, that all conceptual systems are products of human art. Men construct them, guided by some formal selective criteria, however much they also continuously tie them to perception and thus to some controlling, nonconceptual reality. Growing up in a world of concepts (a cultural environment), a child learns the symbols that, by the conventions of his society and its particular language, go with various experiences. He learns to talk and think. His world is quickly an objectified one, for raw perception is transformed into various classes of things, into an intellectual furniture. To a child this is all given, as are also the more complex conceptual systems that he uses to relate these various objects. But individuals continuously alter old meanings and develop new meanings; people come to accept some of these, and all children then learn them. Our dictionaries grow in testimony to man's conceptual inventiveness, or in some cases by almost accidental accretion. It is almost impossible to think about a subject without adding some new nuance of meaning to our concept of it. Vast intellectual systems, such as a particular religion or science, develop by such gradual steps that it is impossible to distinguish all their key moments or all their key individuals. But any conceptual system is still a human contrivance. The necessary raw materials for it are always cultural. They are a developed language, or a body of conventional symbols, awaiting some new arrangement according to some formal criteria. And insofar as the conceptual construct claims to be true about the directly encountered world, it must also utilize a second raw material—perception.

One type of conceptual activity—one that has been pregnant with suggestions for historians—occupies a special status. This is the attempt to use concepts to picture or explain reality itself, either fully or in its most essential features. This is the ontological enterprise.

Here experiential piety serves well as an antidote to any form of metaphysical arrogance. If one accepts the directly experienced world, or the world of perception, as real, and recognizes the selective aspect and the human origin of all concepts, then no conceptual product can ever encompass reality. All conceptual structure is abstract; perception is concrete. There is absolutely no way to bridge the gap so as to make the two identical. This does not preclude selected concepts being tied to perception in a rigorous, unambiguous, and reliable way. It threatens neither objectivity nor existential truth, unless these terms are tied to some copy theory of knowledge. It is so tied when historians moan about the inability of their concepts to do the impossible—to exactly mirror some heretofore hidden historical reality.

To accept our inability to do other than selectively and partially conceptualize reality does not preclude knowledge. In fact, this humility may be a necessary prelude to defining knowledge. Valid knowing, in any area, is just a selective conceptualization of some experiences, even when, as in history, our knowledge refers beyond the focal experience that supports it. The nature of some hidden reality does not determine the cognitive validity of our chosen concepts; rather, this validity depends upon a relationship that we establish with an experienced reality. Man's inability to frame a completely adequate conceptual ontology in no wise threatens his ability to construct valid cognitive systems either in history or in the generalizing sciences. The lack of any determinable one-to-one relationship between reality and concept does not mean that all valid relationships are impossible between the two or that all concepts are, by this limitation, rendered totally subjective or even without any ontological status. In the poetic language of George Santayana, we can learn much about the workings of God in the world without discovering the ultimate nature of God. To want more than this is to want something other than knowledge.

The very conditions of knowing mean that all cognitive inventions have a human stamp upon them, just as do other arts. Being imaginative inventions, cognitive concepts are less than the encountered reality even when they are faithful to it. By brilliant conceptual invention, man may validly interrelate all his experiences, but in doing this he has to ignore almost all the striking features of each experience. To relate more and more, he must exclude and ignore more and more.

Although in one sense there is no universal science, there may indeed be a universal science of some selected aspects of experience. Limited as we are to the varied accounts we compose about reality and as fruitful as experience is in ever new revelations, only a peculiar type of vanity could lead anyone to affirm a finished ontology, an exact model of human nature, a complete science, or a universal history. And despite the much-discussed speculation of Charles A. Beard, we do not have to leap blindly into these impossible labyrinths and opt for one or another competing position in order to deal objectively with reality. In fact, such blind leaps into metaphysical cubbyholes involve the very type of "subjectivity" that precludes valid knowing.

The most basic division of constructive conceptualization is that between the cognitive and noncognitive, or between those constructs that claim something about existence and those that do not. Even constructive conceptualization excludes much, if not most, linguistic behavior, for it requires some formal criterion, some ordering, some art, whereas much of the time we are absorbed in spontaneous and unstructured thought, in reverie, dreams, or idle imagination. And in artful conceptualizing, the noncognitive probably exceeds the cognitive and often provides more satisfaction. Intent, not form, separates the cognitive and noncognitive. Imagination plays the same crucial role in both. And in this particular form of imagination, the image developed is one of ordered words, with an awareness of their meaning but a near complete suppression of the object images suggested by them. Man shares imagination with other animals. Dogs probably relish images as much as we do, although they do not have our ability to induce images by symbolic stimuli. Since a dog does not have a symbolic language and thus never has the direct experience of talking and thinking, it cannot possibly image patterns of words and, with them, related patterns of meaning. As soon as a child learns a language, he can do just this and open to his fanciful or creative imagination a world closed to any other animal.

In imagination we variously, purposefully, artfully associate words, or concepts, forming various patterns from them. One pattern, and not another, may be thought to parallel a pattern that holds for objects open to direct experience. When we intend concepts to match up to such an existential realm, they are cognitive. Very often, we do not assume the pattern to be existent, but believe that by certain efforts it may become so. Here the concepts make up an ideal. When the concepts intend to express a pattern of *possible* relationships in existence and a pattern possible because of a certain present structure in existence and a pattern that can be realized by utilizing this structure and manipulating it in a certain way, we have one type of meaningful but unverified scientific hypothesis, a type that leads not to discovery but to creative induction. Here the ideal and cognitive use of concepts almost merge. Noncognitive conceptual constructs can be produced with great freedom. But the avoidance of evidential limitations does not excuse inferential sloppiness.

There are two broad polar categories in noncognitive conceptual construction. In one, the concepts are those that express the particular nuances of experience. Here the language of passion and emotion, ambiguous as it may be, alone seems adequate. The conceptual patterns have to do full justice to experience as a human possession and to the way it is experienced more than to the exact object experienced. Then, our conceptual imagination focuses on the distinguishing aspects of experience and thus on what always seems a peculiarly subjective perspective simply because of the admission of the whole range of qualitative uniqueness, of unrepeatable and unrecoverable feelings, and thus of the very aspects of an experience that are personal and, often, also of most value to us. Here, in a literary form of imagination, one pushes abstractions as far from conceptual art as is possible, and accepts only the necessary generality of concepts, of class names. Often, in such rich construction, as in some poetry, the artist tries to wring from language even more than these concepts can ever bear; he does this by metaphoric suggestion and through expressive and rhythmic effects. He does not see the ambiguity of a word but its expressive poverty. He constructs a conceptual product that is a great deal more than conceptual, joining with other, nonlinguistic arts. There are ever recurring moments when we all resent the abstractness of any concept, including one that tries to represent intense emotion. At these moments we stop talking and seek more direct, more overtly sensual forms of expression. We dance in our delight or roll in our torment.

In contrast to such expressive concrete, imaginative constructs are equally free but completely abstract constructs, mathematics being a prime example. Any perceptual moment may have features common to other such moments; some minimal similarity of this sort permits experience-relevant class names. But the ultimate in generality, in universal usefulness, is numerical identity. A tree and a unicorn are equivalent in one respect—their oneness. Quantitative relationships are abstract. They denote few of the perceptual qualities present in existential objects and often display an order never duplicated in events. With no direct homage to perception, one can work out all types of numerical and geometrical patterns and all variety of manipulative rules, using unambiguous but perceptually barren symbols. Insofar as one can discover in the perceived world any constant and widely distributed features, he can correlate them with his abstract imaginative systems. By such abstraction one can unify quite diverse objects and discover certain invariant relationships that hold between them. He can, in other words, bring the precision and inferential exactness of mathematical reasoning into his account of existence. By being selective enough, he can rationalize his world. This, by a good classification, is the work of the scientist.

As it should now be clear, cognitive conceptualization can take the same polar forms as noncognitive concepts. On one hand, one can seek the most detailed and qualitatively exact description of an object or event and thus encompass not only the aspects that are widely present and often repeated but also the most particular and unique features—those that make each event different from all others. On the other hand, one can search out and describe the common features of an experience—those that are the most general and recurrent. And such description almost always requires the guidance of some already developed general knowledge, some relational system, some laws. Also, if one seeks such generality he will have to be quite selective. In the common-sense world, we almost always variously merge qualitative uniqueness and selective abstraction in our concepts. Only with the modern sciences did some men, at certain times, reliably unify far reaches of experience and thus construct the broadest possible classes of phenomena. But, except possibly for physics in its broadest definition, no existential science has a universal subject matter; in fact, all utilize descriptions that are less than fully general. Yet, within however restricted a universe of inquiry, the scientist looks for the most general, the most unifying, and in an instrumental or predictive context, the most useful features of experience.

Thus far, the analysis might suggest that history stands as a cognitive opposite to the generalizing sciences and as a formal twin to literature. Such is not the case. History is closest to common sense

and occupies the treacherous middle ground between concrete particulars and abstract relations. Being a true story, a history has a literary
form and contains much nongeneralizable content. In fact, the distinctive content of history—the humanly significant, culturally con-
ditional aspects of the past—never permits any time-neutral or open
generalizations. But significant events do have many aspects that are
recurrent, widely shared, and, within a limited time context, regular
and predictable. By his selective criteria, a historian may often be
most concerned with these recurrent and enduring aspects of the past,
so that his focus is quite narrow and somewhat abstract. In fact,
historians rarely join the novelist and poet in trying to communicate
the full, qualitative richness of an event. If they did attempt this very
often, they would dwell endlessly on a few events. The historian
rarely tries to relive a past; rather he tries to think about a past in a
valid and instructive way. In certain contexts, he may emphasize, or
even try to describe, the human feelings, the pain and suffering, the
joys and elations, that were part of, or a result of, certain past events.
Some histories are quite evocative. A true account of the past that,
by selective choice, focused primarily upon feeling, even over a very
short but thematically unified period of time, would be a history. But
such a history would be narrowly selective, and it does not represent
the norm for historians. Presenting the exact nuances of feeling, even
when this is remotely possible (rare indeed), is at best only one
permissible emphasis in historical construction.

Because a history is a story of the human past, it at least must
relate to feeling and value. And here a parallel exists between the
historian's use of quantity and quality. Only some historians choose
to recount the history of a particular science or often remark the more
general and repetitious features of past, humanly significant events,
but all historians assume some regularity, some abstract structure in
things. In an at least partially ordered world, the historian plots out
certain sequences of gross events which involve many types of ordered
relationships, standing at the crossroads of many transformative
series. These events make up a story, for they relate sequentially and
reflect some pattern or unity. On an assumed background of more
or less generalizable order, which he may not look for, emphasize,
or try to extend, the historian performs his art.

Likewise, he assumes feeling, or a qualitative dimension, in all the
events that he selects for his narrative. Each historical event must

relate, even though at a distance, and by way of many causal connections, to some human experience, which is never qualitatively
neutral. Pain and bliss, even as structure and law, are always involved.
In fact, quality or value is a key criterion for locating the domain
of the human, as contrasted to the natural, historian. This backdrop
of qualitative experience does not mean that the historian must dwell
endlessly, or even at all, on the way something is experienced. He
may, and most often does, recount what men have experienced and
in what ways they have reacted to experience. Since structure and
value are a part of human experience, they are both implicit in
history. In a selected context, either may become explicit in a historical narrative, but neither need be explicit and neither usually are.
As a subject for historical treatment, generality, or law, is a subject
only because of its relationship to human value. The history of a science
is the history of a human art, never a history of impersonal forces; a
history of man seeking and finding ordered relationships, never the
tracing out of such relationships.

There are few specific limits on a historian's subject matter. The
human past is immense. Within it the historian selects according to
some purpose. He tells the particular story he wants to tell. His story
will be an imaginative product, necessarily formed from concepts and
sharing their abstractness and generality. But being about man's past,
it cannot exclude the qualitative and concrete aspects of human
experience. In many contexts, the historian must report the gross,
particular events that men suffer or effect. He cannot escape the
world of common sense and of ordinary experience. His concepts
must never be so abstract as to lose some of their contextual coloration, their ability to suggest variant nuances that often are more
important to man than the general content. The historian must relin-
quish to the generalizing scientists any exclusive concern with narrowly
selective, recurrent, quantitatively regular features of human experience. It is not the historian's task to isolate these more abstract
aspects of human experience (he may indeed tell about the imaginative, value-pregnant, artful isolating of these abstractions by
scientists), for in doing this he would not only be leaving the world
of ordinary experience, he would also be turning away from a time-
conditioned past. The more abstract conceptual objects of a physicist
are barely open to experience, and then only after long inferential
journeys and through elaborate technical aids to the senses. The

world of electrons is not the world of most human experience but a very special conceptual rendition of such a world. Yet increasing numbers of people are physicists and do experience such abstractions; and these particular abstractions have enabled men to change the world, drastically altering all manner of ordinary human experiences. The development of modern physics is an excellent subject for historical treatment, for it is a fascinating as well as a vital story. It is a story resplendent with value, with joys and frustrations in the effort as well as in the results. But it is a story of a deliberate attempt by man, for his own ends, to formulate very precise concepts that necessarily exclude all reference to value.

Other aspects of our definition of history beg many issues but none as basic as the ones suggested by the word "human." Yet, the "truth" and the "pastness" of a historical narrative implicate some of the most controversial issues in present historiography. The problem of truth relates closely to the much debated issues of objectivity and value judgment, which will be treated in Chapter 11. Suffice it to say here that the historian's subject matter presents certain methodological problems, but there is no logical reason why he cannot tell a story that is as true as any scientific hypotheses. Truth, in either case, requires hypotheses, correct inferences, and evidential support, requirements which the historian not only accepts but successfully applies to his work. Of necessity, the word "truth" is here used in one of many arbitrary ways. It is simply the goal of any existential inquiry. If truth stands for something else, for some exact copy of some unknown or intuitively grasped reality, for some internally consistent relational system, for full and complete accounts, or for some final, fully certain hypothesis or story, then obviously no existential proposition can qualify in history or anywhere else. But these conceptions of truth have no methodological relevance. When they are pulled into a methodological context, they distort and confuse all the crucial issues, as they have done over and over again in historiography.

The pastness of a historical narrative implicates the major themes of the next two chapters, or generality and causality. A historically significant event is not only unique (all events are) but time conditioned. It has a significance and is selected by a historian because of its temporal context and, usually but not always, because of some of its particular and unique features. Thus, two events quite similar in many respects, but occurring at different times, often have greatly disproportionate historical significance. Where an event fits into a series of events and how it relates to other events are important in a history (this is equally true of natural histories). To the historian seeking some causal pattern linking two events separated in time, the most particular and exceptional aspects of an event may be crucial. The historian of the American War for Independence, in the context of a particular story he wants to tell, may not be concerned with the episodes that clearly fit some accepted definition of a revolution or that conform to known behavioral uniformities. The key events for him may be quite particular and exceptional. On the other hand, a social scientist seeking an analytical model of a revolution or looking for enduring uniformities in human behavior would discount these historically significant episodes. He looks for aspects least conditioned by time and least burdened by momentary accidents and eccentricities. However much he uses human and value-laden data from a past age, his selective interest may not allow time or value to play any role in his conceptual constructs. His is then a nonhistorical discipline.

At the level of immediate, relatively indiscriminate perception, and of the loose concepts by which we ordinarily objectify or name it, every object is almost overwhelmingly individual, unique, and wayward. The only obvious relationships are temporal and spatial, and these are rooted in aspects of immediate experience and not in some type of analysis or inference. But aided by quite precise and discriminate concepts and guided by accepted generalizations, we can analytically dissect much of our gross experience and slice perceived objects into such uniform and general descriptive constituents as elements, cells, atoms, and electrons. As experienced entities (an atom can be "seen" indirectly), these have the specificity—the temporal and spatial contextuality—of any perceived objects. Each atom is different from any other atom, at the very least in its spatial and temporal coordinates; it is always a potential character in some natural history.

Even the indirect perception of an atom is a value-laden human happening; it is an episode in some human history. In theory, the movements of an individual electron (granted some limit conditions set by quantum theory) can be traced and its history told over a period of time. But as a highly analytical, barely experienceable entity, an electron usually has significance not in its individual peculiarity but in its formal, abstract, invariant qualities and in the regularities of behavior it displays. Even when an electron is crucial in an experiment, no one cares about its remote past history or about its idiosyncratic career. It makes sense to speak of the French Revolution of 1789 but not of the "Smith electron of 1946." The word "revolution" denotes a connected series of roughly unified, partly classifiable, but always contextually variant events and cries out for contextual or historical qualification—for the when and the where. This is true of most complex wholes, for by greater complexity, by the inclusion of elementary simples of many types, there is an almost inevitable decrease in generality and in behavioral order. But *any conceptualized experience, any object,* can be viewed as an individual surviving through time and thus as part of some history, natural or human. And even the most complex events, such as the French Revolution, can be viewed as exemplifying some discrete class entity or some asserted behavioral pattern. The conceptual use may be indicated, but never dictated, by the object. Ultimately, purpose determines use.

Even granting that every thing has a temporal (or spatiotemporal) context and that where value is also present there is subject matter for human history, one can still view the telling of true stories about the past as an inferior conceptual activity, as a secondary path to understanding, and as at best an interim substitute for general knowledge or lawlike forms of explanation. Just as it is usually foolish to view an electron historically, just as natural history is often a poor substitute for theoretical synthesis, so it may be foolish and archaic to view man historically. Why not, in all cases, move away from history to a true science of man, to an unambiguous human nature and to universal and necessary laws that such a nature obeys? This raises issues that reappear in subsequent chapters. Such a challenge, at the very least, requires a historian to vindicate his storytelling by demonstrable uses not served, or not served as well, by the generalizing sciences. It also raises the central issue of the next chapter. Can cultural phenomena—can the distinctively human world of symbolic communication, of purposes, ideals, and final causes—be fully encompassed by general types of description and explanation? Or is there here a subject matter that only permits a genetic or historical treatment?

If all culturally conditioned events could be fully described by their more elemental and universal constituents and explained by invariant and unchanging laws, then the temporal coordinates of human events would seem to have little intellectual significance. In principle if not in fact, one could transform any history, with no cognitive loss and much gain in precision and scope of understanding, into empirically valid generalizations and laws. The historian feels compelled to reject this view and to present good reasons for rejecting it. But he must not overextend his claims for history. He does just this if he suggests that any event, including a culturally conditioned event, ever fails, under some possible, narrowed description, to conform to one or more empirically verifiable generalizations. By careful discrimination, any perceived object has features that are also present in other, possibly all other, objects. If one looks for similarities, again guided by general knowledge, he can always find them at some level of abstractness. But if he wants, and without all the intellectual effort, he can also find the particular and the unique, and between these poles he can find all manner of limited sameness and rare but not unique particulars. All experienced objects are not electronlike (almost none are); not all involve inexpressible floodtides of feeling.

There remains an unremarked alternative. Could not history become as lawlike and as predictive as physics? Why not use the past to unravel the invariant and universal laws that govern man's journey through time? In the clear light of such a universal history, of such a truly superscience, one could dissipate the apparent particularity, the contextual relativity, of human events, not by a deliberate and selective abstraction as in the present empirical sciences, but by making each and every particular event a lawful and necessary part of a grand scheme. Then our histories, ever unfinished and partial, could yield to a universal view, one equally relevant to past and future. We could finish all our accounts and tell the story of the future. The past then only serves us in revealing a heretofore hidden pattern. Our fumbling stories, however laboriously constructed, are only prefatory and henceforth inferior, not to the specialized, generalizing sciences, but to a vast, essentially ontological schema. Of course, all this begs the crucial question: is there such a schema to be discovered? Few working historians believe there is. Past endeavors in the speculative philosophy of history, from Isaiah to Hegel to Toynbee, have lacked both precision and persuasive evidence and have involved both logical and methodological illusions. This, of course, does not prove that all future attempts have to fail. But the wide gulf between past aspirations and almost complete failures in execution, plus the diversity and the complexity of cultural phenomena, nourishes both a profound doubt that such an overarching pattern exists or, even if in some sense it were meaningful to say that it might, that it could ever be open to human understanding.

A more critical objection is that such grand schemes threaten history or even doom it. For they render pathetic its laborious techniques, so humble beside laws that determine all that has happened and all that will happen not only in appropriate areas of selective abstraction but everywhere. The specialized, empirical sciences pose no real threat to history. Often, in more direct and dramatic ways than history, they serve man. Their very abstractness, their selective bias, removes any possible conflict, for what they select in no wise threatens the temporal contextuality or the genetic determinants of all individual events. Some speculative philosophies of history are quite imaginative; many represent great and challenging products of the human mind. But they, in all their formal completeness, and not our hesitant, unsure, ever partial and quite selective stories about the human past, are subjective affirmations. As such, these grandiose but fictional stories can never be told by a historian. His poetry has a more demanding discipline and can never break into such wanton and impious excesses.

Chapter 9

HISTORY AND THE GENERALIZING SCIENCES

Long before man developed any of the present sciences, he was already telling at least crude stories about his past. History was a prescientific form of conceptual construction. But the storyteller must always have recourse to some conventional conception of order and structure in things; otherwise, he can scarcely construct plausible narratives. In fact, historians have usually relied upon accepted generalizations, in rare cases upon the most recent and innovative generalizations, about the world. At times scientific knowledge has seemed threatening to the historian. General knowledge, when pushed too far or when turned into fashionable ontologies, has seemed to deny a place for historical man and has left no humanistic subject matter for the historian. Unfortunately, in overly defensive retaliation, historians have minimized the success of the generalizing sciences or have urged a type of historicism that elevated historical knowledge to an especially privileged position that it hardly deserves.

Contemporary conceptions of scientific inquiry scarcely predate the Renaissance. Only then were scientists such as Kepler and Galileo able successfully to tie nonteleological, rational, mathematical forms to experience. They used internally consistent, precise theories to relate formerly diverse phenomena. Descartes grasped the implications of such ordered and lawful relationships and gloried in a great, impersonal world machine. The fully lawful and determinate world of matter encompassed every phenomenon except mind, a noncorporeal and ghostly substance that usually inhabited the fully material bodies of men. Except for this ego-salvaging concession to man,

151

Descartes finally and completely deanthropomorphized the universe. Soon it was at least possible to suggest that man also be deanthropomorphized (incongruous as this seems) and conceived as fully part of a single, physical continuum.

In Newtonian mechanics man had a fully mature science of great scope and value. Surely here was the ideal explanatory system, an ideal to be sought in all empirical sciences, including those concerned with man. David Hume tempered the early enthusiasm engendered by such a rational system. He stressed the empirical foundations of all scientific laws and challenged the legitimacy of any a priori importation of certainty or ontological revelation into existential propositions. Kant, standing at the crossroads of so much of modern thought, accepted at least a part of Hume's skepticism. He also denied any metaphysical reach for the existential sciences. But to him the formal aspects of scientific explanation (primarily mathematics) were analytical elaborations of given constituents of mind. By emphasizing the a priori or rational side of science, he tried to minimize the skeptical import of a rampant empiricism. In a path followed by later analytical philosophers of science, he also clarified a logical model of explanation, a model which stressed universal and necessary laws. But this model, as any, could become tyrannical as well as useful.

Both historical knowledge and immediate experience provide antidotes for conceptual myopia. Looking back, we cannot miss the variety of, and the continuous changes in, both metaphysical and empirical concepts. Whether structural or functional, the generalizing sciences have fragmented into many diverse subject areas and have displayed many different conceptual systems. Each major conceptual system subtly induces quite distinctive patterns of thought, as witness the quite different intellectual styles of physicists as compared to experimental psychologists. Even the common methods or explanatory models shared by different sciences are not, as logical formalists too easily assume, either a priori or coercive in all inquiry. Methods of inquiry and forms of explanation are cultural products; they developed through time and through successful use. They can now, belatedly, be analyzed by logicians. In a different way, a close inspection of immediate experience discloses the selective nature of all generalizations with empirical relevance and the particular features of experience taken as focal for the various sciences. Since selective abstraction is clearly present in all cases, then any explanatory system, however complete and determinant, still unifies only a fraction of the rich quality directly present to us. No empirically validated explanatory concepts can ever be all-inclusive, for they relate only the aspects of experience to which we adapt them.

Since there seem to be no empirical laws governing the total historical process, the historian cannot work within a tight, selective conceptual system. He does not apply historical laws to individual cases or show how one can deduce individual historical events from such laws. Even at the less general level of class terms, it is hard to find any classifications, except possibly rough chronological periodizations, that are peculiarly historical. The concepts and the words used by a historian are usually those of prescientific common sense. Thus, he disciplines his constructs by esthetic criteria and by evidential requirements, but by no arbitrary and precise symbols (no jargon), by no clear, defined manipulative system, by no master explanatory concepts or models. This both invites sloppiness and encourages breadth. The historian often lacks even simple precision in his terms or rudimentary inferential rigor in his causal statements; yet he almost never displays the narrowed, experientially selective, overly abstracted outlook of many scientists, who too easily assume that reality is simply a further projection, in form and content, of their own conceptual tools. It is easy for a historian to assume that all concepts derive from experience and that they must never claim more than experience justifies. Conversant with many conceptual forms, historians easily view experienced reality as multidimensional. They thus accommodate their thinking to diverse categorizations of phenomena.

For anyone who loves order and symmetry, the most intellectually satisfying knowledge, and in many contexts also the most useful, is the most general. Kant stressed universal and necessary laws and in so doing set the goal for any empirical science. But the very goal determines the conditions. Only those aspects of the perceived world that are ever present, that are ever similar in form, that always reveal invariant, precise relationships, can meet this standard. And it seems, although there is no way ever to be sure, that every phenomenon does contain this regularity, however narrow, selective, and abstract it is. A minimal but ever present order seems to underlie all events. This pervasive order makes up what we call the material world. In broadest definition, physics is the science that encompasses it. The old word "matter," stripped of all its metaphysical meanings, stands for this structure.

Matter is seemingly present as one feature of every event, although one may not remark or notice it. Only selective interest leads us to look for it. In fact, the material aspect of most experience is so narrow, so small a part of the qualitatively rich whole, that it took centuries of discriminatory refinement in concepts before man could isolate and characterize matter; and of course the detailed characterization still goes on. But in an age when almost everyone is aware of even some of the details, it is well to remember that matter, basic concept that it is, remains a human invention. It is a characterization of certain irreducible aspects of experience; it is not an ultimate substance finally discovered (or being discovered) in all its ramifications.

Physicists have developed the most discriminating as well as the most general concepts yet attained by man. But generality has come at the expense of complexity and concreteness. Many conceptualized physical objects are only remotely perceptual, and a few useful ones are not perceptual at all. This abstractness has served a good purpose. Only at this level, it seems, can there be firm, invariant relationships of great scope. Only at such an abstract level can we unify in rational, coordinate systems at least some aspect of every experience (for reasons given later, one need not assume that all physical systems make up one supersystem). And only by such conceptual systems can we develop almost unbelievable power over physical events. And power over the physical aspect of events also gives man some desired control over the occurrence of more particular, more valued qualities.

A purely physical world, itself a selective conceptual construct, is a world without quality, without feeling, without purpose, and without history. It is a human conceptual creation deliberately constructed to exclude everything distinctively human. In such a world, all gross material objects include simple constituents which observe invariant laws. Subject to the laws of motion, this world reflects continuous transformations but no agency. Given sufficient knowledge, one can trace chains of these transformations endlessly backward or forward, with neither direction having any physical significance. But to talk of such tracing—or even to talk of past and future and with it of a unidirectional perspective—is to leave the conceptualized world of matter and to revert to the godlike creature who invented it and who uses it to make such tracings into the past or to predict some future. By physical concepts alone, neither life nor cultural phenomena can even be located, for they involve other than simple physical aspects of experience and have to be differently conceptualized. Of course, since physical processes are ever present, and in this sense universal, correlative physical attributes are always present with organic or cultural phenomena. But only by reversion to a form of conceptualization that discriminates life from nonlife, or symbolic mental functioning from organic and physical processes, can we ever isolate the exact physical correlates. When our vision is limited to the abstract, material skeleton, we have no clues as to whether any flesh covers any of the bones, much less any guide to what the flesh is like.

In man's expressive as well as in his conceptual arts, abstract forms are simple, universal, and difficult to come by. Their discrimination requires great mental discipline or a willingness to exclude those aspects of experience with the most immediate value to man, those nongeneralizable qualities that make one experience more enjoyable than another. Thus, rigorous physical concepts, being abstract, are almost all late-comers. Men only slowly abstracted them out of common-sense conceptions that always had some place for quality and for at least vague concepts of life and mind, to focus on the two other most obvious, major characteristics of our experienced world.

A great fallacy can distort understanding of the generalizing sciences. Perhaps because of a rational bias, or an esthetic mystique that favors unifying scope over perceptual richness, one can view the more abstract and general concepts of the physical sciences as not only more useful (a function of precision and explanatory scope) than the loose concepts of common sense but also as closer to reality. But if by "reality" one means that qualitatively varied world directly encountered in perception, then just the opposite is true. Physical concepts are further from experienced reality (and they surely have no power to create some new reality) and also encompass much less of reality than common-sense constructs. But they encompass the very aspects of experienced reality that are most subject to rational control—the regular, lawful, predictable aspects. History must utilize some of the loose, rich concepts of common sense. It is not, because of its lack of precise, predictive concepts, less real, or even necessarily less valid or true, than the generalizing sciences. It is, in fact, closer to experienced reality and can be true to broader dimensions of reality. To sacrifice generalizing reach is to open up the possibility of greater reach in other directions. Which way we want to reach is, or should be, controlled by our purpose.

Historically, conceptions fitted to more complex, less general relationships, such as conceptions of mind and life, came before precise
physical concepts. In fact, early men conceived all reality as mindlike,
as willful and whimsical. But, as we try to decipher an evolutionary
pattern of development on our earth, simple physical relationships
came first, then organisms, and only belatedly culture, or the type of
interpersonal unity made possible by shared meanings. Culture is thus
a belated and rare phenomenon, for it exists in only a minuscule
portion of the universe that we have so carefully objectified in our
physical sciences.

Either life or mind, however primitive their origins as concepts, can
be rigorously defined, although in their complexity they present great
hazards to generalization. It is difficult to find empirical justification
for any enduring and universal structure of a distinctively organic or
mental type. At least, no generality even in the organic world can
have the scope of physical laws, for organic material is quite limited.
Without doubt, organic phenomena, such as adaptation, reproduction,
or nutrition, can be rigorously classified and organized. Yet, rarely in
the biological sciences does anyone try to isolate or maintain pure
biological theories; instead, as in contemporary genetics, scientists
work out composites of biological and physical theory. Biological
phenomena, discoverable only within the conceptual horizons of
biology, are always open, thenceforth, to purely physical analysis, and
thus to correlate types of explanation. In many cases today (if not in
most), about the only role played by biological concepts is the isolation of phenomena for physical explanation. The end products of
biophysical or biochemical inquiry will be physical uniformities
correlative to biological universes and not properly biological explanations at all. Yet, without a biological conceptual perspective, no such
physical problems could be isolated. Reproduction is not, by any
chemical conceptualization, an isolatable phenomenon. Despite some
recent, quite complex speculation by physicists, no one has successfully reduced such biological concepts to physical terms without some
loss of meaning. The replicating features of reproduction, viewed
even in molecular terms, cannot be completely subsumed under any
physical laws, although reproduction does observe certain physical
laws and certainly does not violate any such laws.

For the historian, the all-important characteristic of experience is
mind, the concept that best stands for functional traits that man does

not share with other animals. The human past is always in part the past of man as a creature of culture, as a developer and user of symbolic meanings, as a product of existing cultural forms. Only his possession and use of such symbols allows man to be historically as well as organically and physically conditioned. This emphasis upon culture, or upon mind as a transpersonal and enduring body of meanings, does not require an idealistic form of reductionism. Mind, as so defined, is only a fit characterization of some aspects of experienced reality. Such a position is fully consistent with some forms of naturalism.

Although cultural phenomena lend themselves to analysis, classification, and comparison, it is difficult to conceive of any empirically valid, transcultural propositions, or of any valid generalizations about man as a product of culture. If the word "generalization" denotes not only universality (propositions of the form "all X is Y") but also temporal and spatial openness (*"always, everywhere,* all X is Y"), then cultural man can never be the proper subject of general statements. But this does not preclude intracultural patterns that endure over long periods of time and allow valid, reliably predictive but time-limited summary judgments ("in this century all Americans sleep in beds"). Such judgments, at the risk of linguistic confusion, may be called *closed generalizations,* for such assertions require temporal or spatial qualifications. Such closed generalizations can be correctly asserted about the most restricted universes, including ones that encompass only one individual and for only a brief period of time. Possibly, the organic and behavioral sciences are also limited to time-conditioned and thus to closed generalizations, closely tied as they often are to correlative physical structure. This would suggest that all empirically valid generalizations are physical statements.

Even the acceptance of valid generalizations in the physical sciences begs some complex issues. Physical scientists do generalize. Their statements have this formal property. But the form of their statements is not necessarily the form of things. Thus the structure in physical concepts is only a structure in the language used. To assert more than this is to make an ontological leap of some sort. By an analysis of concepts, the logician can enjoy a nice, agnostical retreat; he need affirm nothing about reality. But neither does the scientist. Pragmatically, the concepts and laws of the physicist can be amply vindicated. They serve man very well. And even if metaphysically unanchored, these generalizations do unify experienced phenomena and enable men to predict and control events. They work. They can be empirically validated.

With all the perils of generalization even in the physical sciences, it is as much a relief as a threat to find that cultural phenomena do not lend themselves to general statements. Open generalizations about man (people assert them all the time) *as a cultural entity* cannot be empirically verified. In other words, and despite all the possible (and usually exaggerated) methodological implications of quantum theory, general statements of the strongest type can be empirically vindicated in physics (they work) but not in any cultural study. Of course, as one must continually stress, matter is omnipresent, and thus cultural phenomena always parallel generalizable physical events, including physiological events.

Many historians have been unhappy with these conclusions and have sought either some general structure or framework present in all cultural phenomena. Ernst Cassirer sought a science of symbolic forms to provide the same backdrop to cultural studies that Kant's transcendental esthetic (or mathematics) provided for the physical sciences. Claude Levi-Strauss now seeks necessary patterns in social relationships. Linguistic and semantic inquiry may reveal some formal boundaries for all symbolic communication and thus provide a trans-cultural perspective on culture. So far, such efforts have not been unambiguously successful; they have produced only the most vague formal schemes. Even a successful analysis of the necessary formal properties of all languages, and thus of all cultures, would only set certain broad limits within which one could look for cultural phenomena. It would be a science of possibilities comparable to mathematics and not to physics. Such a formal system would in no wise determine any specific cultural patterns or serve as a lawful structure from which any specific cultural phenomena could be deduced. Even given such a formal backdrop, one would still have to seek the particular ideals and purposes that give some unity and distinctive character to a given culture. These cannot be completely transformed into, deduced from, or reduced to, any universally lawful order. All attempts to do so involve an unnoticed move from focal and authentic cultural phenomena to some organic or physical correlate, a procedure often quite useful but one that must be recognized for what it is.

Then how does one explain, or understand, man? The question

begs great precision in words like "explain." If explain means the subsumption of distinctively human phenomena under some deterministic structure, under general laws, then man, as a creature of culture, is beyond explanation. He simply cannot be understood in some of the ways physical objects can be understood. And this is not even remarkable, since any physical object is a conceptual product, as are all the laws by which it can be put in its correct place. But man is not just a product of conceptualizing (although man does continuously define himself and try to put himself in some correct place); he is also conceptualizer. Is it really surprising to suggest that, even though man can grab his own tail in his conceptual teeth and endlessly gnaw away at it, he really will never quite succeed in swallowing himself? Could he consummate this awesome task, he would kill himself. Reduced to a physical object, firmly and fixedly in its place, man would be only a thing and no longer man at all, for he would no longer be conceptualizer, master of symbols, creator of worlds, ever open to new definition as he creates new cultural forms.

But even though man, as a product and as a creator of culture, cannot be fully understood by generalization, this does not preclude such an explanation of all regularities of physique and behavior that he exemplifies. All such regularities are correlative to culture and to his humanity, for they reflect simpler characteristics of experience than mind. But they are indeed correlative, and this we must not forget or deny. As correlates, we isolate them by reference to culture; but henceforth we can, and in fact must, investigate them by the conditions set by physical and behavioral concepts. But no such delimited inquiry is possible without some conception of such distinguishable phenomenon as thought.

How can one relate himself conceptually (we will temporarily dispense with such loaded words as "explain") to the world of culture? In an age of ascendancy for the generalizing sciences, the normal response is to seek some way of generalizing about man—to find his nature and the laws of behavior such a nature obeys (an excellent tactic for all the subhuman attributes of man, none of which he loses by learning to talk). But this approach stops short at the cultural threshold, where one must turn to comparative classification and ideal characterization. Human societies can be compared and can be more clearly or more fully perceived in all their nuances as a result of such comparison (properly a task in such disciplines as cultural anthropology and comparative linguistics). Or a given society (and by implication the individuals who share its meanings, beliefs, or culturally conditioned habits) can be described, in better than a haphazard listing of features, only by the purposes, the ideal ends, and the established valuations that provide some distinctive unity to it. But one who offers such comparison and description, if pressed for some larger scale on which to view a society, has to turn in one direction—to history—and not to the generalizing sciences. The only way to clear up any puzzlement about man as man, not as some small chunk of the physical world, is to produce a genetic perspective (one form of "explanation"), to tell a story of his past. What he has been, rather than some coercive lawful structure, conditions what he is and what he will be insofar as he is a participant in culture. Thus history, as a discipline, is uniquely tied to the rarest phenomenon in our experienced world—to mind or culture as a body of ever expanding symbolic meanings. Telling a story of man's past offers the most comprehensive conceptual tool we have for understanding him as a product of culture. This remains so despite the fact that historical knowledge is not general, not rigorously predictive, and does not have the same type of utility as general knowledge.

One can still be dissatisfied and seek a more determinate and universal knowledge of man. If one does so, however, he will have to leave the abstractive, generalizing sciences, whose reach is simply not sufficient for the problem, and turn to some intuitive insight or revelation not given to ordinary man. Even in theory, such determinate knowledge of man is logically impossible, for, being more than a temporally limited, historically conditioned characterization, it violates what is distinctive to man—conceptual fertility and unending cultural elaboration guided by ideals or final causes. Those who want determinate knowledge of man are really, in some way, dissatisfied with man. Using terms drawn from a literary and nonscientific psychology, they reflect a type of cultural death wish. They want to be exempt from history.

A reductionist outlook is quite prevalent today. Some students have great difficulty grasping a multicharactered perceptual world and, therefore, the parallel idea of correlate explanation. Note the following example: a man raises his hand in a gesture of greeting. By the gesture he roughly communicates the following verbal message: "Hello, I am very glad to see you." Surely here the gesture has a wealth of symbolic content; it is clearly a cultural phenomenon. It is not merely a signal that triggers some instinctive or learned response, although it is also that and might be so explained by a psychologist. In fact, the arm movement not only exemplifies aspects of modern learning theory but the changes in physical components exemplify quite determinate physical laws. But physical laws explain only mechanical motions, isolated from the vast world of such motions only by an organic concept—arm. Such mechanical laws do not explain the gesture, with its symbolic content, or even arm movements as a form of organic or animal behavior. Likewise, theories about behavioral conditioning, which may account for the animal behavior, the perhaps habitual arm-raising when a certain positive reinforcement is present (the glimpse of a friend), are also correlative to the gesture, for they do not explain the symbolic content that turned a signal, of a type common to many animals, into a gesture. In fact, the symbolic content, being subtle, expressive, qualitatively rich, and, because of cultural determination, particularistic (in a slightly altered cultural environment, the gesture might express extreme distaste), has to be excluded from any true science of behavior (that is, from any body of open generalizations).

Both the physical and psychological explanations are true. They lawfully explain muscular tensions or habitual arm motions. But there is no way to move from either explanation to the fact of a gesture. The only way to answer the questions—Why the gesture? Why did the arm movement mean what it did?—is to show how such an arm movement developed such a symbolic meaning in a given society— to turn to history. And here one cannot show why such a cultural form had to develop as it did. In fact, many quite similar arm motions, even in the same society, are not gestures (symbolic acts). Some may be involuntary flexing of muscles; some, well-conditioned responses to nonsymbolic or external stimuli. The only way to isolate arm motions truly correlative to a gesture is to locate, on other than physical grounds, what is quite clearly a gesture. This requires cultural knowledge of a society. The operative physical laws explain why the arm raised and, given a gesture, they supply a complete physical correlate to it. In some cases, puzzlement about a gesture, and what we want to know about it, may be entirely at such a correlative level. Then we might, with some imprecision, assume that we explain the gesture by the physical uniformities present in it. Note that one can always move from the level of broader, more complex relationships (from mind and life) to simpler, more universal relationships (matter). But there is no possible upward movement. This shows the absurdity of simple reductionism but does not assign any ontological priority to any level, including the cultural, a mistake made by too many idealists.

Nor does this position necessitate or even imply some notion of free will or vitalism. In fact, the classic battle between free will and determinism, like that between body and mind, is only another example of the operationally meaningless (but experientially vital) antinomies that ever develop from ontologizing selective, conceptualized bits of experience. Many hard determinists (there are at least three levels of determinism), in their intellectualistic myopia and experiential ignorance, try to compress all experience into the narrow, mechanical mold of an often outdated physics. The traditional advocates of free will, impressed by the expressive and qualitative aspects of experience, seek a similar impossibility—a modicum of agency, a rare phenomenon, exempt from any law or even any cause, and thus under the control of either pure chance or some strangely demonic, esoteric entity called, by an atavistic psychology, a free will. Obviously, such uncritical ideas have no place in a serious analysis of history. But note that some types of determinism are quite consistent with choice, responsibility, and a type of freedom. Such determinism does not threaten cultural phenomena and true final causes. And such causes do not have to be viewed as unscientific renditions of transformative laws, which a rigorous materialistic reductionism would require. Although deanthropomorphizing was a *sine qua non* for the development of the generalizing sciences, it cannot be required in the nongeneralizable world of culture. Anthropomorphic concepts are necessary in talking about man, but this does not mean that even the social sciences should return to Greek essences. Just the opposite. But man still talks by means of these essences; in all their teleological glory they cannot be driven from the human temple.

From a material perspective, culture is additive. The gesture could or could not exist with the arm movement. Without in any way distorting or finding exemptive escapes from the conceptualized world of the physicists, any conceivable elaboration of cultural phenomena is possible (of course the concepts of the physicist are one such phenomenon). The physical correlates ever present in a cultural event in no wise determine the event. The world of meaning, here and there complexly and partially relating large numbers of people, does not require for its existence some loopholes in the physical world, some random events, some miraculous spontaneity.

There is, here, one meaningful problem. The world of culture, it seems, has directive power over the physical world, not only in the sense that it gave birth to the very physical concepts concerned, but in the sense that human choice, made possible by teleologically pregnant symbols, is able to guide natural processes. Few historians, or few people, practically ever doubt some efficacy in choice, even when they view these choices as necessary expressions of some ultimate, metaphysical design, including either the laws of God or of some universal history. But, even if there is no physical efficacy in choice and thus in cultural phenomena (and here there are extremely subtle issues involving the tie between choice, conceived phenomenologically, and the ever present physical correlates of choice, viewed in a stark behavioral perspective), culture could still exist in (or "on") a physical world. But then final causes would operate, not in redirecting natural energies, but only in reshaping human affections, in changing tastes; the world of culture would be a strangely aloof, detached world, despite its inescapable ties to biological and physical correlates.

Thus, if final causes do somehow govern physical objects (and thus culture is effective rather than merely affective), such causes cannot be fully correlative with a certain physical construct, that of *one* world machine in which *all* parts are related to all others according to completely determining laws. It is quite consistent with an all-pervasive materiality and to unexceptional physical laws of a transformative type. But it conflicts with a single, all-pervasive structure. Of course, a phenomenological insistence upon the selective aspects of physical laws assures only a partial, if universal, order. But here the universality, even though selective, cannot be determinate in any absolute sense. There must be interactive, only intramurally determinate transformative series, but not one total, coimplicative whole. Now, as a matter of fact, the machine metaphor, and with it a form of hard determinism, was always speculative, for only limited systems were, or ever can be, empirically traced. And such have been the subtleties introduced in modern physics that neither the machine nor classic concepts of lawfulness are very useful even for explaining limited physical universes; in quantum mechanics, they can be distorting and irrelevant. Except for this one qualification for a correlative view of culture and matter, the two worlds, representing conceptualizations of two quite different characteristics of our experience, make no compromising demands of any sort upon each other.

The example of the gesture helps differentiate the logical form taken by all general explanation from the genetic approach of a historian. But the varied references to psychology suggest one further qualification. Is not psychology the science of mind? Can we not find here generalizations proper to man as a thinker, as a product of culture? Assuredly not. No scientific, as compared to some loose speculative psychology, can in any sense be a science of mind. No legitimate, empirically verifiable generalizations in psychology can include "mind." Such concepts as mind have to be excluded if psychology is to attain the status of a generalizing science, with rigorous, predictive knowledge. But behavioral psychologists establish their limited universes of inquiry by necessary reference to nonpsychological concepts determined by cultural phenomena, such as the common-sense word "mind." Such ordinary words as "mind," "human," and "social" imply culture and lose almost all their meaning when reduced to fit some generalizable conceptual system. They are descriptive only in qualitative contexts. But except for their role in isolating a subject matter, there would be no way of tying any truly scientific (generalizable) psychology to the historically conditioned world of culture. Thus, even the valid generalizations in psychology are correlative to culture (usually at the level of animal behavior) and have a generality that reaches far beyond the most distinctive forms of behavior exhibited by man.

The social sciences, insofar as they reflect either physical or behavioral laws or uniformities that encompass man, are also correlative to culture. They are narrowed branches of physical science (climate correlates with aspects of culture) or, more often, of a general behavioral science or psychology. But again, they too must establish their narrowed universes of inquiry by use of cultural and value-laden concepts, even though they must exclude any of these from their generalizations. If they do not exclude them, they can never have clear, operational, verifiable or falsifiable generalizations at all. Of course, much of the work done in disciplines now modishly defined as "social sciences" is not scientific at all, in the sense of relying on rigorous generalization. Some of it is clearly intracultural and primarily comparative and descriptive, but it uses statistical tools and explicatory models often much more rigorous and revealing than simple reporting. Many so-called social scientists still seek time-conditioned, culturally relative but enduring regularities in human behavior (closed generalizations) and use these for predictive purposes. These are similar to the enduring cultural patterns so often remarked by historians. If these are used, a social scientist should acknowledge a historical rather than a truly "lawful" backdrop for them. Finally, some moral philosophers still exist. They continue to work out ideal constructs and often try to alter the culture by the modification of taste and purpose rather than by the creation of predictive or manipulative tools.

All of this is not to argue that some people, and possibly even some self-professed psychologists or social scientists, do not try to generalize about man as a cultural entity, nor that some psychologists have not worked out what they professed to be the laws of mind or psyche. But such attempts have either been plagued with imprecision or non-verifiable speculation or have been confused and unremarked misuses of correlate generalizations about the workings of the brain or about uniformities in animal behavior. In various cults of depth psychology, beginning with Freud's, men have attempted to isolate the general structure of the psyche, importing at least the form of physical concepts into these murky waters. But their terms have been elusive, their affirmed structures too imprecise and too speculative for unambiguous testing, and their concepts too metaphorical, too literary, and too phenomenological for other than loose clinical or suggestive speculative uses. Thus, any rigorous psychological science will be physiological or behavioral in subject matter and empirical (not introspective) in method. In a similar, loose way, professed social scientists have, at times, combined history, correlative generalizations of a physical or behavioral type, and loose assertions about human nature that are, even if unrecognized, always culturally conditioned. Many of the generalizations of the nineteenth-century economists were of this sort. But note that these generalizations about human nature or even about the psyche are formally similar to those in the physical sciences. Such generalizations can easily be asserted; they cannot be clearly tested and, in fact, are rarely very precise.

Although the historian tells the story of the human past, his subject matter is not limited to the narrow world of mind or culture. The historian's subject matter is, indeed, restricted to culturally related objects—to those things that have had some significance, some value, to man in a given cultural context. But anything may be or may become so affected with value. At a given time, any river or mountain may be a boon or an obstacle to man and figure large in a history about man. Almost any generalizable characteristic of the experienced world can be of human significance. In any case, it may enable man to develop some extremely useful science. And the generalizable structure that, by our most rigorous methods of inquiry, seems to be present in our world, also provides a stage, an ordered backdrop, on which human events can be related and patterned.

Although a historian seeks no open generalizations (there are none to be had within his special subject matter) and although he is not, as a historian, concerned with the verification of generalizations (he is very much concerned with their verity), he nonetheless makes use of such generalizations all of the time. He consumes scientific products, not in the usual manner of putting them to work in order to control events, but as aids to his story telling or his causal analysis. He may use the latest hypothesis about hurricanes to make clear some otherwise inexplicable complex of weather that was a determining condition in a major historical event.

Perhaps some historians still dream about some elusive class of phenomena that is both distinctively historical and fully generalizable, and which only the historian has a license to deal with. But his dream is empty unless some fully determinate laws govern the development of societies and the course of human history. The historian may attend to any conceivable class of phenomena, so long as it relates to a cultural context. But these phenomena, apart from the cultural and valuative context, are never in any distinctive sense historical. They are always potential subject matter for one or another of the generalizing sciences.

These distinctions, along with much of the content of both this and the following chapter, directly relate to the most prolonged and complex contemporary controversy concerning history. The controversy began with a 1942 article by Carl G. Hempel,[1] who stressed the universal applicability of a well-developed model of scientific explanation, particularly to history. Without attending to the subtleties of his

1. Carl G. Hempel, "The Function of General Laws in History," in Patrick Gardiner, ed., *Theories of History* (Glencoe, Ill.: The Free Press, 1959), pp. 344–356.

model, suffice it here to say that, by it, one can explain single events, in history or in any other discipline, only when he can deduce their occurrence from some empirically verified law. Only by showing how an event exemplifies a universal law can one show why it had to occur. Anything less than this, such as showing some necessary conditions for its occurrence, does not constitute a satisfactory or full explanation. This model, in all of its detailed logical development, and as supplemented by a less satisfactory but often required probability model, has not been accepted by all philosophers of science. Its detailed development was one of the most complex and critical issues for philosophers of science in the World War II period. However, the issue for the historian is not the exact logical adequacy of any such model, but the relationship of such scientific explanation to the historian's task.

When Hempel first published his article, he in effect issued a positivist manifesto against certain lingering forms of idealism and historicism. Even as he tried to demolish any idea of a special type of historical explanation, other logicians tried to overturn the related idea that historians have a distinctive method of inquiry or a unique road to truth. Given the intrenched strength of historicism, particularly in European historiography, the devastating arguments against some of its more extreme positions seemed in order. In retrospect, Hempel's 1942 article seems both truistic and dated.

Surely, if one wants to explain why something had to happen, he must try to subsume it under some empirical law. But two questions are always in order. Can a particular event be so "explained"? Even more important, in what contexts does one generally want to so "explain" it? But if he does attempt such explanation, clearly the historian is in no sense exempt from the formal requirements of an adequate explanation. Much of the earlier analysis has indicated that cultural phenomenon, as such, cannot be so explained, for they do not permit valid generalizations of the strongest type. One cannot subsume them under a fully lawful structure. But every culturally conditioned phenomena has its organic and physical correlates. At least the physical correlates can be scientifically explained. To repeat, one cannot show why a gesture had to occur, but in principle at least he can show why the arm had to move.

The problem for the historian is not a logical one but a functional one. When should a historian incorporate an accepted scientific hypothesis, either in the form of a covering law or a probability equation, into a historical narrative or into more restricted causal analysis? Obviously, he should do so when a historical event or series of events seems implausible or mysterious according to the conventional wisdom but quite clear by a better scientific understanding. Arthur Danto, an American philosopher, has shown how historians, at points of puzzlement or incredibility, work a skein of overt or implied general knowledge into their stories.[2] But in most cases the events recorded by historians do not require such explanation. Both the historian and his audience assume an underlying organic and physical order. They assume the "explanability" of events. Any historian who spent pages giving the mechanical equations of an arm movement would rightly be dismissed as a fool.

There is a special form of myopia that can infect even the more discriminating philosophers of science, particularly if they are most conversant with the physical sciences. Here Hempel is not immune. If one refuses to deal seriously with the problem of culture, and if one fails to distinguish correlate forms of conceptualization, he almost inevitably falls into a vicious methodological reductionism (or even by implication an ontological reductionism). Such a reductionist assumes that all phenomena can, in principle if not in fact, be "explained" (be subsumed under some law). This position permits little respect for the nonlawlike causal relationships that historians so often search for and use. Historical narration then is merely a way of ordering events that still await proper "explanation." Historical inquiry, if directed only toward such narratives, has value and intellectual stature only as it provides either subject matter or data for the true scientist. These issues will be analyzed in detail in Chapters 10 and 12.

Methodological reductionism often feeds on a simple failure to distinguish between formal and substantiative issues. Obviously, since assertions in the form of general laws can be made about any phenomena, they can be made about man as a cultural product. In loose ways, such assertions are made all the time. Here the problem is not formal but cognitive. Can such assertions be verified? If not, they are useless. Even if some such assertions are verifiable in principle, they must have explanatory scope to be of any practical usefulness. Under some description, any event can be fitted to some general statement, but often for no good reason except, possibly, for the purpose of

2. Arthur Danto, *Analytical Philosophy of History* (London: Cambridge University Press, 1965).

logical analysis. "John Jones raised his hand in greeting to a young lady" can seemingly be made the deductive consequence of some general law and thus of some asserted social structure. One could assert that "all normal Americans greet ladies by raising their hands." Such a statement may be both revealing and useful, but as a valid generalization or law it is suspect on several counts.

First, the word "normal" is vague and imprecise. What specific class of phenomena, what specific social structure, does it refer to? If it means anything significant, that meaning depends on some unspecified social structure in America. It must not be a class name for the particular behavior observed; if it is it would add nothing to the original description and would involve the following sophistry: "John, an American, raised his hand to a lady. Therefore, to do this in America must be normal behavior. John is a normal American. Therefore he had to raise his hand in such a situation."

More critical from the standpoint of culture and history, unless chronologically qualified such an asserted law governing John's behavior may be either demonstrably false (colonial Americans never used such a greeting) or may become false in the near future. But if it is chronologically limited, it ceases to be a proper or open generalization and loses its predictive value in any rigorous sense. It may or may not apply tomorrow, for it depends not on universal physical laws nor on universal behavioral patterns but on a changing cultural pattern. Being circumscribed by time, it cannot show the necessity, or even the specific probability, of any gesture anytime in the future. Of course, any generalization *may* not hold in the future. But in the context of recognized cultural change, all statements must be time qualified and understood in a historical, nongeneral context. Our experience, at least, does not suggest such changes in physical behavior. This is why, with great confidence, we explain physical phenomena by general, nonhistorical laws.

Both in his numerous contacts with the generalizing sciences and in his frequent references to general knowledge, the historian gains much more than helpful devices for navigating serious gaps in his narrative. Often, he learns from scientists how to use words with greater precision and the value of quantitative exactitude. In other cases, subtle relationships that he would have missed become visible in light of some hypothesis or model. In other words, the best scientific knowledge variously fixes the historian's attention and improves his vision. But the relationship should not be overemphasized. In topically and chronologically narrowed histories and in much contributory causal or structural analysis, the historians may develop a very close tie to a peculiarly relevant science. In broad, sweeping narratives the tie may scarcely exist at all, since the historian utilizes the conventional wisdom on most issues.

Always, the historian's subject matter is broader than the generalizable aspects of it; hence, it includes much that cannot be related to any science. Even if a class term like "revolution" could be made completely rigorous and exact and some determinant behavioral laws could be formulated that would hold true for all revolutions (whether any ever occur is beside the point), the historian would still write the history of the American Revolution very much as before. He would still look to the distinctive, nongeneralizable features that made it an American event and that made it of particular significance to Americans. If the rigorous term became accepted usage and was, as it would almost inevitably be, too restrictive for his subject, he would blandly write his history of "The American War for Independence." If the term, despite the monumental odds against it, did fit, then he might economize a bit in his description, allowing the class term to suggest to his audience much of the now analytically available details.

Generalizations, whether rigorously scientific (a methodological as well as a formal criterion) or loosely commonsensical, present certain problems to a historian. Since he uses and endlessly implicates borrowed or commonly accepted generalizations, the historian's first problem, theoretically simple but practically difficult, is which generalizations to use. It is easy to assert that he should use the best ones, those that are the most rigorous and most scrupulously verified. But this demands of him much greater critical ability in many specialized sciences than he can ever hope to have. Thus, all too often the historian's attempt to follow this approach leads to a superficial modishness, to an infatuation with new, popularized, or striking theories, particularly in such scientific borderlands as clinical psychology, economics, and sociology. Our recent historical literature is full of metaphorical Freudianisms, loose psychological labels, and imprecise class and status concepts. Rather than offering naïveté advertised as sophistication, the historian might better remain loyal to commonsense wisdom, parochial and ambiguous as it usually is. Then indeed he will flatter many existing prejudices and leave his audience in as great a scientific ignorance as he found them. Yet, even within these conceptual boundaries, he may tell very suggestive and true stories. Most great works of history have been of such a type. And at least certain narrative demands are most easily met at the level of conventional understanding. Whenever a historian introduces a new, unassimilated scientific hypothesis, he must at least spend some time explaining it and may have to sacrifice some of the esthetic unity that he craves for his story.

The historian easily relates to the scientist as student and consumer, but only with great difficulty as critic. He may, from a broader perspective, condemn the myopia of a specialized scientist but he can scarcely make critical judgments about the merit of his specialized work. Yet, even without this being his intent, a historian plays a crucial role in disseminating scientific knowledge or, when he remains blind to it, in preventing its wide, popular acceptance. Here he joins with journalists and novelists. Ideally, a historian should be well trained at least in the common methodology of the generalizing sciences, be able to detect overt frauds or fuzzy and misleading popularizations, and be cautious in the use of the specific generalizations that allow him to find new, significant meaning in past events, even if this means he has to explain them at great length.

A second problem concerns the historian not as a consumer of generalizations but as a producer of them. Historians, quite infrequently, but almost without exception, do make general assertions of their own invention, or at least assertions that do not fit into any of the developed, generalizing sciences. These general statements are often loose and perhaps similar to ones shared by ordinary people in a society; in many cases, they fulfill a rhetorical rather than a cognitive function. The historian is rarely aware of having made such a generalization. What can be said about these?

First, the greatest peril lies in generalizing about the whole course of human history. Universal historians who try this are in a class by themselves and are not properly historians at all. But more limited generalizations are the only type common among most historians. Save for their prevalent looseness, these generalizations are of the same type as those developed by scientists. Many seem to be allegations about man or about human nature. But here man variously stands for physical regularities, behavioral patterns, and assumed invariant cultural forms. The first two are legitimate, but the historian rarely has any competence for worthy generalization in either; the last is illegitimate. As a functional distinction, such generalizing could be classified as a nonhistorical activity that is occasionally and often incidentally indulged in by historians à la amateur scientists. True stories about the human past can be told without recourse to new, *ad hoc* generalizations, and probably told better. Obviously, a historian who casually asserts some new generalization will never attend to it to the extent of clarifying it analytically and indicating the type of evidence necessary to prove it, much less going to the trouble of seeking inductive support for it. If classed as scientists on the basis of their typical generalizations, historians would surely be among the world's worst. If a historian falls in love with some new generalization and spends his time trying to verify it, he becomes a practicing and possibly able scientist; certainly, one individual may be both historian and scientist. Such, in fact, is the relaxed maturity of history, as a professional discipline, that few historians are methodological puritans. Most historians quite unselfconsciously do other things than tell or perfect true stories. But more often than not this extradisciplinary fun takes the form of moral preachments, not generalizations.

A typical form for a historian's generalization is as follows: "Human nature being what it is . . . ," followed by some description of some human act, such as "he fought back." Such statements reduce to assertions such as "it is the nature of man to defend himself" or "it is the nature of man always to seek security"—a very prevalent form. Often such statements are only shabby rhetorical devices to hide a lack of any empirical evidence. When one lacks any other support, human nature is a convenient device for justifying almost anything, but it explains nothing at all. Since a vague conventional wisdom also accepts such sloppy explanations, a historian can get by with them. But the argument that all men seek security, given the normal looseness in the word "security," is a near truism within America. When a historian makes such an assertion in a history of the New Deal, he most likely does not intend it as a scientifically accurate generalization at all. He uses it as a verbally loose but contextually clear way of summarizing some empirical evidence about how Americans behaved in the 1930s; at best, he intends only a closed generalization. Thus, the general form should rarely be taken too seriously. Patrick Gardiner has clearly shown the divergence between scientific language and the language of ordinary people, which is the language of historians and the language which allows such a loose form for summary statements about evidence.[3] Such general assertions could be perfected by needed class and temporal qualifications: "all middle-class Americans sought security in the 1930s."

To summarize a long and involved chapter: history is a non-generalizing form of knowledge, for its key subject, man, insofar as he is a product of culture, does not display uniform and invariant structure. Therefore, cultural man cannot be understood by generalization. Culture, or mind, is a legitimate characterization of a scarce but quite distinctive feature of our directly experienced world. Cultural phenomena always exist with more extensive biological and with ever present physical phenomena. At least the physical phenomena, including the part correlative to culture, can be successfully generalized, but any correlate generalization is not an explanation of cultural phenomena. Yet there is no opposition between culture and matter, and there is no need to seek some nonphysical chinks in reality in order to sneak in culture. Finally, the problem of generalization, to the historian, is the problem of critical choice among the various generalizations that claim verity. Specialized scientists develop generalizations with greatest rigor. Their work can be a valuable tool for any historian.

3. In *The Nature of Historical Explanation* (London: Oxford University Press, 1961).

C hapter 10

CAUSATION

Too often we link generality and causality as if they were insepa-rably related. But in the oldest sense of the word "cause"—in the sense that it is still most often used by historians—the very opposite is true. Generality excludes causality. Historians assume and often explicitly refer to a general order in events. But they do not often, and never by necessity or by reason of their historical task, invent or try to verify generalizations. However, historians continuously use causal statements. In fact, history is the one cognitive discipline that does correctly emphasize the same type of causation present in ordi-nary, undisciplined, common-sense propositions.

On occasion, historians use causal relationships to link together events and to give a sense of development to their stories. A diplo-matic history of Europe between 1870 and 1914, for example, may involve a tracing out of causally related events which build toward a climax. Truly epic events seem to demand such causal treatment. But most often, historians do not use causes as organizational tools; rather, they use them to account for events that cohere because of some continuing identity in a subject. In a more typical and genetic perspective, the historian begins with the birth of a person, a nation, or an institution and traces its varying development through time. His focus may be more on the form, structure, or style of his subject than on the various, possibly unrelated, causal conditions that influ-ence its development. If the present is the cutoff point, his emphasis may be upon origins and survival—upon those attributes of past events that still remain in the present.

The concept of causation was, in origin, a simple inference from human volition and action. A person desired something, rearranged some objects, and attained his goal. His act was the cause of some effect. With great precision, Aristotle first analyzed the full implications of such causation, which is clearly based upon human or divine agency. He isolated four distinct aspects or perspectives in causation, including the efficient cause, or the actual energy that lies behind an effect, and the crucial and determinant final cause, or the end toward which one directs action. In Aristotle's perspective, man is an agent and not just an isolated complex of mass-energy states in endless transformation. One can view him as the efficient cause of many effects, but such efficient causes are only the inverse side of operative final causes, of ends which such efficacious acts serve. There is no way completely to sever efficient and final causes; they require each other and are only analyzable aspects of a more complex whole.

Thus, in origin, and most often still in ordinary language, the idea of causation involved agents and teleology. This usage is best illustrated by a near archaic use of cause as a synonym for end or ideal ("he is committed to the *cause* of peace"). Whenever causal judgments can be so translated, they are necessarily being used in a teleological sense. Thus, a historian may assert that, among other things, British violations of American naval rights *caused* the War of 1812. This is another way of saying that the United States as a collectivity, or the American people as individuals, embraced the *cause* of neutral right on the high seas. Very often causal arguments that include abstract entities or historical forces ("American imperialism caused the war in Vietnam") are clearly teleological statements, but with an emphasis upon the often unconscious nature of the commitments (hence, the translation: "whether they recognize it or not, Americans are committed to the cause of imperialism").

When so used, causal language is tied to an almost obvious and inescapable common-sense account of ourselves as end-directed agents. In this original and conventional understanding of causation, any causal agent has an enduring identity which is not radically altered by any effect and, above all, is never transformed into an effect. John Smith may cause all manner of effects, but he is still John Smith. Imperialism may cause twenty wars. In such causal analysis there is no requirement that a designated cause (John Smith) be the sole determinant (he never is) of an effect; there is only the requirement that in one perspective the cause be a necessary condition for an effect, which is all that it can be.

Likewise, any particular event may be viewed as the effect of different contributing causes, or of a whole range of such teleologically pregnant causes, starting at a proximate necessary condition and ranging back to broad, sweeping cultural forms that conditioned the proximate act ("the man died because the angered boy shot him, because a father gave him a loaded gun, because the family loved to hunt and had numerous guns, because the society approved of hunting and the use of guns, because the society tolerated all types of violence, because the economic system reflected a generalized expression of capitalist aggressive traits, and so on"). This causal series does not conflict with other judgments that contain causal language in a seemingly nonteleological sense ("the man died because of a bullet which pierced his heart"). This example excludes a direct reference to any purposeful agent but implies a continuing identity in the bullet. It is either an elliptical causal statement, with an agent implied but not identified, or else a poorly worded or incomplete statement of physical transformations. In the latter case, it might be restated as follows: "a given physical complex, in contact with an external physical force, was transformed into a different state." Here there is no agent and no ends; thus there is no cause in the ordinary usage.

With the development of the modern physical sciences, traditional causal relationships, being imbued always with teleology, had to be slowly eliminated from man's most rigorous cognitive concepts. If they had not been eliminated, a science with wide scope, reliable prediction, and great utility would have remained impossible. In place of causes, the scientists sought nondirectional types of transformation in an unbroken continuity of states. But in a quite new use for an old word, scientists often used "cause" to designate any arbitrarily isolated state in a transformative series that immediately preceded an arbitrarily defined subsequent state, and "effect" to designate the subsequent state. According to this definition, a cause, rather than being an unaltered agent, was a state of affairs which, in the next instant, became another state of affairs. And, without a quite arbitrary, human isolation of points in a continuum, neither cause nor effect could ever be discriminated. Any cause was, from a slightly altered perspective, also an effect. Obviously, calling this relationship causal was to invite all types of verbal confusion. The confusion has been largely dissipated by perceptive philosophers, but it still haunts the historical profession and renders ambiguous much historical language. One could help eliminate the confusion by avoiding causal language in any clearly generalizable context.

But very often causal judgments do not clearly reveal either purpose or a generalizable order. They seem to lurk precariously in between. The bullet that caused the death is a good example of such a judgment. Here, in the least complex use of the word possible, a cause is simply a prior event somehow necessarily related to a subsequent event, at least in a given perspective. It need not be, and in common language almost never is, a fully sufficient condition or a complete cause. But any such cause is, at least under some possible description, a participant in transformative physical systems and thus part of some fully sufficient condition (the A that becomes B). So conceived, such a cause is not infected with value or with ends of any sort, unless one affirms some hidden divine purpose or design behind all physical behavior. If one does so affirm, then final causes are, as Aristotle affirmed, ultimately all-pervasive and fully determinant. Every event, under any possible description, involves such final causes, and our full understanding in any area would require their identification.

But even without such a cosmic teleology, a causal object (the bullet) may nonetheless reflect identifiable final causes. That is, the purposes of a true agent may be present in it. In behalf of some perceived good, in service to some cause, a person may have fired the bullet. More indirectly, the bullet itself and the gun that fired it are clearly products of human art created in behalf of some human purpose. Thus, the bullet could be explained either as part of a lawful, transformative system (the usual goal of a scientist) or as part of a world of culturally conditioned events, or a world of *causes*. This world contains policemen committed to the cause of justice and societies committed to the cause of social order (and thus in both cases to the use of guns and bullets). Since the historian's subject matter is always suffused with culture, his identified causes, as he describes and uses them, almost always implicate the world of final ends and purposes, not the generalizable world of lawful transformations.

Too often the very idea of final causes suggests the Aristotelian world view, some vast cosmic design, or some prime mover or ultimate good toward which all things aspire. Then final causes seem to lurk in every event, whether the event directly relates to human purpose or not. At the other extreme, final causes suggest a narrow, subjective perspective. They seem to require exercises of volition, or self-conscious choices by individuals. Then one can appeal to final causes only when acts are quite deliberate. Habitual behavior, and even human acts in which the hidden thought component, if any, cannot be known, both have to be dismissed as mysteries or else explained by transformative laws that are only correlative to human acts. Thus, on one hand, one can generalize final causes completely and make them the crux of a mindlike account of all reality; on the other, one can push them into a narrow, subjective limbo, scarcely open for objective investigation of any sort.

As argued in the preceding two chapters, a transpersonal body of meanings, or a culture, is a legitimate characterization of one prominent aspect of our experience. Common meanings and with them common, learned habits, link large numbers of individuals together and allow them to act with a common purpose. In fact, an individual becomes human only as a participant in a world of conventional meanings. It is only with socially acquired symbols that individuals project their previsions of the future, their anticipations, their carefully articulated images of achievable possibilities. They plan. But the conscious use of symbols in imagination and volition does not exhaust the role of symbolic meanings. Most human acts are not deliberate but habitual. It is in the forming of human habits, in the giving of some definite if unthought-out form and order to human arts, that developed meanings play their largest role in human affairs and therefore become the subject for historical inquiry.

To push final causes beyond subjective volition—to broach a world of symbols which, rather than being a whimsical and unsubstantial outpouring of capricious individuals, is a determinant in almost all individual behavior—is to move very close to the idea of an objective mind or spirit and thus to the central doctrine of objective idealists. And much is valid in the idealist position. Final causes are not solely subjective. If they were they would be of no great cognitive interest and could be dismissed as unreal apparitions reared on real, transformative organic and physical processes, which alone would be worthy of serious investigation. But the transpersonal scope of meanings—the objectivity of final causes—does not justify the idea of some unified higher mind or the extension of final causes to the physical and organic worlds, where there is no evidence at all of purpose, conscious or unconscious. Final causes are observably present where meanings or mind is present; thus, they are apparently present only in man. By pure speculation, one may posit a cosmic mind behind all events and some far-off divine purpose pulling the universe toward some glorious future. Such an assertion allows no evidential proof.

Thus, true causes (efficient and final) are always separate from but fully correlative to noncausal, generalizable physical and organic structure. In any context where man needs and desires instrumental knowledge, or some new ability to guide events in certain directions, he should seek the general features, the transformative laws, not efficient and final causes, not agency and purpose. He should deliberately abstract, moving his attention from the value-laden features of his experience, from the valuations of himself and his society, and look to the regular, uniform features that allow generalization. Of course, he does this as an end-serving agent, as a product of culture, and for culturally conditioned purposes. For this reason, cognition of any sort is necessarily relative to value. But only when, as in a history, final causes furnish the very key for selecting a subject; are always present in the subject matter; and provide some of the unity, the coherence, and the continuity that permit a subject to be traced through time, are values at the very heart of a discipline.

Only when one locates final causes in an objective, cultural context and not primarily in the volition of individuals can one grasp the great breadth of true causal relationships in the human past and see the potential for causal judgments by historians. Any person is a product of some existing culture. He learns to talk within its social groupings, uses its symbols and grammatical forms, and first makes sense of the world by means of its generalizations. In his personal loyalties and institutional ties, he soon reflects his captivity to myriad valuations that have long since ceased to be matters of focal awareness and conscious choice but that remain as controlling ends or final causes in that culture.

Of course human thought continuously modifies the meanings that make up any culture. At the point of such modification, of such focal and conscious awareness, meaning is always individual and, in that sense, subjective. Any person may, at times and in a few areas, become aware and critical of existing habits and institutions and of the ideal ends which they serve or loosely reflect. Any culture changes, either by circumstance or by design, but such change is always in the form of further elaboration. The past sets inescapable conditions for change. Insofar as change is a product of successful criticism rather than of accidental circumstances, it has to be, in its ideal aspects, in its intended purposes, a product of historical knowledge even as the instrumentalities of change will most likely be the predictive knowledge provided by the generalizing sciences. In fact, the stories men tell of the human past are, whether intended or not, prime determinants of cultural change. What one selects as significant in the past and seriously thinks about in the present surely shapes the direction of change. What, by lack of present interest, one ignores in the past will, by the very neglect, have ever less impact on the present and the future.

When new meanings, new concepts, new and brilliant hypotheses, lofty new ideals, or, correlative to this, new experiences and new types of behavior, remain the uncommunicated or uncopied possession of a single individual, they have only a minor and brief cultural impact. Such private intellectual possessions are of vital importance to the owner and would figure large in his autobiography. But from any broader perspective they make up a very tiny, scarcely noticeable episode in any society. Very few historians, save parochial family historians, would ever select these topics as a part of any history that he would want to tell. But just the opposite is true if these new forms of behavior and new ways of thinking and valuing become socialized, if they are widely imitated, if a whole society slowly absorbs them. As the new ways of acting become common and habitual, no one thinks them. They are scarcely a part of anyone's symbolic experience or of anyone's conscious desires and goals. But they will still be an aspect of the implicit belief and thoughtless behavior of everyone, awaiting only the interested future historian who will, perhaps to everyone's surprise, so tell the story of that particular past as to make his audience aware of what they are, of the ends they unconsciously serve, and of what, in focal self-awareness, they may now gladly affirm or scathingly reject.

Such an analysis as this is in all ways consistent with a behavioral perspective on man. Thinking (or talking to oneself or using symbols) is a type of behavior, and even though seemingly unique to man, is still open to physiological and behavioral investigation. Such verbal behavior is often an adjunct of other types of habit formation, but of habits in this case conditioned not only by physical and organic necessities but also by a repertoire of acquired symbols or meanings and, in a larger sense, by a whole environment of such meanings, or by mind in its social or transpersonal sense. Habits formed in part by the aid of a symbolic language are not different as habits, although at one point they accompanied some overt belief, some conscious assessment. And, in turn, the symbols used, the beliefs present, and the values asserted were at least in large part the bequest of a cultural environment, with its unifying ideals and final causes. Very often we form habits by direct conditioning experiences, without symbolic accompaniment, without language. But even here those who direct or control the learning may be conscious believers, directly and intentionally transmitting a cultural inheritance. Finally, even habits formed without any conscious control by the operant and without verbal awareness in the learner may be cultural products. They reflect nonconscious group habits which, at one point or another in the past, did develop in part through symbolic reflection. At that point, such habits directly reflected projective goals and purposes which may again become objects of critical awareness.

Thus, the realm of final causes (and of all efficient causes) is almost as broad as human behavior. By correlate generalization one can chart some physical and organic limits to behavior. But only by causal analysis, by looking to efficacious human acts, to human goals as they operate over long periods of time, can one account for the diversity of human behavior and the remarkable variety of cultural elaborations. Without reference to real final causes, the variety of human behavior—all within limits set by physical and behavioral uniformities and none in its particularity predictable by any generalization—is quite simply a disturbing miracle. It is a miracle that some social scientists, in their fear of teleology, can scarcely acknowledge. Man is often a most disturbing phenomenon. He will not fit neatly into any transformative system; he will not submit exactly and completely to any universal or necessary laws. He alone cannot be completely deanthropomorphized and objectified, for he alone lives in a world of causes.

Man is a true agent and not just an apparent agent in some foreshortened or insufficiently informed perspective. Thus, it is the causal nature of all the cultural aspects of human behavior that prevents it from being explained, other than correlatively, by any general, noncausal structure. But what about the behavior of a dog? By easy analogy, and one ever appealing to common sense, one can find final causes operating in his dog's life and thus affirm that he, too, is an agent. By the same pathetic fallacy (and one surely often justified despite its parochial dangers) by which we assume the same feelings or desires in another person as we ourselves have whenever the same external conditions prevail (he feels as I do when he cuts his hand or craves the same foods when he has not eaten for many hours), we assume the same things about our dog, who is hurt even as we are hurt and desires companionship even as we. Apart from a valid distinction between man and dog, a distinction that accepts many behavioral similarities, we have no option other than to extend final causes into the lower animal world or to deny final causes at the human level. Historically, psychologists have taken both paths. Only man's use of a symbolic language separates him from the dog. Dogs have no culture and, bereft of symbolic language, they have no capability for developing a culture. But they may, nevertheless, exhibit time-conditioned behavior, or behavior that fits into a natural history but defies any open generalizations.

In causal judgments in either history or common sense, one may focus either upon an agent as the energizing source of some effect, or upon efficient causes which implicate but do not necessarily reveal final causes. But when the agent is the focal point of our concern, we are rarely satisfied with efficient causes. Either directly or indirectly, we try to identify the final causes that are present. To say that President Franklin Roosevelt dropped Henry A. Wallace as his vice-president in 1944 may be sufficient in a history of the presidency but not in a biography of Roosevelt. If Roosevelt's purpose was not contextually clear, we would emphatically ask "why"?

But this example suggests many difficulties. Often, as typically in cases like that of Roosevelt and Wallace, historians do cite immediate, presumably conscious reasons or considerations that led to a particular decision. They introduce conscious purposes into their narrative, although they have to infer these from indirect evidence. But one could always challenge their account. Roosevelt was an experienced politician, with sound political habits acquired over years of political life. He continuously exhibited a quick, almost instinctive pattern of decision-making. Maybe he did not think very much about the Wallace candidacy or consider many of its implications. However reasonable and justifiable the decision, it may have reflected a non-conscious habit. In any case, only a type of mind reading could reveal the actual mental processes that he followed. Even his retrospective accounts to cronies or to a diary would be misleading, for these would lead to some reflection and the development of conscious and good reasons for the choice. He might even be quite sure that the good reasons were present in the choice. And surely, in a sense, he would be correct, for they were operative in the decision, even when unconscious and nonfocal.

Thus, since even a subject's firsthand accounts rarely reveal actual mental operations, the historian, working with no better and usually less reliable information, can rarely do more than suggest possible thought processes. We can know the product of what, at one point or another, must have been a reasoning process, but we are not privy to such a process, whether rational or irrational. When the historian feels burdened to mind read, as is often true in biographies, he should at least acknowledge the evidential perils even as he exploits the literary opportunities. If he does not see the perils, he may fall into a methodological error that has long afflicted many accounts of historical inquiry—the belief that a historian can substitute direct, intuitive insight for the warranted inferences from evidence that, almost always, reveals only human behavior and not the internal secrets of deliberation. Even carefully articulated beliefs are end products, deposited records, of unrecoverable mental operations.

Any human behavior, individual or group, rational or irrational, habitual or willful, that reflects the result of some intentional thought —particularly thought used in behalf of prevision or imaginative projection and thought carried out either in the present or in the remote past—can only be accounted for by causal statements and never by generalizations. Any human act, as distinct from an animal movement, allows a causal explanation (and here the word "explanation" is used in a nongeneralizing context). Such causal explanation is not, at least by necessity or in most actual cases, either a form of mind reading or restricted to a precarious subjective world. Culture is both pervasive and objective; so, therefore, are caused events. It is no wonder that historians, in dealing with the human past, resort so often to causal explanations (without falling into the confusing and absolutely incorrect assumption that causal explanation relates to, requires, or should be transformed into general or covering-law type explanation) or that, along with classification issues (periodization, ideal types), causal controversies take up so much of historians' time and energy.

True causes, whether stated in efficient or in final form, can never provide sufficient conditions for any event. A cause can only be a necessary condition for an event—and even this only in a given perspective. This does not mean that identified causes do not have any predictive power. Given a knowledge of physical circumstances (these make up a relatively constant state of affairs assumed by most historians) and given some stability in either a personality or an institution, knowledge of operative final causes—of ends, purposes, and dispositions—provide quite reliable bases for predicting certain future events. Of course, there are almost always other unremarked necessary conditions that have to be assumed. If not prevented by unanticipated physical obstacles (disease or death) or frustrated by unlikely cultural events (a revolution or coup), John will vote Democratic in the next election. But any sufficient explanation of John's actual vote would have to go beyond all causal conditions, beyond preferences and established habits, and encompass all manner of biological and physical conditions. A sufficient explanation, in other words, would have to take the form of some transformative law and thus embrace some complete state A that necessitated some subsequent state B. If a cultural event allowed this type of sufficient explanation, it would have to be reduced to a moment in a timeless series of transformations. In the process all distinctive, particular, valuative, time-conditioned aspects of the event would have to be filtered away. In other words, to seek sufficient conditions for human events is to seek ways of dehumanizing the event. Again, one is driven to correlative explanation and away from any explanation with cultural reach.

True causes are in time and conditioned by it. Being adjuncts of culture, of man-created worlds of meaning, habits, and institutions, they come into being, develop, and finally cease to operate. Some endure longer than others. Final causes that, despite a conditioning backdrop of cultural forms, develop almost in whimsy and lead to only slight changes in behavior, are most ephemeral. To focus on these and on the spontaneity, unpredictability, or seemingly unconditioned aspect of human choice is to get an altogether subjective view of causal phenomena, or of any subject of a teleological sort. Surely, in such a whimsical area, one cannot find any objective, classifiable content, any prospect for fruitful cognitive efforts, any truth. This may lead one to repudiate history as a cognitive discipline, to flirt with wanton forms of relativism, and to embrace deliberately subjective, nonevidential, intuitive types of insight.

But a polar emphasis upon the stability of culture or upon the endurance if not permanence of culturally conditioned habits and institutions may lead to a loss of any historical sense at all; it may even lead to false assumptions of true universality in human events. In areas of well-established behavioral patterns, where conscious human purpose seems remote or even nonoperative and where analytical descriptive models have reliable predictive uses, the historian may join with cognate social scientists in attempting to turn stable patterns of culture into time-neutral scientific generalizations (this happens most easily in economics). Then the so-called historian will view artifacts from the past, not as cultural monuments of possible value, but as evidence for or against some hypothesis of a lawlike form. He may even deplore the lack of rigor, or predictability, in other areas of history.

The legitimacy for history of causal rather than of general explanation, a central position of many idealists, has been given new respectability by William H. Dray.[1] He has shown how often historians try either to reveal how a subject reasoned his behavior or to indicate how his behavior conformed to some reasonable criterion ("he ran because he wanted to get into the dry"). By using such causal language the historian indicates that a subject's behavior is normal, that he does what one would expect. When a historian can give such a reason for an act, he satisfies all the requirements of a story. He needs no further reference to a controlling psychological law even if one is possible. Dray calls this "rational explanation" and uses it to demonstrate an alternative to Hempel's covering-law model; in fact, Dray's alternative is much closer to the actual practice of historians than is Hempel's.

Dray's "rational explanation" is simply one form of causal explanation, with the full focus on cause in a final rather than in an efficient form, on a purpose rather than on an agent. In fact, in his emphasis upon rationality, goals and purposes are clearly in the forefront and may even be quite conscious. Such emphasis upon conscious considerations, or at least upon behavior that seems to reflect reasoned reflection, can conceal the full scope and the usually nonpersonal and nonconscious operation of final causes. Overemphasis upon deliberation and choice too often diverts attention from the final causes that are deeply embedded in cultural forms, such as slow-changing institutions. In the few cases where final causes are conscious, they are usually in

1. William H. Dray, *Laws and Explanation in History* (London: Oxford University Press, 1957).

process of change and are also difficult to identify. A historian cannot mind read. The final causes that are most often evident to him are no longer operating at a conscious level but are operating through well-established habits, including habits of thought. He thus searches for them not in hidden deliberative processes of an individual but in relatively stable patterns of behavior (institutions) or in relatively stable belief systems (ideologies).

Too much emphasis upon overt thought and upon conscious intent can also force the historian into an overly subjective posture. Historians may then try to do the impossible—to relive and rethink some part of the past. This is not to deny that all subject matter for a historian does have some direct or indirect relationship to human thought but only to make clear that in most histories the actual thought is not focal. The historian is usually properly concerned not with thought processes and feeling but with immediate or belated products of thought. As a convenient but partial perspective, the products of human thought may be viewed in their abstract conceptual form (as beliefs) by intellectual historians. But with equal justification, they may be viewed in narrowed behavioral and institutional forms by other historians. To push historical accounts beyond these effects of thought is to move close to a methodological never-never land, in which inferences from observable evidence requires an added, intuitive faculty, or an ability to leap into another person's mind, to commune directly with hidden worlds of feeling and quality. Rather, the historian must honestly describe and relate events always affected by feeling and quality. He wants to know the past, but above all, he does not want to relive it or rethink it. Knowing involves a conceptual rendition, not a recapturing of specific experiences. The historian thinks about the past; he does not become it.

Thus causation, if understood in both its traditional and common-sense usage, is intimately related to man and is a major aspect of the human past. Causal relating of events is always a legitimate, and may be the focal, part of telling a story of this past. In no extensive history can human agency, and thus causes, be avoided. But some historians are still apprehensive about causal judgments and prefer other than causal relationships in structuring their stories. Perhaps they are wise. Causal relationships are difficult to establish. Many causal claims made by historians reveal ambiguities in causal language and confusion about different types or levels of causation.

As a beginning, historians should be aware of, and on occasion distinguish, at least the following four uses of causal language: (1) To denote decision-influencing conditions—either physical, organic, or cultural—and thus the conscious considerations that led to a decision ("he halted his troops *because* they were too tired to attack"). (2) To identify certain nonconscious but fully cultural conditions necessary for an event ("*because* of prevalent strategic habits, he always formed his troops in massed formations"). (3) To identify, among clearly generalizable phenomena, certain necessary but clearly not sufficient conditions for an event ("*because* it rained, he lost the battle"). (4) To refer to fully sufficient conditions for an event and thus to identify the generalizable order that necessitates it ("mustard gas *caused* the death of his men").

Unfortunately, historians rarely make any distinctions between agent causation (true causes in the traditional usage) and generalizable order. They rightly assume some generalizable order and then use causal language to indicate sufficient conditions for a physical event of human import ("because of the build-up of pressure the mine exploded, with great loss of life"). *Because* of such unanalyzed usage (incidentally, this is a typical causal judgment, using the same language as above for a necessary condition of a cultural type), historians often confuse the meanings of "cause" or mix two meanings in complex statements. One obvious temptation is to cite necessary but insufficient conditions without proper awareness and then to fall into the modes of thought that fit sufficient conditions (exclusivity, universality, and thus a type of scientism). Sometimes one intermixes physical order and human purpose in causal statements, "Because of slight stature, John could not scale the wall." Although the statement is full of intent, and even suggests frustration and rage in John, the causal judgment still refers to physical conditions that limit the options open to an agent. Here a physical state B could not occur because a previous state A, containing the sufficient conditions for B, was not present. In a quite different sense, physical or biological limitations influence human choice and lead to the following causal statements: "Because of the driving rain, he disengaged his troops," or "Because of the severe winter in the north, more people than ever before vacationed in Florida, with great impact on its economy." Here the physical conditions are in no sense sufficient conditions for the designated effects. No relationship of a physical, transformative type exists. The physical circumstances are only decision-influencing considerations in human choice, and thus we here have the rational type of explanation defined by Dray. Compare this with a true physical statement, such as "Because of the cold, he died."

Subject to a lot of qualification, it is true that historians can make unambiguous and truly causal judgments, even of an exclusive sort, judgments that they can support by good logic as well as by ample evidence. As an example, and begging all the problems surrounding the event, the following statement is quite clear and, given enough evidential support, also true: "Lee Harvey Oswald shot John F. Kennedy and caused his death." In a true causal perspective, the act by Oswald was *the* cause of the death and, through it, the indirect cause of many other consequences. But being a true causal judgment, such a statement cannot indicate the sufficient condition for the death. A pathologist might provide such an explanation and even use causal terms, but he would have to use the terms in a quite different way. The shooting by Oswald was not an isolated, unconditioned, or spontaneous event (we have no compelling reason to believe there are such events, although we often know none of the determinants or conditions). His act also was caused. If known, we might cite one of these causes, and, in an indirect sense, even assert *it* to be *the* cause of Kennedy's death. Thus, one had best claim only that there are single, exclusive, proximate causes and that an almost limitless number of ever more remote conditions cannot falsify such a causal assertion. Typically, the causal judgment about Oswald and Kennedy is not very ambitious. The causal judgment does not indicate what, if any, conscious reasons lay behind Oswald's act, nor does it reveal any mental operations that preceded or accompanied the act. These we cannot know. It does assume that Oswald was an agent, that some physical force did not jerk the trigger in spite of himself, that he was not under hypnotic control and thus acting for someone else, or that he was not insane and thus incapable of responsible behavior. It also assumes the obvious, that there were various cultural determinants stretching back from the act. Further inquiry may disclose some of these remote causes, many of which may become quite significant in a history of wider scope.

There are no end of conditions, physical and cultural, that con-tributed directly to Kennedy's death. Why select Oswald's shots from myriad necessary conditions? Even if one leaves out all generalizable aspects—all purely physical necessities—there still seems no clear reason to select Oswald's act over that of someone else. After all, Kennedy would not have been killed by Oswald if he had not made the decision to go to Dallas. Could one not correctly state: "Because Kennedy went to Dallas, he was assassinated and the whole nation plunged into grief"? This strikes at the heart of any claim that, in simple events, exclusive causes can be established, for any number of truly causal (not physical) conditions could be cited and, in a certain frame of reference, made the focal or significant cause. Still, there is a rather obvious way of distinguishing Oswald's act from all other culturally conditioned causes.

But first one must concede that the history one writes does set up criteria for selecting causes. If one were writing a history of the tragic career of John Kennedy, showing how innocent, even idealistic choices often led him into totally unexpected and unforeseeable misfortune, then his choice of the Dallas trip would be of focal interest, and in this context it might be cited as the cause but not properly as the exclusive cause of his death, in much the same way that it would also be cited if a thunderbolt had struck him down in Dallas. But here the story being told involves Oswald only incidentally. It is a story of misfortunes that afflict a person. This is quite different from a history of the Kennedy administration or a history of recent American history, in either of which the Oswald explanation would most likely be relevant. Often, extended events with one label but numerous and variously emphasized aspects, such as a war, reflect a near infinity of necessary conditions. Here a diversity of causal arguments often reflects quite different stories being told and different simple events being accounted for.

The earlier judgment about Oswald is a proximate causal explanation with some exclusivity to it, for there was a feature in Oswald's act that was not present in any of the other necessary conditions that one can imagine. His was not only an act by an agent (so was Kennedy's choice of the Dallas trip) but an act displaying intent appropriate to the result. At least, his act seemed to display such intent, although almost no conceivable evidence could conclusively prove it (he may have been hypnotized). No causal judgment, particularly when it involves human agency, can ever be certain. But certainty is another issue than exclusivity. Such emphasis on intent appropriate to the result parallels the idea of direct legal or criminal responsibility.

In the assassination only Oswald was legally subject to a charge of murder, although such causal judgment in no sense depends upon any legal guilt. Oswald's act would still be *the* cause of Kennedy's death even if no criminal law applied.

From the perspective of Kennedy, the act by Oswald was an unexpected calamity to be suffered, much as an unexpected thunderbolt. None of Kennedy's choices displayed any intent at all appropriate to the terrible outcome. His contributory acts, such as riding in an open car, had no intentional connection with the murder. But because of intent, Oswald had a distinguishable type of responsibility for what happened. This does not preclude other types of responsibility. Perhaps some Secret Service agents should have anticipated some such attempt and taken greater precautions. They may have displayed poor judgment, for which they might be expected to suffer some professional punishment. But no such dereliction can be said, in any intentional sense, to have caused Kennedy's death.

In isolating a special category of necessary conditions or causes through intent (impossible in many situations where such intent is not present), one assumes that such causal acts are volitional or voluntary. But one need not assume that they are, always or even usually, carefully planned or even immediately conscious (surely Oswald's act was both of these). Again, many final causes become embedded in habit, and in numerous events of lesser moment than Oswald's we all do habitual things for which we are responsible. In fact, we usually accept such responsibility and would not like to lose all the praise that comes from such beneficial activity. Much that we do is truly our acts, voluntary even if unthought, for we have in the past been conscious of such acts even as a structure of habits formed. In other cases, we have formerly been conscious of certain habits and thus in a position to criticize and modify them. Particularly in more complex, group behavior, at a community or national level, intent often lurks, well hidden, in long-since established ends now thoroughly embodied in institutions. It cannot even be discovered by polls of citizens, for almost no one is consciously aware of these ends.

The tie between cause and responsibility (a rather obvious connection when one correctly views all efficient causes as dependent upon final causes) does not necessitate moral judgment. But, by most any conception of morality, the location of responsibility is a prerequisite for moral judgment. A historian can assert that Lee Harvey

Oswald caused the death of Kennedy, that he was legally responsible for the death according to existing criminal laws, but without any desire to place the act against some accepted scale of good and evil. Even if the historian reacts in a moral way to the act, and even if he expresses his admiration or distaste, the causal judgment still stands. Oswald killed Kennedy. The historian knows that such causal judgment, such fixing of intent and responsibility, invites moral judgment from his audience and that much of the interest and fascination of history lies in this moral pregnancy. Now, in fact, historians often reveal their own moral verdicts and thus try to guide the audience reaction. But although such overt moral judgment is quite proper for a historian and is often valuable in fulfilling noncognitive purposes (interest, relevance, involvement, sympathy), it is still extrinsic to the causal judgment. The historian is, thus, always trying to construct correct accounts in areas full of valuative content. In fact, any subject matter completely value neutral to man is not historical subject matter at all.

When an event, such as a duel or the outbreak of a war, involves antagonistic intent by two or more agents (and thus two interacting series of intent causes), the assessment of cause easily becomes, in fact, an assessment of blame; it is a moral judgment of the historian concealed in causal language. Causally considered, a duel almost without exception would be the result not only of an array of conditioning circumstances but of many intentional acts by two people, some of which may be appropriate to the final results, some surely directed at very different results. In a loose, quantitative way, a historian may, with some peril, try to determine the causal weight to be given to the acts of each protagonist ("John's angry statement was the largest single cause of the conflict"). He may also try to determine to what degree one side misinterpreted intent on the other and thus seek elements of tragedy in such conflict (without ever desiring such an eventuality, a person may be forced to defend himself or face death).

But, too often, the historian falls into the moralistic trap not only of evaluating the issues at stake (as a moral person he can scarcely avoid this and should not try to avoid it) but of letting the evaluation determine the alleged causes (really, he means blame rather than cause). Thus, he turns the evil agent into the asserted cause, and he turns the good agent into a suffering and innocent recipient of some causal act. After all, the good person only acted out of self-defense; he did not "cause" the fight. The causal agent was the only aggressor. Such ascriptions of blame, cast into the form of causal judgments, plague all intensely emotional conflicts, such as the American Civil War or the recent cold war, both much too complex for anything close to exclusive causes based on intent. In neither case can the historian do more than isolate some of the necessary conditions, including varied intentional acts, almost none of which lead to intended results. In fact, whenever a historian asks questions such as "*Who* caused the cold war?," one can routinely expect a moral evaluation rather than a true causal judgment.

Another distinction that must be made by a historian, if he is to avoid ambiguity, is the difference between proximate causes (such as Oswald's shot) and more remote conditions (physical or cultural) that explain the proximate cause. Why did Oswald shoot Kennedy? This opens up a labyrinth of possible causes of one type or another. By either asserted generalizations about human behavior, or by citing various acts by other people stretching far into the past, it may be possible to argue, in a most plausible manner, that Oswald had to shoot Kennedy, that he could not have done other than he did, and hence that the assassination was inevitable. Since Oswald had to do it and since there was no reasonable way for Kennedy to anticipate and avoid the bullet, the event takes on a fatalistic dimension. And, indeed, historians often exploit this tragic element in human affairs, usually by turning away from proximate causes and their immediate context to remote causes which seem to so determine events as to leave no room for individual options and no place for moral judgment.

But terms such as "inevitable" or "could not have done other" are themselves ambiguous and are often interchangeably used in two different ways. For example, to use the familiar old issue, was the American Civil War *inevitable*? According to possible meaning of the word, it both was and was not inevitable, as different historians have amply demonstrated. As in all human events, retrospective analysis shows ample reasons why varied participants chose as they demonstrably did choose. They would really have had to be different men, with different characters, to have done other than they did. In fact, their behavior shows what character they had, and no one can escape this circular, retrospective argument. In this sense, not only the Civil War but all human events are inevitable, and stress upon the determinants of human choice invites a commendable sympathy and pity in our stories of the human past. But the word "inevitable" here has a soft or moral meaning, not a strong or mechanistic one. It does not, in fact, lead one to sufficient conditions for human acts, to any past state of affairs that, by the working of uniform laws, of necessity becomes a later state. No mechanical necessity, no determinant laws, forced any of the human agents to act as they did in the pre-Civil War years. No physical force compelled Oswald to pull the trigger.

Thus, despite remote and even seemingly fully determinant causes for a human act, an individual is still, in one sense of the word, free to do other than he does. No physical impediments block his act; no transformative laws compel what he does (even though the act necessarily exemplifies such laws). For this reason, such an agent, whatever the cultural backdrop, is still rightly held responsible (or else the idea of responsibility has no real meaning at all). A "hard" use of "could" and "could not" applied to the participants in the Civil War shows that they clearly could have done differently. They had options of all sorts, and if they had been better men they would have taken them. If one wants to cast moral stones, then one rightly casts them at their lax character, their manifest incompetence. He blames them for not being better men, for not being able to make better choices. In this sense of the word, the war was not *inevitable*. Only physically determined events are inevitable. And in making this judgment, the historian does not, of necessity, assert some standard of conduct of his own invention. He need only emphasize the moral standards affirmed by the participants, the ideals they surely wanted to achieve. One does not have to import valuative judgments from the present to assert that these men failed. They acknowledged the failure themselves. From this perspective, by this sense of the meaning of words like "inevitable," the war becomes a case history in human failure—a failure that indeed seems more tragic when we place it against a larger, causal perspective.

By these somewhat subtle distinctions, the Civil War was both inevitable and could have been prevented. The two seemingly contradictory perspectives are not in conflict; they do illustrate the need for greater precision in the causal language used by a historian. And this precision can be found, not in the methodological subtleties of the physical sciences, not in textbooks on logic, but in age-old distinctions made in moral philosophy, by far the most relevant discipline for clarifying causal confusion among historians.

All the confusions about causation in history cannot be settled by making a radical distinction between transformative physical relationships and human causes, by asking historians to be aware of two quite different perspectives for causal language, or by an even more treacherous attempt to distinguish, and give a preferred place to, effect-intentional human acts, or to a special category of causes. All too often the historian must make causal judgments which reveal no clear intent and must, for reasons of economy if no other, isolate one or only a few causes out of many necessary conditions for an event. Assume that the bullet that killed Kennedy had been fired by accident and from some distance away. No intentional act at all appropriate to the end result allows a historian to set up an exclusive and preferred cause. If he wants to explain the event in causal terms, he must turn to quite varied, almost inexhaustible conditions, proximate or remote; for eventually every institution in the society may be implicated. He may, in a given selective context, allege that the failure of Kennedy, or of the Secret Service, to select a bulletproof automobile caused the accident or, much more remote and embracing, that the gun laws in America caused this and many other useless killings. Obviously, one writing a history of the Secret Service would select the first cause; one writing a history of violence in America would prefer the second. Such causal statements are not only context determined but also carry with them an unwritten qualification: "this was only one of many necessary conditions for the event."

Causes of this selective type involve no methodological or cognitive issues of great import. Given the above qualifications, they allow no crucial subjective inroads. The historian, by his own intent or interest, chooses the story he will tell and within it selects and emphasizes certain things, including certain causes. As an empirical fact, different historians use varied criteria for selecting causes. These criteria may be analyzed, as by Morton G. White,[2] and such an analysis may be of help to historians. In some situations, historians with a certain bent always assume the constant state of affairs and select as causes the unexpected events. Thus, "Kennedy really died because

2. Morton G. White, *Foundations of Historical Knowledge* (New York: Harper & Row, 1965).

a boy accidentally discharged his hunting rifle." But another historian might emphasize a more constant state of affairs, such as gun laws. In an instrumental context, one may stress the curable or eradicable condition over other conditions impervious to our action. Often not only historians but almost everyone gives the unexpected, the extraordinary, the rare condition a preferred place. If they make no special claim, such a selection abets a good story, providing interest, surprise, shock. Here, of all places, the historian should not be confused with a scientist, who always has to seek a sufficient and fully determinant condition, or come as close to this as possible. The historian almost always gives a selected cause for a selected event. In a narrative a historian correctly cites a cause if it is one necessary condition and if he neither makes nor implies more sweeping and exclusive claims.

Possibly the distinction, made by Ernest Nagel[3] and by others, between a constant state and unexpected or abnormal events, has some relation to two words used (not very clearly, one must admit) by many historians in a seemingly causal way: trends and forces. It is dangerous to try to sum up even what most historians mean by these terms. But they could mean by a trend (or is it a tendency?) a steady increase in choices of a certain type within a group. This would indicate that some unifying social goal or purpose, some new and significant final cause, was becoming ever more operative in a society and, for some people, perhaps already on the way to becoming a part of their working habits. Thus, one might predict an increase in formerly rare or unknown choices or modes of behavior. In this sense, a historian might say that a society exhibited a "clear trend toward individualism" (whatever that means). Likewise, force could be used to denote relatively fixed patterns of choice and behavior. Then, statements such as "because of economic forces beyond his control, he did so and so" would indicate stable economic institutions, well-intrenched economic habits, and, perhaps so unconscious as to be beyond criticism, certain internalized goals and purposes. After this all too neat definitional legislation, one might make almost meaningful statements of the following form: "because of economic *forces* beyond his control, he had to accept the feudal system before 1688, but by then a clear *trend* toward individualism enabled him to launch a new entrepreneurial venture."

3. In *The Structure of Science* (New York, 1961).

Even so brief an analysis has at least demonstrated the complexity of causal judgment in history and possibly has clarified the following propositions: That any single, exclusive, and fully sufficient condition for any event, even when cited by a historian, implies some lawlike generalization, some non-time-conditioned or ahistorical order, and, however related by the historian to cultural events, must itself possess no cultural or distinctively human traits. That true causal judgments, involving real agents, can never provide such sufficient explanations for an event and thus can never involve anything more determinate than necessary conditions for an event. That primary (and in some cases exclusive) proximate causes of this type can be isolated, out of numerous necessary conditions, only by the presence of agent intent appropriate to an event. That, beyond these distinctions, only the topical context or narrative demands can guide the selection of certain necessary conditions out of a vast manifold of such conditions. And, finally, that there is no conflict between proximate causes and more remote, more inclusive causes, although remote causes seem to dissipate options and thus lessen the sense of responsibility.

C hapter 11

OBJECTIVITY AND VALUE

The so-called problem of objectivity continues to plague historians. Unfortunately, it is not one problem but almost as many problems as there are meanings for the word "objective." Not only is the word "objectivity" used in many ways; so are other terms that follow in its wake, such as "value," "relativism," and "presentism." On no other issue have semantical issues been so central and real substantive issues been so peripheral.

Can a history really be objective? It can be, but only when the term "objective" has a practical and very restricted meaning. Neither history nor any other cognitive discipline can be objective if that means such impossible things as certain truth or an exact correspondence to some hidden reality or such unlikely, undesirable, or absurd requirements as complete neutrality, impersonality, and detachment. Also, history cannot be objective if objectivity requires sufficient conditions for all events or if it requires the subsumption of all events under covering laws. If it has any bearing on history at all, objectivity means that the clearly cognitive (truth-claiming) parts of a historical narrative, even as the lawlike hypotheses of a generalizing scientist, must specifically refer to, and be inferable from, some perceptual evidence of a public sort, and it means that the cognitive claim must go no further than this evidence seems to allow. If it does go further— if one gives evidential weight to nonpublic, personal, intuitive data or to preferences and wishes—then a purported history is not objective. This is true even if such a history proves later to have been more valid than a more restricted, misleading, but evidentially disciplined account. Thus, objectivity is a criterion for establishing true propositions, but it is not a synonym for truth.

The demands of objectivity do not preclude a historian's personal interest in often quite selective historical subjects and in highly creative and imaginative constructs that are never identical to any past reality. Objectivity is quite consistent with numerous noncognitive, esthetically or morally suggestive, personally or culturally revealing, judgments within a narrative. After all, being objective, or even being true, is not the only goal of most historians; it is never the sole aim of any good historian.

A history is a story about the past; it is not the past itself, although the word "history" is often used for this unrecoverable thing. Whether one draws a history from the guidance of memory or of monuments, it cannot exactly mirror some directly experienced past nor the feelings and perceptions of people in the past. We can never, with any adequacy, conceptualize even our feelings, articulate without ambiguity our beliefs, or recount much more than the outlines of our actions. There simply is no equivalence between existence and concept. This has a double import. First, we can never adequately conceptualize our experience of symbolically rich human artifacts that seem to represent past human efforts, but at least, in some carefully selected areas, we have to do the best we can if we are historians. Secondly, inferences from these artifacts to past human feelings are hazardous, so hazardous that historians should avoid such inferences whenever possible. The experiential past is largely hidden and lost. But inference can be made, almost conclusively in some cases, to the concepts and acts of men in the past, to their articulated beliefs and to the ends operative in their behavior. In fact, we can infer ends that they served without knowing it, or momentous events that they scarcely heeded, for we have the advantage of hindsight. Without it there could be no history.

Often the most momentous events of our life go unnoticed at the time they happen. In rare cases, we die without having recognized them. The accidental meeting that led to a job, the enjoyable meal that led to illness, the blind date that led to marriage and a family are examples familiar to all. Let anyone tell the story of his life, and these episodes may figure large. Every detail of that blind date will become a cherished family heirloom; in nostalgic analysis, every gesture, every word may take on great importance ("Honey, why did I ask you that silly question?"). If one of the participants can find language suitable to the task, he can turn such episodes, so full of meaning, into family epics, endlessly recalled and repeated. Unfortunately, a good raconteur may do more than memory allows; he may embellish the epic with dramatic flourishes, with imaginative importations of details that should have been present at such a demonstrably momentous event. Instead of simply claiming significance ("Oh, what a glorious and important evening"), he adds a moon that never shone, a brilliant repartee that never developed, a band that never played. And soon, out of a past that never was, he constructs an illusory self that will never be, one that is pathetic to those who know the truth (historical in this case).

Usually through the revelation of symbolically suggestive artifacts, rather than through memory, the historian constructs an inferential bridge to events far in the past, and by another class of inferences he calculates the values, purposes, and ends reflected in those events. He cannot rethink or reexperience the past. But he does think it and experience it as a past. His interest must be selective. The husband and father who remembered the momentous blind date soon forgot a thousand other events and, in most cases, for good reason. They had no recognizable significance for anyone. The historian finds little of interest to himself or to an audience in most of the past that lies symbolically exposed even to causal inference. Thus, he does not think it and constructs stories about it. It is not worthy of his art.

But here and there the historian does find at least bits and pieces of a seemingly compelling past, very often including the past that endures in his beliefs and habits (and who is not interested in himself?) or a past that is related to the pressing concerns of himself, his group, or his country. Here, alone, are the events that he wants to understand and the stories that, given constructive ability and evidential support, he wants to tell. These stories have value for him. But to tell such stories or even to hear such stories is not at all like having had the experiences told about. It is not a reliving of the past but a particular way of living in the present (a historically conscious way). In rare cases this historical experience can be more intense than the past experiences thought about (the husband and wife may find more meaning and more exhilaration in the historical experience of their first date than they actually found in the frightening, insecure first meeting). Historical experience is often charged with drama, with a sense of the vital importance of certain past events. Very often, even in areas of the past long familiar to almost everyone, a historian sees a new causal relationship (some necessary condition formerly ignored) and thus some new significance in an event. This makes possible the telling of an old, old story as it should be told. And in the new perspectives he offers, it is really a new story, a history never yet created by anyone, and often a story never even vaguely understood by any of the actual participants. By such a process, by turning the heretofore forgotten and meaningless into the memorable and significant, the historian both rescues and creates a past. By so doing, he helps in some small way to determine the future. He keeps telling children new secrets about their parents and tries to convert their sweet innocence into mature wisdom.

Such stories of the past have two closely integrated, mutually conditioning types of cognitive content. The personal (if one wants, the subjective) intent, the selective aspect in the choice of topic, and the purposes sought do not play any necessary cognitive role. But any historian asserts something as true about a delimited past (he classifies subjects and events, locates them in space and time, and serially connects them by causal relationships or continuity of identity). Also, if only by implication in the language used, he also affirms something about how such events relate to unspecified events in their future (possibly our present) and to events well outside the temporal span of the story itself. This not usually explicit truth claim also involves either causes or continued identity.

When the father recounts that momentous blind date to his children, he constructs a narrative with a time-limited subject—one evening in the life of John and Mary Doe. But implicit in practically every word is the relationship that event had to many later events, including the very existence of Harry and Susan Doe. Such a then-open future has an indispensable role in establishing a significant past, and thus in selecting a proper story to tell; it also, as Arthur Danto has so effectively argued, has a role in the describing and relating of various episodes in the narrative itself.[1] In the family of our example, the opening telephone call to set up a date became, correctly in a larger context, the first act in the John Doe family epic; it became something that it was not, something that it in no way could be known as, when it actually happened. It is for this reason that even simple descriptions in a historical narrative may contain some temporal spread and causal content.

Almost no one denies that a historian can reliably infer certain

1. Danto, *Analytical Philosophy of History*.

simple, past events from surviving artifacts, or that in many cases
he can reliably date such events according to some conventional
calendar. But simple events, in themselves, are of minor importance
in most histories. One might easily assert that John and Mary Doe
dined in a certain restaurant on that critical evening. But so what?
So did a hundred other couples. We will even assume that John and
Mary duly recorded their visit in a dated guest register. If long afterward a garrulous John Doe were challenged in his epochal account
of that evening, he might even seek out the old register in order to
establish the fact. By this "research," he adds public evidence to his
account and becomes a more exact and rigorous historian. But until
John Doe consulted the register and used it, it was scarcely historical
evidence, for it as yet evidenced nothing and supported no history.
The surviving effects of past human efforts are surely almost infinite;
few ever become historical evidence; few ever achieve symbolic meaning. Only for John and Mary Doe does the old register (deposited in
the local archives) come to life. Only for them does it have weighty
meaning. It bears witness to the most glorious and momentous episode in their whole life, to the very opening of their history as a
united couple.

But one question remains. In referring to a glorious evening, in
going beyond the evidenced fact of such an evening together, is John
Doe being objective or subjective? By a plausible use of both words,
he is equally both and without conflict. What he says is true. It is also
charged with intense, personal meaning. Of course, if without qualification, without any clearly implied and limited context, he had
claimed that the date was then experienced as the most momentous
event in his or in human history, he would be correctly dismissed
as a fool.

There is no way to construct a complete history, either in the sense
of including everything or in the sense of any story being completely
finished. Not only must we select, but we must face the limitation of
being ourselves in process. Even the most ancient history, insofar as it
has any continuing relevance, may have a radically different significance for us next week or next year. For example, John and Mary
Doe may be divorced next year, perhaps as an aftermath of some
serious mental illness and drastic changes in personality. Then he will
tell the story of his first date quite differently, but not necessarily less
objectively. He may remember as keenly and even find new cor-

roborating evidence. With the added perspective given by more recent events, he now sees the blind date not only as a glorious beginning to years of happiness (it is still that, although with a tragic tinge) but also as the first episode in what became, finally, a family disaster. Thus, John Doe's earlier histories were far from being all the truth; now they seem misleading. But they were true. The most crucial knowledge may indeed have been left out, but he could not have such knowledge until other things took place. And unlike more abstract and lawfully determined events treated in the generalizing sciences, many of these most crucial occurrences could not be predicted.

John Doe's plight is typical of the plight of any historian. Judgments in history, even down to descriptive language and class terms, have time qualifications attached to them. The war in Vietnam, now a localized conflict, may to the reader already be seen as the opening episode of World War III. But this type of limitation is not relevant to objectivity; it is relevant only to the temporal context and thus to a special type of fallibility or incompleteness ever present in historical knowledge. Our present judgments about Vietnam may be based on firm evidence. So was John Doe's earlier judgment that, in his life, that first date was the most glorious and momentous thing that ever happened to him. Thus, the historian must not only qualify any proposition with "until new evidence indicates otherwise" but must qualify most judgments with "until new events reveal new significance and permit more reliable assessments."

Another issue suggested by John Doe's history is a great deal more subtle. As he told and retold the story of his blind date, he selected and emphasized some events of the evening over others. In fact, some remembered details never seemed worth mentioning. They were not significant to his story. Thus, a historian is not only inclined to tell stories directly related to present interests and concerns (surely no less a motivating factor for him than for generalizing scientists), but he will also, within the broad leeway allowed by the narrative form, highlight some events and ignore others. Clearly, in doing this, he reflects not only some of his own evaluations ("I feel the struggle for Negro rights is vital and thus feel justified in emphasizing the Negro's role in the Civil War") but also those of his age, his community, and his culture.

This interior selectivity does not threaten objectivity, but it does reveal a critical difference between historical accounts and most scientific hypotheses. In a new context, it simply exhibits the difference between the generalizable and the human, or between sufficient conditions and final causation. Given the value criterion by which he selects a topic for inquiry, the generalizing scientist has not only a methodological discipline that demands verification by public data (even as the historian) but also a formal discipline that demands, within however narrow and arbitrary a universe, a type of completeness (not certainty). This is simply a feature of all lawlike explanation, or of transformative states within a system. Such completeness, such sufficiency, is impossible in disciplines limited by time and concerned with final causes. The historian can never, however restricted his topic, compose a complete or fully sufficient account. His is always, by practical if not by theoretical necessity, a partial story, and he has no formal reason to struggle toward a complete story. He looks for causes but never for all causes. If by accident he isolated all necessary conditions, he would have no criteria for recognizing this rare achievement.

Another way of stating all this, although it may sound sophistic, is to argue that a historian's selectivity never comes to a stop against some discrete topic, like the Civil War. He has no isolable system to explain; rather, he isolates a system as he explains. Every divergent but objective account of events in the United States from 1861 to 1865 is a different history, about some slightly different topic, selected by some different, and in some sense arbitrary, criteria. Many of these related but different accounts may carry the label "Civil War." Thus, there is almost never a common universe of inquiry in history; there are only varied related universes and various overlapping stories. At places of overlap, divergent accounts may be compared and judged by cognitive criteria. On the evidence, which is the true, or truest, account? But almost never can two complete stories, even about purportedly similar subjects, be equated, for they are really about slightly different subjects. Thus, selection of a topic and selection within a topic are scarcely distinguishable in history. From beginning to end, the historian must select, with no formal demand that, at any given point, he stop selecting his universe and get on with the explanation. This is not to deny that, totally apart from formal criteria, historians do face some conventionally delimited subjects and some professionally favored topics.

This selective freedom requires some necessary caution. Even though there are no set entities awaiting complete explanation, this must not mean that subjects actually selected by a historian do not have some integrity of their own. Almost any subject will display thematic unity (a continuing personality, characteristic, or flavor), which may well become the unity of a story about it. No historian could, or would want, to write a full biography of John Doe, with full meaning either all about him (an impossibility) or even a balanced and equal emphasis upon all aspects of his career. Only some part of his life may seem important enough to tell. Because of the significance of his beliefs, one may want to do an intellectual biography. John Doe developed a somewhat coherent body of beliefs, some of which very much influenced his society. But these influential beliefs cannot be abstracted in any complete fashion from less influential beliefs and even from nonintellectual aspects of his career. To be at all accurate, the historian must fit the focal beliefs into a larger whole, apart from which they could make no sense. Any historian accepts a holistic requirement, an obligation to move at least occasionally from more focal fragments to a cohering whole. This is true because the selected few fragments must be understood rather than distorted. And their proper relationship is a part of understanding. If one insists on picking and choosing among unrelated fragments, perhaps in behalf of some immediate use in the present, he leaves the field of historical understanding and enters the area of parochial and polemical pleading.

Thus, even though a selected subject for historical narration does not carry with it a demand for completeness or set up rigid guides as to what must be told, it does determine what is integral to it, what must not be fragmented and isolated. Even to select out of the unity that is any man or any nation some particular and narrow topic, such as ideas or beliefs, demands justification and frequent reference to the nonfocal but always conditioning context. Many true (that is, evidenced) but quite narrow histories (the success of John Doe in one endeavor) can be justified only by a large body of assumed information already present in an intended audience. Otherwise such histories are unbalanced. They easily mislead by omission, and they distort understanding. However selective a historian is, he faces crucial problems of judgment in determining how much background he must bring into a narrative, how much he can assume his audience to know, and how much, even though relevant and unknown, he must exclude in order to finish his story at all. In this area of judgment, fairness and balance are often accounted evidence of a type of objectivity, but it is clearly a type of objectivity that has nothing to do with verification by public evidence.

Thus, there is a vicious type of historical presentism or relativism, to use two very overloaded words. Every history has contextual limitations, not the least of which is the ever unfinished, future-conditioned nature of any narrative. Of course the most pressing contemporary concerns, or at least the areas of present awareness, often govern the infinite selectivity in any history. (No one can write a history of some aspect of the past that, because of present cultural blindness, is not even conceivable.) But a vicious presentism does not guide selection in history; it precludes history. Instead of making careful inferences from evidence, instead of constructing a true story about some part of the past that now seems significant and worth our thinking, we instead project our own beliefs and our own standards into some past, and we end up by revealing only ourselves. Such is not history, for the alleged pastness, replete with dates, is a false camouflage; and the alleged evidence, replete with footnotes, is not really historical evidence but undeciphered relics. This type of presentism, perhaps the most tempting pitfall of the historian, always leads to pseudohistories, which protagonists often use to sanction immediate interests or to buttress naïve and oversimplified criticism. Our present interests and our estimate of what is and has been of greatest significance to man should direct our backward gaze to those parts of the past worth knowing, and of such vital importance that we must dissipate all illusions by knowing them well. We fail this when we let our present concerns blind us to any past that does not mirror our concerns and our prejudices, and thus to almost any past at all.

Incompleteness—lack of any formal criteria for a full explanation —means that historians can endlessly compose their stories, even in narrow chronological or topical areas. There is no limit to the *number* of true, but somewhat different, stories that can be told about the Civil War. But there is a limit to *what* stories may be told about the war, and this limit is, of course, the evidence that supports all such inferences to the past. But this evidence has no assessable limits, for endless objects may, by recognition, become appearances for past events. Their symbolic content is the only evidence the historian needs. And when he seeks out such evidence, he effects a transformation in heretofore speechless and dead objects.

The unending, and more or less arbitrary, selectivity that enters into every history cannot be cured. In fact, there is no reason why one should want to cure it or conceal it. Perspective and personality should be clear, not camouflaged or confused. They both add to the appeal of a story. Obviously, there is no general agreement on what is most important, of most value, in our present world. There can be no single, agreed-upon perspective on the past; in any perspective there may be true accounts. Human tastes vary because of physical differences or, much more often, because of cultural differences. All historians join in finding significance in past events of a cultural sort, or in events infused with value, but this minimal concurrence only testifies to the fact that history is a story of the human past, a past ever replete with meanings and causes.

The only way that judgments of historical significance (of greater or lesser significance, of what should and should not be told) could be fully harmonized would be for all historians to agree on some object of ultimate value, on some final end. Then, perhaps, all human events would have an assessable significance in reference to this end, and limited and parochial judgments could, if desired, be reduced to some universal scale. Whatever its contextual meaning, any event could then be judged on this scale and allotted its significance in a universal history of man. But obviously, because of the very fact of cultural variation, because of the very fact of being historically conditioned individuals, historians do not embrace the same ends and never will. Even to accept the objectivity of value (or, more plausibly, an objective aspect in the determination of goals) does not, with the present diversity of cultures, enable historians to establish any common framework of judgment. Yet, within given ideological, cultural, or national settings, historians do share many common valuative assumptions and criteria; their historical selectivity can be critically scrutinized by other historians and by their lay audiences. Such criticism may be directed, not to cognitive or esthetic issues (is it true? is it well written?), but to the importance of a story (is there really that much significance in this topic? is that not trivial? how did those events affect the future?). Historians ever face the dismal prospect that, in a few decades, they will be adjudged foolish in their preferences, shortsighted in their pressing concerns, and condemned for telling, not false stories, but the wrong ones.

No methodological horrors lurk in the selective criteria used by a historian. This value content does not preclude exact description and valid causal judgments. Surely the valuative aspect of selection, even though in history it operates within a topic as well as in the isolation of it, does not force a historian to write fiction or to bend his evidence to support some cause of his own. And although value selectivity determines the story to be told and what can be evidence (only that which relates in a direct way to the story) it does not produce the evidence or provide any magical means of bypassing it.

But the problem of value is not so easily banished. Those who offer the most cogent arguments against historical objectivity may well accept the distinctions heretofore attempted. They may agree that objectivity is in no necessary way threatened by any personal interest that leads to the selection of a historical topic or to the selection of what to highlight within it, by other judgmental criteria located in the present, or by the imaginative and constructive elements of the story that originate in the thinking of a historian and never leap out of any quarry of facts. They will, rather, insist that value is most compromising, not in selective roles, but as integral to almost all the language and to many of the judgments made by historians. It not only focuses interest; it also in part certifies the final product.

Thus, the question: to what extent do private or culturally determined valuations affect the language and the judgments of a historian? First, and most obviously, a historian reveals his private preferences in the language that he uses. If he tried to eliminate such self-revealing language, he would not only be doomed to failure, but he would destroy the literary merit of his story. Since the historian must tell a story in familiar language, he has no recourse to any neutral, unambiguous symbolism. In fact, he often seeks words in behalf of expressive, rather than of cognitive, purposes. His very willingness to bare personal taste, to show how he feels about a historical person or event, can add immensely to the dramatic impact of his stories. Few historians would want to dispense with *beautiful* vistas, *compelling* speeches, *lovely* people, or even *glorious* revolutions.

Such revelations of private taste need not threaten the objectivity of an inquiry in history or in any other discipline. But to argue this is to force a distinction between the cognitive, or truth-claiming, language in a completed history and the language that fulfills other purposes, such as esthetic ones. The historian, for example, might assert that monarchical greed was a contributory cause of a glorious revolution (a revolution in which his father participated and which led to national greatness). The causal argument, which asserts an existential relationship, is clearly cognitive. Any historical critic could rightly demand evidence to support it. But the historian would rather think his critic a fool if he demanded: "prove that it was glorious." Clearly, in this context, the adjective expressed how a particular historian felt about a particular revolution. In the same sense, a biologist, describing a new butterfly and writing in ordinary language, could or could not give his own personal reaction to its bright colors. He could call it a beautiful butterfly and, in so doing, pose no threat to the accuracy of his description. In fact, his more colorful account would provide an experiential accuracy not usually present in scientific articles (it would reveal how it is for one person to experience such a butterfly). The nature of the historian's storytelling art makes it even more likely that he will frequently exploit such personal and colorful options.

This is not to argue that a simple distinction between cognitive assertions and self-revealing language can always be made by a critic. Our language, again, is just not that precise. Expressions of preference are most innocent when most obvious, and they are often far from obvious. To say that Lincoln was a *great* man may mean, in one context, that one admires or likes him; in another, that he made decisions that drastically altered the future of the United States. The first use reveals the historian's taste in men; the second asserts a causal relationship and begs evidential support. In such ambiguous contexts, the historian has an obligation to make his meaning clear. But there is no good reason for a historian to conceal his own personal reaction to Lincoln any more than there is a good reason for a biologist to conceal his reaction to a butterfly. Surely the obvious warning—that personal reactions must not lead one to ignore or misuse evidence—is almost too gratuitous to mention. What must be emphasized is that the problem of disciplinary integrity is not solved by the deletion of revealing language or by inhuman and impossible efforts at neutrality. Surely no one would suggest to the historian the absurd if not impossible assignment of telling stories only about men, groups of men, organizations, or nations that they neither like nor dislike, about which they have no feelings or qualitative reactions whatsoever. This assignment would limit storytelling to blighted and neurotically insensitive men and, if applied to the generalizing sciences, would have the same effect. The qualitative element is present in any art, including the cognitive ones. To try to suppress it is foolish and inhuman; to conceal it, a mere convention; to express it, a possible adornment; and to misuse it, a crime. In fact, concealment presents the greatest hazards and invites the greatest dishonesty.

The most subtle threat to objectivity—to a history with all its cognitive judgments tied completely to public evidence—is quite another use of valuative language. Even though not compelled by his subject to do so, historians often render verdicts on the acts of individuals and groups. ("His decision was a *wise* one." "His solution revealed his *brilliance*." "The country reacted *rationally* to all the threats." "The abolitionists were *fanatics*.") Clearly, such judgments reflect what is often a very private language. Few persons, even in the same society, mean the same thing by words like "wisdom." But the problem of meaning and thus of effective communication plagues almost all the language of a historian. Here, the critical issue is not meaning (we will assume that the historian can, if challenged, make perfectly clear what he means by his judgments) but the type of support he can offer for such judgments. For in each of these cases the historian intends more than a mere revelation of his personal reaction to events, more than "I feel or think so and so." Each of these judgments can be, at least in some sense, cognitive. They may rest on well-established theories and on extensive evidence, which, at least in a judicial sense, fully justifies the verdict rendered. Yet, in other societies, in other ages, the verdict would be different.

Such assessments primarily implicate not private taste but communal standards. On self-conscious reflection, the historian has to admit a valuative content in all such judgments, and he should claim objectivity only for the public, evidential component, which would be identical with the status of evidence in a court of law. In other words, he could prove that an individual did display the behavior that, in his society and by his own standards, clearly qualified him for the status of being wise. He could not prove that such behavior is "really" wise, for he has access to no universal and eternal standard, to no omnipotent lawgiver, to which he can appeal. Just as in a court, in a context of established sanctions, it is meaningful to ask for proof, so a historian can respond to a requirement of proof for his verdicts. Neither in a court nor in a history is it appropriate to expect proof of the legitimacy of the standards assumed. But some understanding of these standards is a prerequisite for understanding the verdict.

The sum of all this is that the word "objectivity," even when restricted to a methodological standard, may still have two slightly different connotations for a historian. In the judicial context, it requires enough public evidence to substantiate a verdict within a set of culturally determined, valuative standards. In a causal context, it requires enough public evidence to substantiate a relationship, and relationships, as such, are not culturally conditioned (the willingness to value such relationships is culturally determined). Objectivity, in the verdict context, is thus different from objectivity in the generalizing sciences, where such assessments do not occur.

All this chasing after the meaning of an ever more elusive objectivity should not obscure the complexity of a written history. It is a story as well as a purportedly true and objectively based account. Much of the purely cognitive content of any history could be expressed in other ways—as a series of descriptions and as a list of causal hypotheses. But so expressed they do not yet constitute a history anymore than a group of isolated melodies constitute a symphony. A history is not only fact statements but also the complex, time-extended whole that includes them and which, quite often, directed a historian to them. Saying that a history is a story is much like saying that much of modern physics is rational and mathematical. But physics is not all truth; it is only the truth that fits the formal requirements of largely mathematical relationships. And physics is certainly not mathematics; it is only those selected mathematical constructs that fit some aspects of experience. Likewise, historical truth is a quite limited variety of truth, and true stories about man's past are only a minuscule portion of all stories. In both cases, form and verity are complementary, and in their interaction they define the discipline. Isolated but true statements about even past human events ("John killed George in 1892") are not historical statements until they can be fitted into a story, into some history, with a theme and development over a period of time.

One result of all this is clear. A modern physicist must be a mathematician. And, however many historians work at the bits and pieces of a past event or events, eventually someone must be able to put them together to form the story. Obviously, the form of a discipline does not determine the truth of its propositions, although many a scientist and many a historian, infatuated with the esthetic or moral merit of their latest constructs, have wished that it could. Thus, there is no direct relationship between form and objectivity, unless one argues for an ontological rather than for some instrumental or esthetic justification for a given form ("reality really embodies a mathematical order and thus can be described only by a mathematical science.").

As stressed in the first chapter, it is a serious error, in physics or in history, to attribute prior reality to the conceptual product of inquiry rather than to the experiential ground for the inquiry. Once invented, of course, the concepts are indeed part of an experienced reality. The mathematical order of the theoretical physicist is a human invention, but it is an order that can be fitted to parts of experience. Once fitted, once the invented order has permitted us to locate uniformities or similarities in our experience, we too easily fall into the trap of seeing what reality allows as what reality required; into the trap of negating the creative and additive role of our conceptual inventions. They spring from human art, not from physical necessity; in fact, the conceived physical order and the necessity are both useful products of such art. Experienced reality probably allows more physical constructs than we could ever imagine. The same thing is true in history. After finding causes, describing complex wholes, or finally constructing stories and disciplining them to fit evidence, we may come to think of our conceptualized past as a fixed, preexisting structure, awaiting our discovery, rather than seeing any history for what it is—an imaginative, time-conditioned, but evidenced human invention. But reality as experienced severely limits those concepts that intend to explain a part of reality and that intend to bring us into some harmonious, working relationship to that part. And it is in our dutiful respect for those limits that, in any discipline, we are *objective*.

So long as we do defer to these limits set by experienced reality, or by the aspects of reality we select for ordering, we must place objectivity and, closely related, truthfulness, above other criteria in our conceptual arts. We often have to sacrifice esthetic and moral goals. A scientist has to dismiss the very hypothesis that, were it only true, would surely win the Nobel Prize and in addition cure all cancer. It may be elegant and beautiful but yet cannot be fitted to reality. The most instructive and entertaining account of the Protestant Reformation may not relate or unify enough of the surviving artifacts to be convincing, even if it does not directly contradict some known evidence. It may make a great novel, but it should not be advertised as history. In history, more than in any other cognitive discipline, there is great scope for formal invention. Since there are no entities to be completely explained, no causes that are not partial, no area of human experience excluded, no limit to the possible evidence to be sought, and often no alternative but to build on numerous weak inferences, one correctly judges the historian as much for the imaginative, intrinsically valuable aspects of his hypotheses and stories as for their truth or significance. He is a great historian not only because he tells the truth, finds the most relevant topic and the richest evidence, or makes the most brilliant inferences from it, but also because he tells a moving and eloquent story.

The narrative form is not only uniquely fitted to the historian's subject matter (they grew together)—to the distinctively human past —it is also necessary for what the historian is often trying to do. One tells a story about the past not to get some predictive knowledge, not to gain some direct control over events, but to produce, in the author and in his audience, a certain conceptual experience. A historian tries to get people to think a particular past in many of its dimensions, often as much in its particularity as in its generality. The story form embraces not only causal relationships but conflict and struggle: dilemmas that await resolution, ironic and tragic situations, paradoxical and surprising events. To bring men to such an experience of a past is not easy. It certainly requires gifts of presentation, or literary skill. In many cases, a historian's metaphors are more important and harder to come by than is his evidence. Rather than being a handicap, his rich and colorful language is a necessity. If the audience does not become involved in the story—if they do not appreciate it, grasp its significance, and see its relevance—they will lose all that it has for them (no technology flows from the historian's handiwork). In fact, "audience" is a key word for the historian. Unlike many scientists, a historian is not content to record in barely decipherable prose the results of his inquiry so that he will get the credit, so that his work will inform and enrich the ongoing process of inquiry, or so that some immediate practical return will be realized. For the historian, the presentation, in a form for maximum impact on an audience, is all-important, however dependent the finished story is upon what he calls research or however many contributory analyses he may have made in a nonnarrative form.

Because a historical narrative is, or purports to be, true (or as true as possible), it does not necessarily lose esthetic value. It can still be a superb work of art, with many features that have everything to do with it as a construct and nothing to do with it as truth. A gifted historian can create a unified whole out of many disparate parts, which is a problem not of inquiry but of organization. Where complexity confounds, he can find the most subtle words; where ambiguity lurks, the most precise; where drama hides, the most colorful. Even the truth he conveys demands such linguistic virtuosity, for he does not ignore but rather emphasizes qualitative aspects of a past (it was really a glorious battle to the victors). But art has to accept its limits and work its way around the immovable and demanding evidence. For gifted storytellers, this may hurt, but not as much as pedestrian historians imagine. Surely a historian must dig and sweat, count and calculate. But unless he is a horrible bore, he will do most of this offstage. A completed history must be carefully composed and presented; it must not be merely an exhibition of evidence or analysis. Of course, a historian should look well, swim in and through a thousand archives, count carefully, calculate by every strategy of statistical science, let computers grind on for months. But finally he must present his story, now surely as true as refinements of method can make it, surely weighty in significance to justify all the work, and thus in all ways deserving of the respect that only beauty can bestow.

The word "objective" has often been tied, misleadingly, to the idea that historians must tell what happened, just as it happened, even if not all that happened, in some human past. If qualified in a certain way, this has to be in part true. No one would suggest the opposite— that a historian should tell what did not happen. But "what happened" begs some questions. Does it mean all the various experiences had? If so, it is a meaningless, because an impossible, requirement. Does it mean what happened, as conceptualized and remembered, by proximate participants? If so, it might be recoverable, but, unless further interpreted in light of more recent events hidden to participants, it would be a past with little meaning to us and a past that would be full of absurd judgments. Does it mean some selected past that lies partially revealed in artifacts, including the recorded words of participants, and a past that endlessly takes on new significance as time passes? If so (and surely it is so), then historians tell what happened but not just as it happened.

Despite all the distinctive aspects and problems, histories result from inquiry. There is no good way, and no good reason, to set historical inquiry apart from inquiry in any other field, as if it revealed some distinctive road to truth (it is rather a road to a distinctive type of truth). The historian must conform to the same rules of inference (logic) and to the same canons of inductive verification as any other inquirer. Considered in this narrowed context, history presents, to the logician or to the philosopher of science, the same cognitive demands as physics or biology. And there is no one, clear, fully accepted model for such inquiry. Maybe even the elaborate attention given to such models in the last generation is now lessening. The old extremes of rationalism and empiricism are gradually disappearing. Even the most rabid formalist accepts experimentation (even if secondary); even the most rabid experimentalist concedes the indispensable role of rational formulation. Almost everyone recognizes the critical role of abduction or hypothesis invention and concedes an esthetic role here.

The following somewhat generalized model of inquiry illuminates some substantive methodological issues in history. John Dewey first formulated this model, but Karl Popper has subsequently, with slightly altered and more formal emphasis, adopted and refined it. By it, one should be able to say that a historian, confronted with, and in some way baffled or disturbed by, disparate phenomena that seem to give evidence for some human past, begins to construct imaginary accounts or narratives, perhaps including within them several causal judgments, in an attempt to unify and make some sense out of all the confusing phenomena; that he constantly checks each invented story against a residue of acquired knowledge (vicarious verification) as well as against the focal phenomena; that he keeps up this game until he finds a story consistent with what he already knows, and which gives some pattern to his phenomena (or most of them); that his narrative also almost inevitably implicates other, as yet unexperienced phenomena; that he then, either directly or by inferential, deductive chaining (desired phenomenon A necessitates B, and B necessitates C, which if found will have the same evidential significance as A) seeks out the specifically indicated evidence, knowing always that one unpredicted and noncoherent phenomenon will falsify his story; that he keeps restructuring his story until, finally, with the most diligent search of all evidence then available, he has so integrated the original phenomena and the induced phenomena as to have a quite unified, plausible, and supported account (as well as, we hope, an eloquent and dramatic story), although he knows that falsifying evidence could turn up at any time and that, most often, his story is most tentative because of the many probable inferences that had to go into it.

How does this model fit historical practice? Perhaps better than the working historian thinks. The problem-solving aspect, if given quite broad meaning, may be present in any historical inquiry, but of course it rarely accounts for the motives of the historian. But since these controlling motives are usually extrinsic to the inquiry (an assigned dissertation, pecuniary goals), they are not directly relevant to the model. The historian, in the often years' long interaction between evidence and imaginative construction, is hardly aware of the complex interplay of invention, deduction, and inductive verification; he may well reject any formal analysis of his procedure. But this also means very little.

The most crucial problem with the model (or is it with historical practice?) is that very often the historian does not (or cannot) attain the precision in his causal hypotheses, or the coherence in his narrative, to permit clear-cut falsification by one or a few exceptional or unanticipated phenomena. Quite simply, he almost always ends up with lower probability assertions in direct proportion to the scope or importance of his accounts. With near surety, he may say that Oswald killed Kennedy (this is, at least, falsifiable), but, given a series of necessarily weak inferences, what probability and how much precision is there in an allegation that the key remote cause was the violent state of American society? If this causal proposition can be given precise and operational meaning, and if evidence can be found to support it, it is still difficult to argue that, in a sea of necessary conditions, it was the most determinate cause, and thus give a quasi-quantitative weight to it. Yet, such a claim could be strengthened by supporting evidence; it could hardly be falsified by any conceivable evidence. At most, elaborate statistical data might weaken it.

The working historian will almost always respond more avidly to a phenomenological account of inquiry than to a logical account. This is not remarkable; he is the best judge of his own experience and possibly no judge at all in the field of logic. He particularly responds to any account of inquiry that emphasizes creativity and inventiveness. He rarely analyzes the methodological and logical nuances of his own art; he is a good historian as a result of good habits rather than of good rules. He is well acquainted with historical inquiry as a type of experience, with all its qualitative blessings and agonies. Perhaps for this reason he can find the language of insight and intuition, of imaginative identification and vicarious re-creation, of reliving and rethinking, quite persuasive. And, insofar as one can conceptualize a creative process, such language may be both ambiguous and yet quite accurate. Only after long contact with a subject area, long intimacy with potential sources, long and thoughtful consideration of a period, and thus with what seems like the veritable reliving of a past age, can a historian be very fruitful in constructing narratives or in inventing causal hypotheses. Thus, the intuitionist view of history is most closely related to the formal part of history, to brilliant composition and to imaginative leaps, but it is not correctly tied to the inferential and evidential aspects of history.

Even the blanket word "research" covers two quite distinctive historical activities, even if historians rarely distinguish them and even though they are rarely widely separated in time. The historian, seeking some correct story about a past that seems somehow important to him—or, in a more narrow, analytical context, seeking a correct causal explanation for some confusing even if quite narrow problem in well-rehearsed stories of the past—often immerses himself in the relics of that age or in the possible evidence for solving the problem. He goes to the archives; he endlessly reads manuscripts; he takes notes of material that seems to be relevant. This is an experiential, immersion process, out of which comes unifying themes or causal hypotheses. In other words, this type of research contributes directly to fruitful invention, to formal construction, and not to the inductive verification of constructs. Even the materials handled are not, as yet, historical evidence or data of any sort. The word "source" perhaps correctly identifies them as potential locations for finding such evidence. Benedetto Croce was most perceptive in distinguishing the dead artifacts that are dutifully, even piously retrieved and stored, in the expectation that someday, someone, in conceptualizing a certain relevant past, will convert these artifacts into living symbols, finally rich with meaning.

Once the constructive phase of history begins (a schema, a convincing pattern or theme, a crucial causal hypotheses), and it may begin very soon or never, a second type of research becomes possible, and this alone involves true inductive verification. Then, and only then, do questions beg an answer, problems beg a solution, and form demand a specific content. Maybe by good guesses or habitual thoroughness, the historian has dutifully viewed all the relevant manuscripts and transferred to photographs, recordings, or note cards all relevant data. Then the verification process can be carried out at one's desk. Maybe his memory is acute, and he can utilize evidence vicariously, without any recontact at all. In the first, familiarization (a key and precise word in the historian's vocabulary) phase of research, the process seemed one of osmosis, of some absorption or intuitive grasp (like getting to know John Smith, a matter of existential encounter and immediate perception, undistorted by any concepts). This world of immediate experience is the fount of all conceptual invention. And very often, the constructive parts of history—the brilliant narrative patterns or the daring hypotheses—seem all-important. These are in the limelight much more than evidential verification, and they usually distinguish the great from the mediocre historian. Here, in constructive invention, is the outlet for historical genius, for the man who can meet an age in diverse, fragmentary surviving artifacts, and quickly see a unifying pattern and likely connections. The verification process may seem as unexciting and as cold as taking John Smith's fingerprints to be sure of his identity, or administering a physical examination to certify his healthfulness, or counting his money to attest to his wealth, when one already "knows" that he is John Smith and that he is both healthy and wealthy.

But neither in the present nor even more in constructs about the past can we really know without examining and counting. We only indirectly encounter the subjects of our histories and infer their very existence from deposited and surviving effects. A characterization of a friend, John Smith, can be operationally prefaced as follows: "If you will go and meet John Smith and carefully observe him, you will find the following: . . . ." But for a historical John Smith, the same preface has to read: "If you will go and look at these designated places, you will find the following evidence which, with the greatest probability, shows John Smith to have been as follows: . . . ." In this operational perspective, a historical proposition, even though about something that existed in the past, has the same reference to some future verifying experience as any other existential hypothesis, and it has cognitive meaning only in this reference. However brilliant the hypothesis and however loyal to an existential acquaintanceship with some of the sources, it still prescribes some work to be done. If the work orders are clear, the phenomena to be sought of a type in theory perceivable by anyone, then the historical proposition is meaningful, testable, and object-referring. The actual work may be fruitless, the perceptions required unachievable, and the proposition false. But it is of the type that can be objectively tested.

The sum of all this analysis and qualification is probably the following advice to historians: unless you are willing to define very carefully, drop all the conventional methodological dualities from your vocabulary. It is usually futile to talk of "objectivity versus subjectivity," of "presentism versus loyalty to a real past," or of "relativism versus positivism." All such dualities rest on arbitrary definitions and thus become snares for the unwary. Much historiographical controversy involves more heat than issues. No one should doubt that history is a valid cognitive discipline. Propositions about the human past can be meaningful (they clearly indicate the evidence that will vindicate them) and can be objectively verified. Historical judgments can, with ever higher probability, be confirmed by prescribed evidence; and, at least judgments involving clear and precise relationships, can be falsified by counterevidence. More complex, always probable judgments can at least be weakened by counterevidence of a statistical type. Most important, the varied relationships between history and value do not prevent evidenced and reliable judgments or make history a form of fiction.

But some final warnings are in order. Objectivity, a matter of methodological rigor, does not guarantee truth. Despite ever present possibilities of human error or of remote chances for clever forgery or prefabrication of evidence (these are present in any area of inquiry), the historian can conclusively validate the occurrence of simple events, detailed descriptions of events, and even many proximate and simple causal relationships. Here the historian need nourish no more doubts than a physical scientist. But such simple knowledge is rarely a point of controversy among historians; much of it they take for granted. As soon as the historian moves on to complex patterns and to more sweeping, remote causes, he often moves beyond any conclusive evidence, or into an area he often calls interpretation. Here the invention of patterns or hypotheses is all-important. From long acquaintanceship, from moving among the scattered artifacts, the historian feels confident of at least the suggestively approximate validity of his judgments, but he cannot vindicate them with more than a few fragments of ambiguous evidence.

It is easy for a logician to demonstrate the tenuous chain of arguments that mark almost any complex historical judgment. In this sense, much of history is a stab into partial darkness, a matter of informed but inconclusive conjecture. The available evidence rarely necessitates our judgments but is at least consistent with them. Obviously, in such areas of interpretation, there is no one demonstrably correct "explanation," but very often competing, equally unfalsifiable, theories. Here, on issues that endlessly fascinate the historian, the controversies rage, and no one expects, short of a great wealth of unexpected evidence, to find a conclusive answer. An undesired, abstractive precision of the subject might so narrow it as to permit more conclusive evidence. But this would spoil all the fun.

Chapter 12

USE

Any serious consideration of history should end with an answer to the critical question: of what possible use are true stories about the human past? Definition and delimitation are prerequisites for these answers, but they do not reveal them. If history were a generalizing science, with lawlike regularities, transformative conditions, and the power of exact prediction, it would provide the same kind of instrumentality as the physical sciences. But it is not and does not. The quite different uses of history have to be elaborated. Of course, to define history and, on this base, to show its possible uses, is not the same thing as to show how people do in fact use it, misuse it, or even use what they mistakenly think it is.

An obvious, yet in some ways the most complex, use of history is that it provides various types of satisfaction to those who compose it and to those who consume it. Some of these satisfactions are intrinsic to history; others are completely or largely extrinsic. For the historian, much more than for the consumer of histories, these satisfactions variously relate to motives—to the reasons or causes for his being a historian or for his writing the particular histories that he does write. Such motives or apprehended reasons are of no direct methodological import, and they rarely coincide with the extended uses that such a history may have. The private reason for a historian writing a particular book may be far removed from the value that his history, as history, may have even for him, let alone for other people.

People become historians for many reasons. One must emphasize that, today, the decision to become a historian is generally a decision to become part of a well-defined profession; it is a decision to assume a clear social role; and it is thus a decision that may be made with scarcely any reference to particular histories that need to be written or to any broad social purpose that such histories might serve. Few students now enter the profession because of any compelling desire to know and reveal a specific part of the human past.

Not too long ago, most historians still believed that the reasons why a person became a historian or, even more, the reasons he selected certain topics, had grave methodological significance. Thus, they variously confused psychological and logical issues, as is so well illustrated by some of Charles A. Beard's ill-fated excursions into historiography. Few make such a glaring mistake today. But, at least in the American historical profession, there still seems to exist a rather clear hierarchy of more, and less, acceptable reasons for being a historian and for writing particular histories. As used here, reasons do not mean hidden or compulsive causes; they mean the conscious intent of a historian, or the ends he seems to be trying to further. For example, a historian who writes in hopes of bolstering some ideology, of furthering some practical moral or political cause, or of gaining popular esteem or a large income, may risk his professional standing. His colleagues suspect him of being nonobjective, if not completely dishonest. But they honor historians who write because of quite personal interest in some past (curiosity), in behalf of self-knowledge, or even for sheer fun. They believe them more likely to be objective and reliable. They reveal this functional hierarchy by such favored but almost incomprehensible and absurd expression as "history for its own sake" or, to multiply absurdities, "the past for its own sake." Those who use such expressions surely mean something like "history for my sake" or "history for my immediate gratification and enjoyment, without any concern for its further usefulness" or possibly the methodological intent that "history should be vindicated by correctly interpreted artifacts drawn from a past, not by any imposition of present valuations." No historian intends the seeming meaning in such statements: that history or the past have somehow taken on a life of their own and that such personalized entities have ends of their own to serve.

It seems that the distinctions between the varied motives of a historian parallel the many distinctions made between pure and practical scientists. At best, all such distinctions embody only half-truths. No inquiry, in any field, is pure in the sense of excluding all extrinsic or instrumental goals. But inquiry, if artfully pursued, is full of immediate value. It is enjoyable; it may be pervaded with esthetic quality. As one develops skill in any field of inquiry, as he acquires and assumes certain personal goals (esteem, salary, professional standing), and as he soothes his conscience by a conventional assurance that the product does serve some moral ends (even though unspecified), then the only focal and conscious ends served by inquiry may be esthetic ones. The vocation becomes a compelling avocation, completely self-justifying. Then a scientist or a historian might suggest, in all honesty, that he carried out his inquiries out of sheer enjoyment or because of his own love of truth (they might even suggest that any other reasons are ulterior and suspect). And, almost always, the best products of inquiry come from persons who are conceptual artists—from those who respond most fully to the demands of their chosen art form. The worst science and the worst history come from nonartists—from those who seek only extrinsic ends, those who never love the subject, never see its challenges, and never reap its immediate rewards.

Thus, in one sense of the term, historical inquiry is always self-contained. Intrinsic rewards are always present and may well dominate. But such artful and rewarding historical inquiry is not without use, even though the language used to describe it may imply such. More importantly, the returns from doing history are quite a different thing from the uses of history as product: the prime return from inquiry is personal and immediate, and the motivation to inquire is often more powerful because of this return. When a historian lauds truth as the sole object of his inquiry, he really celebrates a form of beauty or something that has immediate appreciative value, something that brings joy in itself and not as a result of any of its effects.

Surely, most historians love their work. It is even conceivable (but very unlikely) that somewhere there is a historical artist who seeks fitting topics not because of any expected use, of any moral purposes to be served, or of any professional or pecuniary rewards to be attained but solely because of esthetic and intellectual criteria—the story that will answer the most intriguing questions, unify harmoniously the most evidence, form the most eloquent story, pose the most creative challenges, and permit the most fulfilling resolution. This does not mean that such a person could escape some of the pervasive concerns of his time and place, for he could scarcely conceive of topics outside this context; nor does it mean that cultural significance does not guide his selection of topic and treatment, for no challenging or broadly unifying topic could fail to reflect this criterion. But his purpose does not extend beyond his completed history, although he may anticipate some appreciation from other historical artists. He does not care a whit whether his history has social utility or whether it will win him a promotion. Now, as a matter of fact, such an artful history will inevitably serve other than esthetic ends. Being a work of genius, it will undoubtedly gain him the promotion and influence thousands of people. It may lead to major changes in a society's goals. But we here assume that our dedicated historian, in his lofty purity, has not been sullied by any prior consideration of these gross facts.

Who has ever known such a pure historian? And is such purity desirable even if remotely possible? There may be a snobbish hypocrisy in those who, even if they do not attain it, still venerate it. But the partial truth is still there: both the intense interest and the esthetic returns are almost indispensable for any dedicated inquiry. Fortunately, the relationship between esthetic and moral goals is never disjunctive, but it is often quite complementary. The moral purposes directly intended by a historian (his desire to tell such stories and in such a way as to change and better the goals, tastes, habits, and institutions of a society) are ultimately only esthetic goals. But they are much broader ones than those of the pure historical artist. Instead of immediate private value, he seeks a society that is more generous in its bestowal of value to everyone. He seeks a beautiful society as well as a beautiful history. Thus, often, the emphasis upon pure history (or pure science) amounts to a form of selfishness, or to some hoarding of intellectual values, or even to a refusal to engage critical but complex moral issues that, whatever the historian's intent, will be somewhat affected by any good history. Conceivably, the pure historian and the morally committed but artful historian might write histories of similar merit, but for different reasons. The morally conscious historian may be the better man, but obviously he is not then the better historian. This only indicates what should be obvious: motivation is, in itself, an issue completely distinct from the merit of any historical product. But it is extremely unlikely that either the skill or effort requisite to great history will be present when the esthetic goals are missing.

Extrinsic goals of a personal type do not conflict with intrinsic or esthetic goals, but neither do they complement them. A historian is also a person with varied needs. He must earn a living, gain self-respect, find security in some social role. If he cannot find these returns in history, or in the *historical profession,* he may not be able to afford the luxury of composing any history at all. If one's preferred art can secure other than esthetic or even long-range moral returns, then one can give more time to that art and become a better (if not a "purer") artist. And in history, as elsewhere, good art is all too scarce. We need more. But "pure" art is unneeded, even if remotely possible.

Extrinsic goals probably play a larger role in the selection of a career and in the selection and treatment of topics than most historians either imagine or would willingly admit. Of course, everyone remarks the books calculated for a student market or jealously condemns other historians for falling for the bright lures of some publisher. But these focal concerns do not begin to match the extrinsic influences exerted by a self-conscious and organized profession. At least since the late nineteenth century, most historians have functioned as members of a profession, usually in some association with professional organizations and journals, and almost always in an academic intellectual role. Today, the product generally labeled history is largely produced in this professional workshop and according to loose but restrictive professional conventions. Here the historian is at one with other merchants of ideas and knowledge. Throughout the modern world, professionalization has standardized products in form and content and, in many ways, has vastly improved the over-all product.

The historical profession largely determines the motives that first lead a person into areas of historical investigation, even into his life work. There may be more complicity than participation on his part. He may write his first book in order to get a Ph.D. and possibly at the behest of a major professor. He may early become involved in interpretative one-upmanship and do yeoman work in order to refute great historians and thus gain recognition. He will look for topics that might please program chairmen for conventions. Even his courtship of publishers will not be so much a zeal for better informed students or even pecuniary rewards as a desire for professional status. Possibly, this professional concern pushes personal interests, esthetic rewards, and moral purpose ever further into the background. This is costly in added pedantry, in too many intramural conflicts of no interest to anyone but the main participants, in the substitution of the form of scholarship for the substance, in an environment that invites selfish career boosting, and even in a quite clear loss of moral concern and moral perspective among historians. But professionalization has helped create a larger supply of historians, of written histories, and of historical publications of all sorts. Above all, at its best, it has helped produce intellectual integrity and rigor in historians, not just as ideals to be achieved but as internalized habits that are followed.

But even when most influenced by extrinsic goals, historians may still respond to intrinsic rewards. Most do. Many people, including some historians, have an antiquarian bent; they enjoy contact with ancient manuscripts. Perennial detectives may enjoy piecing together evidence and finding answers to historical puzzles. Admittedly, neither musty manuscripts nor arts of detection constitute history, but they may each be a part of historical inquiry. Other people, with literary talent, find their reward in the composing of history, in organizing their insights into eloquent accounts. Masters of inquiry may find their rewards in scholarly exactitude, in the marshaling of conclusive evidence in behalf of significant causal hypotheses, or in adding their insight to a growing body of historical knowledge. Finally, such inquiry is intellectually fruitful; it bares new and intriguing problems, begs further thought and analysis, and attracts students with a philosophical turn of mind. When any of these rewarding personal returns are present, historical inquiry at best has the same justification as a fine art, and it always has at least a utility equal to valued forms of recreation and to enjoyable even if pointless intellectual games.

Entirely apart from one's personal motives almost anything one does has some social impact, either in drawing upon the resources of society or, through its effects on the individual, in changing his exact role in society. This is as true of recreation as it is of historical inquiry, recognizably so in most societies, which variously support and control both. Swimming may be indulged in simply because it is fun. But it also incidentally aids good health. Maybe most individuals compose histories for enjoyment or for completely extrinsic reasons (a career boost). Nonetheless, such historical thinking may change an individual and, if widely indulged in, a whole society. Most historians are a bit skeptical about the uses of their product, for they see how often laymen overlook almost all the individual and social benefits that really derive from histories and how often they offer overt justifications of history that are either mistaken or beside the point. This is even sometimes true of justifications offered by historians, usually true of justifications offered by educators, and almost always true of any justification given by politicians, who after all provide many of the resources necessary for the development and dissemination of historical knowledge. Always applauded for the wrong reasons, called upon for the wrong type of advice, denounced for the wrong deficiencies, the historian is indeed tempted to accede to a gigantic fraud not of his own making.

Few historians write or teach for purely personal goals or solely because they both enjoy and get paid for what they do; at least, few think they do it for these reasons alone. They aspire to a more honored social role. Often without rigorous analysis, the historian assumes that the product of his discipline has some value to other people and even to a whole society. If pressed, he will insist that other people enjoy history and will usually vaguely suggest other uses for it. Consoled by undoubted assumptions of usefulness, he may never bother to locate any specific return from his own inquiry. He is doing history. And history, as everyone knows, is important. In a professional context, only a minority of historians choose their career, select topics for investigation, and emphasize certain aspects of topics because of some clarified moral goal that they believe their history can or must serve. But there are still exceptions. Some historians want their work, in specified ways, to form better character in individuals or to influence more desirable policies in a society. Yet, when a historian attains a greater degree of moral self-consciousness and more clearly formulates his goals, he risks censure if his valuations are unconventional (his well-evidenced stories may provoke critical doubt about some revered belief or institution), but he may gain popular praise for more conventional causes (national histories written to induce loyalty and patriotism). Surprisingly, in either case, he may provoke professional suspicion, particularly if he seems to be making a special plea, possibly in behalf of some ideology. From this perspective one might conclude, somewhat pessimistically, that historians are most professional when they leave purposes to the professions, to the established order of things, and look to their own immediate tasks and carry out their own assigned role.

There are complex issues here, and issues treated in large part in chapter 11 (on objectivity). Just as a historian may deliberately reveal overt, clearly identified personal valuations, so morally self-conscious historians may become so concerned about how their histories can or will be used that they try to influence that use by overt sermons, by drawing the moral of the case. Such sermons are not necessary to history and, of course, are not cognitive or subject to proof. Convention, which keeps the scientist from emphasizing desired uses, does allow the historian this option. In any case, such is the transparency of a historian's language that explicit moralizing usually only clarifies what is obviously already present, perhaps in the form of clearly implied policy guidelines. But two qualifications are here in order. The desired moral use must not play any evidential role in inquiry. This is obvious, but there is a very narrow line between moral purpose correctly guiding topic selection and illegitimately guiding the search for evidence. But the topic selected and the hypotheses about it do necessarily guide this search. Finally, no historian has very much control over the use of his product. Use cannot be calculated by such a simple expedient as pointing out preferences. Just as the scientist does, he must suffer the agony of what he may well conceive to be all manner of immoral and mistaken uses of his product. Given the diversity of belief and purpose in a society, a true story of the past may have many divergent lessons and may seem to support many different policies.

History is rarely a magical tool for achieving any of our fondest goals. In fact, quite often historical knowledge seems an impediment to what we desire. Some of our desires may be of such a nature that no existential truth can justify them. If we want to get rich on quackery, then medical science is a hindrance, although some pseudoscience may be our prime resource. If we wish to exorcise some detested habits or institutions, we may falsely attribute to them an illegitimate or dishonest parentage. Then, historical knowledge is an impediment to our purpose; fantasies about the past are excellent armament. And historical quacks are not easy to detect; they too easily camouflage their deceit or blindness or too often share it with their audience. The point is clear. Much that purports to be history is indeed fantasy, but it is valuable propaganda nonetheless. Yet in some cases, history—history as true as evidence permits—may be good propaganda. There is no way to establish the integrity of the product by surveying its uses. Clever deceit almost always takes the form of impersonality and detachment instead of fervent commitment.

And one can at least hope that serious commitment will foster the integrity that eschews illusion and that, whatever the short-run cost, embraces an often hard truth.

History has probably been most misunderstood and most abused as an allegedly simple tool for justifying personal and public decisions. This is the history (or pseudohistory) that is always "proving" something. Indeed, if there were a constant, generalizable human nature, then accounts of past human effort might be unambiguously instructive. But even without such, there seems to be a certain logic in trying to use history to prove things. Surely, on the basis of past experience rather than of chemical evidence, one can suggest the inutility of ingesting arsenic or of trying to do without liquids for thirty days. The example simply illustrates a type of nontheoretical empiricism leading to a loose physical generalization. The examples drawn from the past, although related to human values and policies, only show, by a few examples, the probable relationship between certain chemicals and the human body. Given some policy, such as the preservation of life, such low-level scientific knowledge can indeed justify policy decisions, but only in the same way that any scientific knowledge, in clarifying means and consequences, allows informed decision-making. In no sense is such a generalization historical; it reveals an invariant relationship of a chemical sort, a relationship not conditioned by time nor by meanings nor culture, even though data drawn from a past can verify it (much scientific knowledge can be verified by data from the past; the date of evidence has nothing to do with its verifying role).

No human choice can be proved *true,* for choice is not a cognitive issue. But a choice may be justified or rationalized by a twofold reference—to the end it is intended to serve and to the adequacy of the means to be used to attain it. The end served does implicate history and can often be clarified and understood only by some historical inquiry—by finding out how it came to be. But it is nonsense to say that clarification in any meaningful sense proves an end. By clarifying an end, one may be better able to judge critically its relevance to experienced value and thus its desirability. Unlike the end served, the means contemplated implicate relationships that hold between events; they can be justified only by some type of scientific knowledge, which can indeed be proved true. But to validate relationships is not to validate choice, although choice that does not consider invariant and necessary relationships is blind.

More often, history is alleged to prove something in a somewhat different sense. Thus, many allege that the Munich Conference of 1938 proved the effects that flow from appeasement. Here there is the minor problem of definition and the major problem of correct analogy. As used after Munich, the word "appease" has no clear class meaning. It is now dangerous to use it in any other context than that of Munich. It no longer suggests some general feature of diplomatic negotiation but only a set of particulars found at Munich. As such, it is a time-conditioned word, a historical label, much like "Renaissance," and we may soon begin referring to *the* appeasement with complete accuracy.

The problem of analogy is much more complex and revealing. If Munich has taught us anything, it is because it does reveal certain analogical features shared by other diplomatic conferences. And surely there are analogies. It is a foolish mistake to overemphasize the nonrepeatable or unique aspects of any complex historical event (after all, no events, in their entirety, are repeatable) or to ignore similarities between historical events. But it is the height of wisdom to indicate the complexity of historical events and the minimal chance that some of the features will ever be repeated. Any two diplomatic conferences will reveal both similarities and differences; but all too often the similarities have little policy significance, or they reflect common features already assumed by any policy-maker (an example might be the well-justified rule that nations usually seek what they perceive to be their self-interest). Almost always, the most important policy guidelines are in the particular and contextual and unrepeatable features of an event, and these cannot be anticipated by any historical knowledge. When politicians use Munich to prove the certain results of appeasement, they invariably generalize non-analogous features and assert them to be true of all diplomatic conferences. They illegitimately transform the actualities of Germany and of Hitler into concealed, lawlike propositions about the behavior of nations, ideologies, dictators, and even all mankind.

This does not mean that, in diplomacy or anywhere else, historical knowledge is irrelevant to policy-making. But it does mean that it bears a very subtle relationship to policy. Both personal and national behavior can often be predicted with high probability. All foreign policy today is based on a detailed knowledge of other nations. Much of this predictable behavior depends on physical determinants, such as geography and climate, which may be understood by scientific generalizations. But much is tied to cultural influences, and this can only be accounted for or explained by a particular history. If one is to predict what John Doe or France will most likely do tomorrow, he has to know not only universal laws, not only generalizations about how people or nations act, but quite particular things about a person or a culture; in other words, he has to know about final causes, purposes, and goals, some quite recent in origin. In a narrow context, such knowledge is descriptive and analytical; in a broader context, it is historical. Historically blind description—however sophisticated in data acquisition and interpretation, however aided by ingenious models or behavioral theories—is much like limited, nontheoretic empirical sampling in the physical sciences. Only a backdrop of theory, of already assumed conditions and possibilities, allows a judgment in one case that fifteen repeated occurrences do not a rule make (or, more likely, only a trivial rule make) while in another that only two repeated occurrences exemplify a rule of great scope and highest probability. Thus, only historical knowledge can rescue policy studies from a tragically blind empiricism, from an empiricism that can be adorned by all manner of formal and statistical aids without losing any of its blindness.

History in itself, and particularly by analogy, never justifies, let alone proves, any policy decision. There is never a built-in assurance that any particular aspect of the past will repeat. All aspects cannot repeat. But the past relates to the future, and, at least by setting limits and conditions, does determine it. Without a specific past, some human events are impossible; with a particular past, others are impossible. Before historical knowledge can correctly relate to policy decisions, it must be supplemented by the most exact possible knowledge of the decision context. No stories about the past can provide this knowledge; at best, they provide only a framework for making better sense out of such knowledge, for interpreting and applying it. Statesmen should interpret their intelligence in light of diplomatic history, including Munich. Given the various "lessons" mislearned from Munich, they at least may expect, in carefully defined contexts, certain behavior from nations such as the United States. Even though Munich did not prove any rule about diplomatic conferences, it very much changed subsequent conferences.

To relate historical knowledge to policy is a bit confusing. In one sense, now the more typical sense, policy-making takes place within an assumed valuative context; it is a matter of proximate goals and correct means. The backdrop for such policy is a vast, slow-changing culture, with habits reflecting goals that few people have thought about for generations; such goals rarely come under review by anyone, much less by policy-makers. Nonetheless, any new programs adopted must relate to this backdrop, and in some minor degree each new policy may imperceptibly help to modify it. On occasion, either within a policy-making context or without, we recognize some of the more foundational beliefs and habits and openly affirm or challenge them. At this point policy-making becomes much more than a matter of conventional decision-making; it is searching and fundamental ethical and philosophical criticism. Such broad criticism encompasses the more restricted policy-making and may undercut it at its most vulnerable point—the ends it uncritically serves. At the level of ethics, of moral philosophy, of esthetic appreciation, the specialized policy studies all have to stand in judgment before a higher court.

Many of the traditional arguments for the social utility of history have stressed its role in abetting rational decision-making, either at the individual or at the group level. When most history was politically oriented, it was supposed to foster citizenship in an individual, statesmanship in politicians, and wise policies in government. In a context of overarching cultural values, themselves rarely questioned, it surely did play that role. But even here true stories about the past, as well as rigorous general knowledge, can only provide the backdrop for, and never become the substitute for, quite detailed, contextually comprehensive description. Both law and history are implicit in any policy decision; each requires its due, whether recognized or not (and nonrecognition may be a prelude to disastrous choice). But lame historical analogies cannot identify the relevant laws or habits; we can determine these only by the most rigorous and thorough analysis of the present context. Indeed, without some prior knowledge of law, the empirically analyzed context could never reveal any such laws or, along with them, policy guidelines. The same is true of the historical background of cultural phenomena. A political adviser, unaware of the varied effects of the Civil War on voting behavior—on habitual preferences and political goals—might remark a statistical correlation between corn prices and Republican pluralities in an Iowa congressional district. He might then leap to the conclusion that he had located *the* essential condition, rather than a minor condition, for Republican successes and, as a result of this misapprehension, completely mislead a prospective candidate who wished to develop a winning platform. At the very least, only extensive empirical investigation could clarify what a little historical knowledge makes obvious: many voters in the district will vote Republican despite corn prices. But not all will so vote, and possibly not enough to assure a Republican victory. Without quite an array of supporting empirical data, no historian could cite the effects of the Civil War on voting patterns as the sole, or even as a major, condition for a recent Republican victory. Thus, in justifying policy, the relation between historical knowledge and detailed description is always a complementary and interactive one. Neither can stand alone.

The unraveling of this interaction not only reveals one valid use of history but further clarifies definitional problems in the vague area loosely called the social sciences. All these disciplines have at least one common point of reference—man. Beyond this definitional agreements end. For example, some political scientists and economists retain an ancient interest in moral theory; they continue to invent normative models of an ideal political economy in the hope that their essentially philosophical labors will lead to criticism at the most fundamental level of policy, or at the level of ends and purposes. Some social scientists still describe human behavior against a backdrop of historical and cultural understanding. But most reflect not only the analytical sophistication of this century but also some of the disciplinary fads of the present. Just as social thinkers in the eighteenth century looked to physical determinants such as climate and geography, and in the nineteenth century to culture and history, so they now turn to behavioral theory, which is drawn from psychology. They look for the generalizable aspects of human behavior and are often more oriented toward the definition of their fledgling sciences than to immediate policy uses. But at least many social scientists are incurably addicted to policy goals; they actively advise or serve governments or hope that their research and teaching will directly influence governmental policies.

Abetted by an ever more narrow topical and chronological specialization, many historians work very closely with such policy-oriented social scientists. In fact, their work variously overlaps. For example, a political scientist (the label is here a loose one) who works in a culturally conditioned area of human behavior (and politics is one such area), needs a historical perspective for many of his problems. When he cannot borrow it from a historian, he may become a historian himself and unravel a particular story about the past. Likewise, a political historian, trying to make sense out of his data, may utilize statistical techniques developed by political scientists, may see new nuances of meaning in his data by relating them to some borrowed analytical model, and, finally, may want to compare a past context to a present one—only to find no adequate contextual description of the present. In another context he may need a model that makes past behavior understandable—only to find that no one has invented it. In both cases, he will probably do the work of the political scientist and even utilize some of his research techniques. The more closely a historical specialty correlates with a social science, the more intimate is the possible interaction. Unfortunately, the interaction can be narrowing as well as broadening. A historian who tells very selective stories and ties them to a cognate social science hardly provides an extensive backdrop for social analysis; he may even unconsciously reflect some of the most myopic products of this analysis.

With the decline of epochal national histories, and with more specialization and professionalization, more and more academic history seems to have a rather narrow policy orientation. But even though historians may deny it, much economic, political, diplomatic, and even social history is policy oriented. The changing topical fashions indicate this; in some histories the policy guidelines are quite explicit. Post-World War II historical monographs in the United States deal endlessly with such focal policy issues as imperialism, collective security, the welfare state, economic growth, business monopoly, the party system, minority rights, and constitutional safeguards. Certainly the interpretive perspectives vary, but not as much as historians often think. Either because of methodological convention or because of a lingering ideological naïveté or provincialism, the values assumed are not usually explicit. But today such growing fads as comparative history and assertive histories composed by young radicals seem to be pushing more and more historians out of the area of proximate policy and into a more fundamental and more critical area of heretofore assumed ends and purposes.

The development of a strong nationalism was one of the ends served by many nineteenth-century American historians. They helped

unify the diverse states and regions and surely aided in the transformation of newly arrived immigrants into "good" Americans. But
since 1900, an increasing number of historians have been largely
concerned with the better working of our national institutions, as
have many social scientists. Only with the end of World War II
have ideological issues, and with them some searching concern with
ends, moved a few historians to a careful and subtle examination of
the final causes that lurk in our institutions—of the beliefs that, at
one time, were conscious and overtly loved. Actually, few historians
have been able to operate at this level of conceptual criticism.
Instead, they have struggled at a less demanding task—to keep up
with the social scientists in techniques and theory. Even today the
average historical monograph is a labyrinth of undefined ideological
labels, of liberals and conservatives *ad nauseam,* but it reflects a
careful and thorough search for evidence and a careful statistical
weighing of its importance. At least the historian is now disseminating,
in a more popular guise, some of the latest tools and findings of the
social scientists. And his technical proficiency in using evidence, his
orientation toward policy, when coupled with either ideological naïveté
or disinterest, even more allies him with contemporary social
scientists.

Whereas much contemporary history is policy oriented, much
nineteenth-century history in both Europe and America was identity
oriented. This quite legitimately suggests another use for history, a use
that is probably more significant than policy use. History, as a source
of ego identity, has no necessary functional tie to the social sciences
or to any other discipline. In a quite personal way, a remembered
past becomes a crucial part of our self-image. We may or may not
like what we have been and thus what we inescapably are. We can
add but never really erase. One may not like being male or white,
but these are physical and unchangeable facts. One may not like
being a southerner or an American, but, although he can condemn
both or deny loyalty to them, he can escape neither of them, for
they are part of him, essential to his self-definition and inseparable
from his self-image. If concerned, he might learn a good deal from
psychology, physiology, or anthropology about being male or white.
By analysis and by history he can learn a great deal about the South
and about the United States (and thus about himself), whether this
brings solace or despair. Recent students of American history reflect

about as much despair as solace in being American, perhaps in part because of a similar ambivalence among historians. But even a few decades ago, most American historians had few doubts about America. They expected to bring to diverse Americans acquaintance with an often glorious past and, at least for those who suffered some of the newly discovered dilemmas of being American, both solace and self-confidence.

A confident national history may be dishonest and in part mythical; it may even be a deliberate and hypocritical device for garnering loyalty and sacrifice. At best, even though evidenced, a glorious past is narrowly selective and thus unbalanced. Much national history as well as local history is parochial; it affirms, but neither defines nor defends, basic beliefs and commitments. These are so confidently held, so secure, as scarcely to need rationalization. The historical parts of the Old Testament—the most influential national history ever written—are a clear example of parochial history combined with sermonic goals. If believable, affirmative national histories flatter those who share them. Such history may expand oneself, give new and affirmative meaning to one's life, inspire one to great efforts, and provoke both self-assurance and community loyalty. Even the most balanced history of a group of people, of a nation or village, or of a church or party helps create a community, for it broadens the area of common experiences and brings solace even in group penance. Many people need an expanded and clarified past, not to make better choices nor as an adjunct of policy, but as an object of one's appreciation, as a certification of some meaning in one's endeavors, or as evidence of one's membership in a community.

Earlier, we found that history is a tool for essentially philosophical criticism; in this role it may serve a more fundamental purpose than sheer enjoyment, limited policy clarification, or even the buttressing of personal and group identity. This is not to suggest that history is now more often used in a critical way, but rather than when so used it has a much greater impact on a society, reaching as it does to the most hidden but most determinate assumptions and goals.

A faint recognition of this critical role is present in the now-popular justification of history as a tool of self-understanding. It is somewhat ironic that with a seeming increase of policy-oriented history, avowed and immediately practical uses of history are in bad repute, whereas such vaguely humanistic uses as self-knowledge have never been more acclaimed. The term "self-knowledge" can be quite misleading, particularly if it suggests some complete and almost impossible isolation from policy at any level. But there is no doubt that many do use it with such an intent and want to repudiate anything broadly practical and moral.

Self-knowledge has at least two aspects, the purely personal and the shared. For the most part, self-knowledge is only an arbitrary emphasis, since the designated knowledge is, by necessity, a knowledge of many other selves. Most that we are (and in part, all that we are) is a product of culture. We share it with other people. Only this type of socially pregnant self-knowledge can be gained through the stories of the human past that historians are wont to tell. Of course, in a very private context, each man continuously rehearses his own past, and this private history may indeed illumine aspects of character that are unique to the individual. Unless the person is famous, a hero or a leader, this private history will remain private. Even if advertised, few would be interested in it unless, again, it turned out to be more than private—common to many, respresentative, typical, prophetic. Even the uniquely private past, as told on a psychiatrist's couch, can lead to self-knowledge, to more effective functioning in a society, to a clear self-identity, and to stronger character. This type of purely private and particularistic self-knowledge has little to do with written history. But even the most private facets of self-knowledge have social implications. Improved individuals mean an improved social order. There is no legitimate and complete separation of a private sphere (an often useful abstraction) and a public sphere (another abstraction).

Circumstances and change are unavoidable. For men, so is choice. When choice is tied to knowledge, it may direct change and utilize circumstance. The circumstances that set conditions for human choice are physical, biological, and cultural. The physical and biological circumstances are constant, or nearly so. The cultural circumstances are time conditioned and historical, although they are often quite stable. At great peril, we choose in ignorance of either of these circumstances. Without knowledge of the invariant relationships in matter, of the uniformities of organic behavior, we usually choose futility. Without an understanding of causes, of cultural determinants, we usually choose rigidified convention; thus, we nullify rather than exploit the freedom that is present in choice. Accident rather than purpose then determines the ceaseless elaboration and development of culture. Even choices made solely in the light of general knowledge, or laws, or in the light of well-intrenched causes which are falsely taken to be general and unalterable, are rational only with respect to means, not with respect to final ends; in these circumstances, ends are not consciously involved in choice but unconsciously operate nonetheless.

Thus, historical knowledge not only reveals enduring and stable patterns of culturally determined behavior, providing a needed backdrop to many types of social analysis, but, much more importantly, it clarifies the ends, the causes, that operate in our choices and in our most intrenched habits and institutions. Or it clarifies alternate ends that operate in other cultures. In such a role, history supports reevaluation at the most basic level. Through awareness, it permits a critical judgment on our purposes. In some cases, we see articulated ends as futile and foolish, for they are contrary to scientific knowledge. In other, perhaps more crucial, contexts, they are contrary to experienced value, even when value includes the broadest possible context. Then, historical awareness is a prelude to moral and esthetic judgment. It aids the development of new tastes and new commitments. And in a sense, what we appreciate, what we love, and what we dedicate ourselves to is what we are. At the level of basic causes or ends, historical awareness is the most potent instrument for the rational development of new cultural forms.

The following example illustrates this use for history. In the United States we live under a distinctive cluster of political institutions, although few components are either uniquely or originally American. These institutions developed over a long time, and at least at one creative point or another they reflected, although never perfectly, certain overt assumptions or beliefs about fact and value. The institutions have changed and are changing, often by force of unrecognized circumstances. Meanwhile, many beliefs and aspirations have changed, in part as a result of cumulative changes in circumstance. But the political habits, reflecting internalized, often long-forgotten ends, remain with us. This complex situation opens two possibilities for criticism based on historical understanding. On the one hand, an appreciative and honest understanding (not easy) of the original ends and purposes which our political forms reflected may give new meaning and validity to those forms. But this understanding will also reveal how often Americans have converted these forms to other, possibly unperceived ends, or in some cases even prostituted them to other, perceived goals. On the other hand, an honest understanding of the original ends reflected in our institutions, ends which surely joined with circumstances in determining their form, may reveal what now seems, in the light of new knowledge or by some significant change in taste, the foolishness of narrowness or blinding self-interest of our progenitors. This knowledge will lead us, not to a reinvigoration and repurification of institutions, but to a more radical attempt to replace value-frustrating institutions by new, value-serving institutions.

Although history has its own distinctive and often crucial contribution to criticism—a more full knowledge of existing but largely unconscious ends in our society; a vicarious introduction, in a developing context, of variant cultures, and thus of alternate life styles—it is not the only discipline that permits and abets such critical evaluations. Anthropology offers another comparative perspective. Literature and other fine arts offer imaginative alternatives or help shape qualitative aspirations, contributing to the valuative perspectives necessary for criticism. Ideal models developed by philosophers, by social theorists, or even by utopian dreamers often provide the critical perspective. Finally, whereas historical knowledge is necessary for a perspective understanding of the possible causes present in our society, only a detailed and rigorous inspection of the present context can determine which causes are actually at work. Even when applied to the critical task, historical knowledge cannot be completely separated from contextual analysis.

Although this critical use of history may seem to place a premium on cultural and intellectual history, it should not. It does place a premium on historical accuracy and on historical breadth, whatever the topical or chronological boundaries of a given story may be. All stories of the human past encompass human values and meanings and reflect some aspects of a cultural environment. All histories implicate final causes of some sort. The most narrow history must be told against this backdrop; if not, it will not be told well. As one must ever emphasize, it is almost impossible to know very well any significant part of the human past. It is comparatively easy to refer our present meanings, goals, and assumptions to a past and thus to conceal the true story (this is the vicious presentism earlier condemned). By misinterpreting past-referring artifacts, we can fashion all types of interesting fantasy. Because of an all-too-inviting presentism, many specialized, policy-oriented historical monographs, despite all the forms of scholarship, are scarcely historical at all. Isolated artifacts cannot be interpreted in a vacuum; too often, they are misinterpreted in a present, often hazy and ideologically confused conceptual framework that actually distorts the past. Many Ph.D. dissertations are, in this way, unhistorical as well as unphilosophical (the two almost always go together).

To tell a story truly is to penetrate the symbols of a past and to read them correctly. The recorded words and symbolically rich deeds of past actors often meant something quite different from our seemingly identical words and deeds. In order, therefore, to write history at all— to tell true stories rather than superficially persuasive stories—one must have some ability to deal with semantical and conceptual subtleties; to interpret cultural styles; to see the meaning, value, and intent that lurk in institutions and behind human acts. This skill is far more important than any of the tools, quantitative or otherwise, that enable historians to interpret certain types of data. This skill requires conceptual rigor, ideological sophistication, philosophical self-consciousness, and almost always a long and broad acquaintance with a past age, either from reading good histories or from moving, with growing recognition, among diverse artifacts of that age. Any good historian, whatever his topic, must be able and willing to find the thought content, the ever present even if not articulated meanings, of a past age, even when his focus is upon the functioning of institutions or upon the consequences of human behavior. But except in quite selective contexts, a historian need not focus on *conscious* ends or on *overt* rationalizations. Likewise, the self-conscious and topically selective intellectual historian who abstracts the thought content and focuses on it, and, even more, the historian of ideas, who deals largely with the isolated and usually more artful or rigorous products of human thinking, lose all their perspective unless they remark and use as a backdrop the continuum of intrenched habits, the forms of behavior, that are always interactive with, and inseparable from, deliberate thought.

At this point, the advocate of history may face the charge of naïve optimism. Even to relate history to sweeping criticism, to the task of restructing basic ends, all in behalf of more attained value, of an enhanced quality of life, seems to assume the possibility of real progress, of some possible betterment in man's condition. One could show the utility of history for criticism and at the same time suspect an

ultimate futility behind the critical games that people play. But this
would be pointless. In our day it takes little sophistication to repudiate
the very possibility of progress. Ask any sophomore. Even "history,"
a weapon much used by our children, "proves" the ultimately futility
of moral effort. Over and over again we hear the thought-obscuring
litany of "two world wars and the bomb." Since history proves nothing
legitimately, but everything by selective misuse, it now nourishes our
despair as faithfully as it used to nourish our most foolish dreams.
But the charge of naïveté cannot be so easily routed. For many perceptive people the critical issue today is not finding proper armament
for moral criticism; it is finding the courage, the affirmation, that
makes possible any moral engagement at all. In a tragic world, nobility is the only worthy goal of man, and surely it has never been
frightened by futility.

Most of us live in a disillusioned age. We know tragedy; it is a
growing part of our experience. In the very recent past, particularly
in the American past, our many illusions and our naïveté successfully
camouflaged our dilemmas, our entrapments, our inescapable futility,
and thus the only possible ground for tragic experience. We knew
failure, but not irreducible conflicts of value; sin, but not unmerited
and mocking frustrations and horrors. Once free of illusion and from
the one overarching illusion (that we are the privileged beneficiaries
of some cosmic plan), we cannot, in honesty, ever return to its warm
embrace. Thus, as an experienced and thus peculiarly inescapable
fact, we will continue to confront tragedy. There is no escape, save
illusion, from this phenomenological fact. Thus, we must in some way
deal with tragedy.

There are still the two perennial sources of tragic experience—
nature and culture. Lightning strikes without a semblance of justice;
so does cancer. By what has to be interpreted as chance (even though
we know that it may not be), misfortune afflicts some and spares
others. Our progenitors saw the hidden hand of God, of providential
guidance, in acts of nature. This, we assume, was one of their illusions. We find no redemptive purpose, no deserved punishment, in our
suffering. Of course, we do know more and more about the physical
and organic worlds. We have ever more control over them. Even my
disease is the physician's challenge. We may find a cure for cancer.
But these hopes are small consolation for present victims. They suffer
their affliction with small solace; their suffering is rarely the means

to such cures. Knowledge and a hope of eventual progress can hardly console them; instead, quite often, it has helped remove the solace of past illusions. There is no honest way to dissipate such tragedy for those who suffer it, although some philosophical and religious bypasses are still compelling for many people. But the saint does not suffer; to him, tragedy is impossible. For the rest of us, such tragic experience does not preclude progress. It invites it, and our sciences attain it. It does not teach futility; it offers a challenge—that we bring knowledge to bear on these natural afflictions.

Tragedy rooted in culture rather than in physical nature—in causes rather than in laws—is much more of a challenge to any form of moral affirmation. Such tragedy alone implicates history, as Polybius so long ago argued. Again, such tragedy is an inescapable even if rare experience for most people, or perhaps for any intellectually honest person. We cannot exorcise it by any magic. By the interaction of circumstances and human choices, most long forgotten, men in various societies have come to serve not only contradictory or futile causes in their own society but causes that conflict directly with those in other societies. Particularly in intercultural contacts, but also in internal change, these causes have led to conflict, dilemmas, and often hopeless despair. Often we have literally painted ourselves, or have been painted, into corners. At that point there are no good answers, and there is no escape. We are helpless victims of causes unperceived and beyond our control. However virtuous, we cannot avoid many such dilemmas, at either a personal or a national level. This is even more true in our Hellenistic age—an age of clashing ideologies and cultures, exposed and naked social systems, and lonely individuals. Neither the isolation of parochial communities nor creeds protect us. From too simple optimism and illusioned hope we have often moved to abject pessimism and no hope. Moral achievement seems irrelevant. Where there are no good answers, such achievement is impossible. Where there are no clear values, achievement cannot be gauged.

Causes, even as transformative laws, can be discovered. We can often trace the varied historical developments that clearly account for our present miseries. By this we at least get rid of all demonic and fatalistic explanations of tragedy, including those explanations that rely on some ambivalent human nature. This reduces tragedy from a cosmic distortion to a phenomenological affliction. Historical knowledge shows us that we suffer not from demonic forces but rather from the mistakes of our parents and grandparents (some contemporary youth invest even those progenitors with demonic attributes). But, really, often only we know, or can know, that our parents' choices were grievously mistaken. They often acted in greatest wisdom. They could not have chosen otherwise (here, "could not" means not physical obstructions but that, in light of what they knew and valued, they had to choose as they did). Knowledge of this cannot dissipate our present suffering (perhaps nothing can) and cannot provide good choices for us (there may be none), but it does place our tragic plight in a causal perspective and lessen its often innervating and cynical import.

When trapped, we suffer. We may avoid other traps, but we cannot escape some of our present ones. Any moral philosophy that affirms a magical solvent for all present dilemmas is based on some illusion. The problem of trapped, often futile man is courage, not deliverance. Can he live through (not remove) present tragic dilemmas, and can he possibly escape more tragedy that always lurks in his future? If what grandfather achieved, despite his well-meaning choices, is only this, how can we hope to do better? Look what past generations did to our world. Since better historical understanding will not reveal many devils or conspirators (so simple would it be if it did) but only ignorance and blindness, will not such historical understanding quickly turn youthful commitment (or at least that based on devils and conspirators) into tragic despair (such despair may be wiser than illusioned commitment)? Of course it may, but it need not. And in removing illusions, history invites the maturity that alone can alleviate some future frustrations and dilemmas. Without it we find only the blind, ahistorical naïveté of perennial reformers who see perfection lurking just beyond the final eradication of some favorite clutch of demonic people or forces.

The human past has drama, just as does the human present. It is about men who suffered and knew they suffered, who chose and fully experienced the agony of choice. The human past is haunted by "ifs" —by a sense that it could have been otherwise. Yet nothing is as set and determinate as the past. We know that, in one sense, it could not have been otherwise. In this sense the "ifs" are unreal, except that men intensely experienced them; thus they were phenomenologically real. The past actors, even as we, felt quite confident that they made up their own lines. As historians we agree. They surely did. And they made them up, in part, according to their knowledge of or their illusions about the past. Often they, even as we, tried above all to avoid their father's mistakes and then learned their history lesson much too well (or rather mislearned it by too little attention to all the subtle meanings), falling into a much more grievous error. And here, in a way easily missed, was how the "ifs" were really efficacious. The choices their fathers made became their lesson, and the choices their fathers rejected became their choice: without their fathers' choice and their historical understanding, they could never have made the choice that they did.

Thus, for us in the living present, the drama of the past—of all the contingencies that were present, but really not present—is our drama and our freedom. Every haunting "if" of our father's world becomes a living option again in ours. But their exact choices are, by our very knowledge, forever beyond our choosing. If we follow them, if we choose the same objects that they chose, it is for us a quite different choice, for we know the past and know that we choose again. The past is, indeed, finished, but the historical past—the past thought about by us—is ever suggestive and alive. We cannot, in honesty and proper piety, blame our fathers for anything. Their tragedy, when its meaning is sought, is not only very often the perceived source of some of our tragedy but a vital and now recognized circumstance for our choosing. Being what we are, knowing the history we know, we choose as we must. But when knowing is a crucial determinant, when blind circumstance is driven back a bit, we are free and we are responsible in the only meaningful sense of these two words.

We have no assurance that we choose well. We may reap our rewards at our children's expense. We have no complete, objective, hierarchical system of values by which to determine our choices. And we could not have such and be free, for our freedom means continuous redefinition and unending cultural elaboration—it means new ends, new causes, new tastes. Man never stays still long enough to be exactly measured by any moral yardstick. But insecurity and a lack of certainty do not mean that we cannot choose by objective criterion, by a science that reveals consequences, by a historical understanding that reveals causes operative in our society. Tragedy, as an existential fact rather than as a cosmic distortion, is ever present; it is a component of our freedom, of our being agents. We cannot escape it or escape being the cause of tragic dilemmas for our as yet innocent children. But we can know tragedy for what it is—a product of as yet unknown or uncontrollable physical circumstances or of accumulations of in part blind even though generous human choices. Knowing even this devil, by far the worst of all, we can at least learn to live with him even though we cannot eliminate him.

This ends a quite lengthy list of appropriate and always in some sense distinctive uses for history. The writing and studying of history has other incidental effects on individuals. For example, historical inquiry has some of the same effects, even social and educational effects, as other types of rigorous inquiry. But the uses of inquiry are quite a different thing from the uses of history, for they constitute a more inclusive class. All intellectual activity, as a class of activity, has its appropriate fruits. But this clearly is well beyond our concern.

No person, no historian even, will gain all the possible benefits to be derived either from historical inquiry or from a careful study of completed histories. One who knows not tragedy will not master it by historical understanding. One who never questions his most basic goals will not find history of use in criticism. One quite secure in his community will hardly need it to buttress his identity. Those who never engage areas of even proximate policy, who shirk from politics, will never use it as a backdrop of social analysis. And, alas, those who do not enjoy it, whatever its other potential, will, most likely, never realize any of its uses.

EPILOGUE: SOME PRACTICAL ADVICE

Whatever value they find in it, almost everyone in the Western world displays a keen interest in some type of history. For most of us, to be vitally interested in something is also to be interested in its past. Note the eagerness with which small boys collect incredible amounts of information about the past performances of baseball players or about older automobiles, airplanes, coins, and stamps. Note the families that keep heirlooms, the clubs that annually elect historians and cherish records, the towns that zealously treasure every local tradition. As much as physical nature or social relationships, the past endlessly confronts and tantalizes the human mind.

But a rigorous and successful exploration of the human past is not easy. In fact, history can be the most difficult form of inquiry, demanding greater intellectual versatility and more specific skills than any other discipline. Yet, inferior history can be produced with little effort and no skill. As in the fine arts, the most critical distinction is not between historians and nonhistorians (if there are any such) but between good historians and bad ones. Good history has to be both supremely literate and rigorously true. Unlike the novelist, the historian cannot make it up. Only laborious investigation yields an account that other scholars can check.

Even the investigation may demand almost unattainable skills. The historian's potential sources are vast and far-ranging, from a scrap of stone to archives crammed with the miscellanea of modern governments. These materials of history are both complex and unmanageable. Thomas De Quincey once described the two angels which must guide the historian: one, the genius of research; the other, that of meditation. The two qualities seldom combine in the same person. The laborious comber of archives who must "read millions of dusty parchments and pages blotted with lies" is one sort of man; the artist fired with the imagination and literary skill necessary to breathe life into these dry pages is quite another. The good historian must contrive to be both. But one must add the other roles of the historian: that of detective, wherein he often has to possess the sleuthing qualities of a Sherlock Holmes; of activist, for he should know the world; of adventurer, with the resourcefulness to track down and gain access to elusive sources.

How should historians go about these difficult tasks? There may be something to the view that historians are born and not made ("There are some who are historians by the grace of God," wrote Albert Schweitzer. "No erudition can supply the place of historical instinct. . . .") But clearly those who have a vocation for it must greatly improve themselves by nurturing the talent. The apprentice historian can best do this in specialized research seminars, under the guidance of experienced and specialized historians. Such is the diversity of historical subjects that no specific directions can fit all types of historical inquiry. The requirements simply vary too much. The skills required to authenticate an ancient document, or to infer from it great revelations about a civilization, scarcely match the statistical tools needed to extract meaning from census reports or election returns, or the analytical and semantical finesse required to dissect the subtle array of meanings in a single key word or phrase. Some subjects place a particular premium on one skill and not on others; some require a special application of skills. Yet the historian, whatever his field, has to be skillful in three areas—meaning, inference, and verification. For these are the prerequisites of successful inquiry in any discipline.

Perhaps the most neglected and yet the most critical problem in contemporary historical writing is the lack of conceptual rigor; there is too little attention to meaning. Historians have, for the best of reasons, rejected a highly technical vocabulary or jargon. Such a vocabulary, even though originally a shortcut to clarity, almost always ossifies and, in vulgar form, becomes the favorite camouflage of mindlessness and mediocrity. But eschewal of jargon makes it even more imperative that historians carefully define their terms, particularly broad categories, periodizations, and labels. Too much contemporary history relies on terribly ambiguous labels, such as rationalism, romanticism, imperialism, naturalism, positivism, industrialism, urbanism, pragmatism, liberalism, conservatism, radicalism, capitalism, socialism, and on ad infinitum. The increasingly heterogeneous audience for most history, resulting from the breakdown of parochial communities with common verbal habits, makes it even more imperative that we define in context and subject almost every word to definitional scrutiny. Even "God save the Queen," a clear enough expression in an insular context, now requires qualification. Which God?

Good inference means valid deductions. A historian, just as anyone else, has an obligation to be rigorous in his logic. Logical fallacies haunt almost all our discourse; any text in logic soon frightens us by its endless catalogue of possible pitfalls. Some of these implicate grammar and meaning, for they involve deceptive sentence structure or ambiguities of language. If we are not careful, we argue in circles, or we unknowingly move from class to subclass and thus attempt to characterize parts by wholes or wholes by parts. By shifts in the meaning of key terms, we even deceive by what appears to be a good syllogism.

But most logical fallacies derive from improper deduction, or the drawing of fallacious conclusions from given premises. If we infer wrongly, then no amount of evidence can rescue us. Any history will contain implicative arguments which have to meet formal criteria. Given a plausible proposition about the past, the historian often has to deduce the various implications of its being true even before he can begin to seek out evidence to prove it. In concealed language ("therefores" and "thuses"), historians continually draw simple inferences of the form: "If a, then necessarily b, c, and d." A typical, but fallacious, argument of this sort follows: "In 1933, Franklin D. Roosevelt had to devaluate the dollar in order to achieve higher prices. He did devaluate in April 1933. Therefore, prices rose." And, in fact, prices did rise. It may also be true that they could not have risen without devaluation. The premise may be true. And, as many New Dealers believed, the gold devaluation may have, in some sense, *caused* the price rise. But as stated the argument is still fallacious, for the conclusion does not flow of necessity from the premise. To extend such examples would be an endless task. Suffice it to say that all historians, at one time or another, do fall into logical errors and weaken their lines of argument. Despite this, their final conclusions may still be true. Then only their statements are wrong. But more often than not, logical fallacies mean wrong conclusions, or a wasted use of sources.

Verification, or proof, seems more critical than either meaning or good logic. In one sense it is, for it has a "clinching" quality about it, or a finality not present in semantical and logical achievements. After all, completely untrue propositions may be abundantly clear and allow quite valid inferences. Evidence alone can bestow verity. Yet, without clear propositions and valid inferences, there can be no rigorous inquiry and no real evidence. For sources, artifacts, data, phenomena (use whatever word you want) become evidence only in the context of some question, assertion, or hypothesis that requires it as an answer or as proof. There is no evidence in general; there is only evidence for this or that. In this sense at least, meaning and inference not only precede verification but are necessary conditions for it.

A historian may easily confuse sources (as potential evidence for some question historians are wont to ask) with evidence and thus confuse research of an exploratory, or topic-seeking and hypothesis-seeking type, with the controlled search for verifying evidence indicated by the logical implications of a hypothesis. But despite such definitional confusions, professional historians have rarely minimized the role of evidence and the need for proof. We live in an age of technical expertise, and historians abundantly reflect it. Of course, in history as in most fields we still have our more or less glamorous amateurs, who often rush in where professionals fear to tread. In history they often garner a goodly share of the popular market while perpetuating much ignorance, to the despair of the honest yeoman historian. They pay for their popularity by earning his scorn. The beginning historian should note the quality of technical criticism in the book reviews of leading historical journals and the devastation which results when a William L. Shirer crosses the path of the professionals and the often savage encounters between authorities each heavily armed with erudition. Today it is likely that even a fairly modest contribution to historical knowledge, dealing with a distinctly minor figure or episode, will have been researched in a dozen archives using scores of collections of unpublished papers. This virtuosity in research effort has been encouraged by large graduate schools, a massive growth of Ph.D. programs, numerous large libraries and manuscript depositories, and even the availability of research and travel grants. The very proliferation of source materials has created even greater needs for bibliographic aids.

But skill in finding the way to and through archives does not insure skill in using the materials. A naïve empiricism always threatens. If unaware of the need for a unifying theme or hypothesis, the would-be historian often accomplishes little more than taking from one pile and adding to another. An ancient scholar, in despair, once said that he had made a heap of all that he found; he is emulated by many Ph.D. candidates. A mere transfer of records does a disservice to the advancement of historical knowledge, for students of history may well take an impressively researched monograph as the "authority" in a given field. An industrious culling of documentary sources does not guarantee perceptiveness; the judgment of a highly skilled researcher can be utterly wrong. The alleged law which decrees an inverse relationship between research energy and philosophical acumen may come into play. Grotesque or inadequate interpretations may accompany impeccable scholarship if scholarship entails only documentation.

Yet the unintelligent drone who has burrowed deeply but cannot master his findings is no worse than the clever theorizer who invents striking interpretations (probably revising the received doctrines in order to gain attention) without doing much research. "Without hypothesis, or synthesis, history remains a pastime for antiquarians," wrote the famous Belgian historian Henri Pirenne, but he added that "without criticism and erudition it loses itself in fantasy." Both are necessary. But there is a greater likelihood that professional, academically trained historians will lack imaginative hypotheses than the erudition.

Historians are, by and large, well aware of these problems. They may sigh, with A. C. Bradley, that "Research though laborious is easy; imagination though delightful is difficult." They know which libraries to visit in order to find needed primary sources. Indeed, they have probably had their topic determined for them by the existence of the sources. Senator A or Foreign Secretary B has bequeathed his papers to a library which has capably organized them. Letters of the same estimable statesman, as can be learned from a national union catalogue of manuscripts, may be found in other collections. Before long the fledgling Doctor of Philosophy is off on an interesting trail that may lead him across continents and oceans. It is laborious but easy to copy the contents of these manuscript collections. But what use to make of all the material? No one really tells him this. He is left to his own instincts and prejudices.

Sooner or later, he will see the need for some hypothesis or organizing principle. It may be quite simple and restricted. He does not have to settle cosmic issues. It does not matter whether historians agree on ontological issues. It does not matter whether they decide

that reality is chaotic and must have an order imposed upon it by the
historian or that there is an inherent structure in events which the historian only discovers, or whether it is a little of both or (perhaps most
sensible) that the issue is meaningless. In any case, we can approach
the events of the past only by imagining possible patterns or structures and then checking to see if these can be validated by evidence.
It is true that, in most cases, we cannot fruitfully engage in such
hypothetical reasoning until we have explored the terrain experientially, but then neither can we do so unless we know a good many
things outside the historical theater altogether. At some point we
must frame questions or propose some hypothesis; otherwise, we
wander aimlessly. Perhaps we should go as far as Ortega y Gasset
when he says (*Man and Crisis,* Norton, 1958, p. 13) that "facts
cover up reality; while we are in the midst of their innumerable
swarmings we are in chaos and confusion." We must for the moment
put aside this chaos and imagine an order; then we must compare it
with evidence to see if it can be matched to some experience. If we
find a match, then we have succeeded; we "have discovered the reality
which the facts covered and kept secret." If we find no match, then
we have to do some more hard thinking.

There are obvious dangers. To love a hypothesis too much is to
ignore contrary evidence or to search only in areas where favorable
evidence is likely. All single-minded or monomaniac interpretations of
history, with one primal factor or theme as the key to everything, are
subject to this weakness. No one key can unlock all doors, and anyone who thinks it can simply ignores most doors. Hypotheses must be
applied tentatively and modified when necessary.

Another danger is our inability to break away from long accepted
and seemingly obvious hypotheses. We freeze our perspectives.
Herbert Butterfield, in an essay on the origins of the Seven Years'
War, showed how the solution of the problem was delayed for years
simply because no one looked in the right direction. This often happens. In a richly detailed study of the Dreyfus case, Douglas Johnson
shows how the assumption of the complete innocence of Captain
Dreyfus as the victim of a nefarious plot—a kind of black versus
white, good-guys and bad-guys approach—failed to explain all the
details of this famous case. Yet, such an assumption plagued almost
all earlier historians. Of course, we can never divest ourselves of all
assumptions. Some of our preconceptions are very dear to us and can

be questioned only with a great deal of courage. But a flexible and open mind is an asset in any inquiry.

The skills, the resources, needed by a historian seem frightening in their variety. The historian needs to improve the quality of his mind by wide and intelligent learning in many fields. There is no specifically "historical" data which he masters by historical research. The quality of his mind is involved in every step as he writes history. He may gain valuable knowledge from the social sciences, as many historians now allege. But where can he not seek inspiration and ideas? Poetry and novels deal perceptively with many aspects of cultural man and may brilliantly illumine a period, an issue, a human predicament; and so, in principle, historians ought to know all the great literature of the world. Toynbee, who used world literature a great deal, found his leading theme of challenge and response in Robert Browning and built a theory of civilizational decay on some lines from George Meredith. The historian may gain as much insight from a novel as from academic psychology or from the more speculative insights of a Freud. But if literature can be helpful, so also, obviously, can philosophy; one may argue cogently that no competent historian should be without some working knowledge of the methods of the natural sciences. Nor should he be without wide travel and acquaintance with the practical affairs of the world.

In brief, the historian ought to know as much as he can of everything, so that he can bring to bear the greatest possible amount of wisdom on the materials he handles, in order to shape them into the most illuminating account possible. In principle this fertilization of his mind has almost no limits. It might be thought that a diplomatic historian could profit only from studies in political science, but there seems no reason why he could not derive benefit from a novel dealing with situations of rivalry comparable to those that arise between states, from a sociological analysis of game theory or of the contours of popular belief, or even from an awareness of the precepts of Confucian ethics in regard to statecraft. Many other pieces of knowledge might be applicable to the historical episode or process which concerns him. In his tool kit, almost any knowledge may be useful at some unexpected moment. He must not be a slave to any of his tools or try to force one to do everything. Wisdom consists in knowing when to apply a tool.

But there is a final irony: even versatility and brilliance have pitfalls. History is such a fluid subject, with so many possibilities, that even a small subject offers almost unlimited possibilities in both conception and research. One can see heaven in a grain of sand. And one is never done. The case of what Philip D. Jordan called "the palsied hand" reveals one peril. There are able scholars familiar to all of us, who for some reason never finish a work. Lord Acton was a celebrated example of this; though in fact this great man wrote a great deal of high quality, he never published a major book-length study. His "History of Liberty," for which he long collected materials, remained unfinished at his death, thus becoming, as one wit remarked, the greatest book never written. In Acton's case the trouble lay in his very genius; he was not only an able researcher keenly aware of the value of original materials but also had a subtle and searching intellect. How could such a mind ever finish such an ambitious project?

Other historians, without his brilliance, enjoy research but lack the analytical or imaginative skill to turn their findings into a synthetic whole. Others so value perfection that they cannot publish so long as relevant sources remain unexamined, which is always the case since few topics of any importance can be altogether exhausted, at least not in one lifetime. Finally, there is the richly imaginative person who sees innumerable interesting subjects and develops a fresh enthusiasm each week, flitting from one to another excitedly but never able to fix his attention for long on one. He has to learn to curb his imagination and enthusiasms. Boundaries, limits, rules, and discipline are necessary to all great art. Historians must strike a balance of reasonable completeness somewhere between an unseemly haste to publish and an obsessive drive for complete perfection. The palsied hand is as useless to society as what might be called a compulsion to publish everything. In all these issues, balance and moderation are the rule, along with candid self-analysis.

BIBLIOGRAPHIES

1. BIBLIOGRAPHY ON THE HERITAGE OF HISTORY

General

Basic textbooks on the history of history, all informative but with some limitations, include Harry Elmer Barnes, *A History of Historical Writing* (New York: Dover, 1937); James Westfall Thompson, *A History of Historical Writing* (2 vols., New York: Macmillan, 1942); and Matthew A. Fitzsimons and others, *The Development of Historiography* (Harrisburg, Pa.: Stackpole, 1954). Using these as works of reference, the student may do better to read something more interpretative. The historical part of R. G. Collingwood's *The Idea of History* (New York and London: Oxford University Press, 1946) is the prime work of this sort. T. R. Tholfsen, *Historical Thinking: An Introduction* (New York: Harper & Row, 1969) is actually a short history of historical thought. In *Shapes of Philosophical History* (Stanford, Calif.: Stanford University Press, 1965), Frank E. Manuel supplies brief but discerning lectures on leading frameworks of historical thought from early to modern times. In *Six Historians* (Chicago: University of Chicago Press, 1956), Ferdinand Schevill presents a portrait gallery from Thucydides to Henry Adams, including Saint Augustine, Machiavelli, Voltaire, and Ranke. J. B. Bury's *The Idea of Progress* (New York: Peter Smith, 1960), originally published in 1926, is still of interest. Fritz Stern, ed., *Varieties of History* (New York: Meridian Books, 1956), and Patrick Gardiner, ed., *Theories of History* (Glencoe, Ill.: Free Press, 1959), begin only with the modern period (eighteenth century). Much the same is true of J. R. Hale, ed., *The Evolution of British History: From Bacon to Namier* (New York: Meridian Books, 1964). *The International Encyclopedia of the Social Sciences* is useful both for individual historians and for the articles under History and Historiography.

Ancient Greeks and Romans

J. B. Bury, *The Ancient Greek Historians* (New York: Dover, 1957), and M. L. W. Laistner, *The Greater Roman Historians* (Berkeley: University of California Press, 1947), are two standard accounts which may be supplemented by Chester Starr, *The Awakening of the Greek Historical Spirit* (New York: Knopf, 1968). Arnaldo Momigliano, *Studies in Historiography* (New York: Harper & Row, 1966), contains an essay on Herodotus and several others on ancient historiography, by a noted master of this field. On the great Greek historians, who have been much studied, see Aubrey de Selincourt, *The World of Herodotus* (Boston: Little, Brown, 1963); John Enoch Powell, *The History of Herodotus* (Amsterdam: Hakkert, 1967); F. E. Adcock, *Thucydides and His History* (London and New York: Cambridge University Press, 1963); and Charles N. Cochrane, *Thucydides and the Science of History* (New York: Russell & Russell, 1965). Also on Thucydides, see John H. Finley, Jr., *Thucydides* (Ann Arbor: University of Michigan Press, 1963), and a magisterial essay by H. D. F. Kitto in his *Poiesis: Structure and Thought* (Berkeley: University of California Press, 1966). An able French book on Greek historical thought is *La naissance de l'histoire* by Albert Chatelet (Paris: Editions de Minuit, 1962). Kurt von Fritz, *Die griechische Geschichtsschreibung* (vol. I, Berlin: de Gruyter, 1967), is a recent German investigator; his *Aristotle's Contribution to . . . Historiography* was published as a University of California Publication in Philosophy, 1958. Good editions of the greater classical historians are readily available. C. A. Robinson has edited a convenient *Selections from Greek and Roman Historians* (New York: Holt, Rinehart & Winston, 1963), while not only Herodotus, Thucydides, and the greater Roman historians but Xenophon, Suetonius, and Procopius are in paperback editions (Penguin). An interesting supplement to Thucydides is A. W. Gomme's *An Historical Commentary on Thucydides* (Oxford: Clarendon Press, 1966). The Great Histories series, general editor H. R. Trevor-Roper, in Washington Square paperbacks, with useful introductions, reprints the writings of Herodotus (ed. W. G. Forrest), Thucydides (ed. P. A. Brunt), Polybius (ed. E. Badian), Josephus (ed. M. I. Finley), Tacitus (ed. Hugh Lloyd-Jones), and Procopius (ed. Mrs. Averil Cameron). Two indispensable books on Tacitus are Clarence W. Mendell, *Tacitus: The Man and His Work* (New Haven, Conn.: Yale University Press, 1957), and the longer, rather ill-organized but richly informative work of Sir Ronald Syme, *Tacitus* (2 vols., Oxford: Clarendon Press, 1958). There is also Bessie Walker, *The Annals of Tacitus: A Study in the Writing of History* (Manchester: Manchester University Press, 1960). Tacitus' *Complete Works* are available in a Modern Library edition and *The Annals* in a Mentor paperback excellently translated by Donald R. Dudley. Livy's *History of Rome,* translated and with an introduction by Moses Hadas and Joe P. Poe, is conveniently available from Modern Library; the best recent book on Livy is by P. G. Walsh, *Livy: His Historical Aims and Methods* (Cambridge University Press, 1961). An interesting article on Josephus was published in *The*

Listener (London) by Martin Braun, vol. 56, July 12, 1956. George H. Nadel's essay, reprinted in Nadel, ed., *Studies in the Philosophy of History* (New York: Harper & Row, 1965), "Philosophy of History before Historicism," is a good summary of the ancient outlook on the past. Ludwig Edelstein's *The Idea of Progress in Antiquity* (Baltimore: Johns Hopkins Press, 1967) is discussed by E. R. Dodds in *Journal of the History of Ideas,* vol. XXIX, July-September, 1968.

The Judaic-Christian Tradition

Mircea Eliade, *Cosmos and History* (New York: Harper & Row, 1959), by a master of comparative religions, provides background for the Judaic view of history. Biblical studies are too numerous to count, but a handful with special relevance are: R. A. MacKenzie, *Faith and History in the Old Testament* (New York: Macmillan, 1965); C. R. North, *The Old Testament Interpretation of History* (London: Epworth Press, 1946); E. W. Heaton, *The Old Testament Prophets* (Baltimore: Penguin Books, 1961); and Norman H. Snaith, *The Distinctive Ideas of the Old Testament* (New York: Schocken, 1964). Snaith has an essay on "Time in the Old Testament" in F. F. Bruce, ed., *Promise and Fulfillment: Essays Presented to S. H. Hooke* (Edinburgh: Clark, 1963). W. Taylor Stevenson, "Theology and History: The Relation Considered," *Christian Scholar,* vol. 46, no. 2 (1963), pp. 110-25, sees the biblical view shaping the historian's consciousness in Western civilization. R. C. Dentan, ed., *The Idea of History in the Ancient Near East* (New Haven: Yale University Press) includes chapters on some of the ancient pagan empires as well as on the Hebrews. Martin Buber, *The Prophetic Faith* (New York: Harper & Row, 1960), is by a master of modern religious thought. R. L. P. Milburn, *Early Christian Interpretations of History* (London: A. & C. Black, 1954), is a valuable work; Eusebius' *History of the Church from Christ to Constantine* (Penguin), and Saint Augustine, *City of God* (Doubleday Image book; introduction by Etienne Gilson), are current paperback editions of early Christian historical classics. C. A. Patrides, *The Phoenix and the Ladder: The Rise and Decline of the Christian View of History* (Berkeley: University of California Press, 1964); Herbert Butterfield, *Christianity and History* (New York: Scribner's, 1950); Reinhold Niebuhr, *Faith and History: A Comparison of Christian and Modern Views of History* (Scribner's, 1949); and E. H. Harbison, *Christianity and History* (Princeton, N.J.: Princeton University Press, 1964), may be suggested for insights into this subject.

Medieval

Further on Saint Augustine, Chapter 12 of Charles N. Cochrane, *Christianity and Classical Culture* (London and New York: Oxford University Press, 1957); G. L. Keyes, *Christian Faith and the Interpretation of History* (Lincoln: University of Nebraska Press, 1966); and Theodor E. Mommsen, "St. Augustine and the Christian Idea of Progress," *Journal of the History of Ideas,* vol. 12 (1951), pp. 346-74, reprinted in Mommsen's *Medieval and Renaissance Studies* (Ithaca, N.Y.: Cornell University Press, 1960) along with an essay on Orosius, another strong influence on the Augustinian conception of history. A. Hamilton Thompson, ed., *Bede: His Life, Times and Writing* (New York: Russell & Russell, 1966), is useful on this great early medieval historian, whose *History of the English Church and People* is a Penguin paperback. Robert W. Henning, *The Vision of History in Early Britain* (New York: Columbia University Press, 1966), includes Geoffrey of Monmouth as well as Bede; Geoffrey's *History of the Kings of Britain* is a Penguin Classic. M. R. B. Shaw is the editor and translator of *Joinville and Villehardouin: Chronicles of the Crusades,* another Penguin Classic. In the same series is Gregory of Tours, *History of the Franks. Carolingian Chronicles,* tr. B. W. Scholz, is published by the University of Michigan Press (1970). M. L. W. Laistner, *Thought and Letters in Western Europe 500-900* (Ithaca, N.Y.: Cornell University Press, 1957), includes the historians of early medieval Europe. Further on the Crusade chroniclers, Colin Morris, "Geoffrey de Villehardouin and the Conquest of Constantinople," *History,* vol. LIII, February, 1968, sees the historian of the Fourth Crusade as much like Froissart in his concern for noble deeds of warfare. Froissart's *Chronicles* may be found either in Penguin Classics or in Dutton Everyman edition; see also C. T. Allmand, "Jean Froissart," *History Today,* December, 1966, and G. and W. Anderson, *The Chronicles of Froissart* (Carbondale: Southern Illinois University Press, 1963). Speros Vryonis, ed., *Readings in Medieval Historiography* (Boston: Houghton Mifflin, 1968), includes Byzantine and Muslim as well as Latin historians in selection. Michael Psellus' *Fourteen Byzantine Rulers* is a Penguin paperback. On Ibn Khaldun, see Muhsin Mahdi, *Ibn Khaldun's Philosophy of History* (London: Allen & Unwin, 1957); Walter J. Fischel, *Ibn Khaldun in Egypt* (Berkeley: University of California Press, 1967); and Franz Rosenthal, ed., *The Muquddimah: An Introduction to History* (3 vols., New York: Pantheon Books, 1958; an abridged edition in one volume is a Princeton University Press paperback). See also Rosenthal's *History of Muslim Historiography* (Leiden: Brill, 1952). Norman Cohn, *The Pursuit of the Millennium: Revolutionary Messianism in Medieval and Reformation Europe* (New York: Harper & Row, 1961) interestingly surveys a significant tradition. Otto, Bishop of Freising, *The Two Cities: A Chronicle of Universal History to 1146,* ed. C. C. Mierow, has recently been printed by Octagon Books (1967). So has *The Chronicle of Bury St. Edmunds, 1212-1301,* ed. Antonia Gransden (New York: Humanities Press, 1964), a good example of a monastic history of the type so common in the Middle Ages.

Renaissance and Reformation

Francesco Guicciardini, *History of Florence* (Harper & Row, 1969), is the chief work of probably the greatest Renaissance historian. The Great Histories series (Washington Square) includes volumes on both Guicciardini and Machiavelli, with useful introductions. Felix Gilbert's *Machiavelli and Guicciardini: Politics and History in Sixteenth Century Florence* (Princeton, N.J.: Princeton University Press, 1965) is the best secondary work, an extremely illuminating introduction to Renaissance historiography; Gilbert also has an essay on "The Renaissance Interest in History" in Charles H. Singleton, ed., *Art, Science, and History in the Renaissance* (Baltimore: Johns Hopkins Press, 1967). See also George Huppert, "The Renaissance Background of Historicism," *History and Theory*, vol. 5, no. 1 (1966); Myron P. Gilmore, *Humanists and Jurists* (Cambridge, Mass.: Harvard University Press, 1963); and the review of the latter by Julian H. Franklin in *History and Theory*, vol. 4, no. 3 (1965); William J. Bousma, "Three Types of Historiography in Post-Renaissance Italy," *History and Theory*, same issue; also Herbert Weisinger, "Ideas of History during the Renaissance," *Journal of the History of Ideas*, vol. VI, November, 1945. Eric Cochrane, ed., *The Late Italian Renaissance* (New York: Harper & Row, 1970), contains an essay on historiography by Giorgio Spini. Gilmore has an essay on "The Renaissance Conception of the Lessons of History" in W. H. Werkmeister, ed., *Facets of the Renaissance* (Los Angeles: University of California at Los Angeles Press, 1959). Peter Burke, ed., *The Renaissance Sense of the Past* (New York: St. Martin's Press, 1970), is a collection of documents. Donald J. Wilcox, *The Development of Florentine Humanist Historiography in the Fifteenth Century* (Harvard University Press, 1969) is a recent monograph. Gerald Strauss, *Historian in an Age of Crisis: The Life and Work of J. Aventinus* (Harvard University Press, 1963), deals with a late fifteenth-century German. A good introduction to the subject of history in the Reformation is E. H. Harbison's *The Christian Scholar in the Age of the Reformation* (New York: Scribner's, 1956). Paoli Sarpi is included in the Great Histories series (Washington Square). Bruno Neveu, *Un historien à l'école de Port-Royal: Sebastien Tillemont* (The Hague: M. Nijhoff, 1966) carefully studies a representative Catholic historian. J. G. A. Pocock, *The Ancient Constitution and the Feudal Law: A Study of English Historical Thought in the 17th Century* (New York: Norton, 1957) is outstanding; it may be supplemented by F. S. Fussner, *The Historical Revolution: English Historical Writing and Thought 1580-1640* (New York: Columbia University

Press, 1962), and by Levi Fox, *English Historical Scholarship in the Six-teenth and Seventeenth Centuries* (London: Oxford University Press, 1956). Christopher Hill has an essay on "Ralegh and the Study of His-tory" in his *Intellectual Origins of the Puritan Revolution* (Oxford: Clarendon Press, 1965). For the French school, J. H. Franklin, *Jean Bodin and the Sixteenth Century Revolution in the Methodology of Law and History* (New York: Columbia University Press, 1963), can be sup-plemented by the interesting essay of Donald R. Kelley on "Baudouin's Conception of History" in *Journal of the History of Ideas,* vol, XXV, January-March, 1964, and also by Kelley's book, *Foundations of Modern Historical Scholarship: Language, Law and History in the French Renais-sance* (Columbia University Press, 1970). Bodin's *Method for the Easy Comprehension of History* has recently been reprinted (New York: Nor-ton, 1969). "The Cartesian Spirit in History" was excellently analyzed in an essay by Lucien Lévy-Bruhl in R. Klibansky and H. J. Paton, eds., *Philosophy and History* (1936, reprinted by Peter Smith).

Eighteenth Century

John B. Black, *The Art of History: A Study of Four Eighteenth Cen-tury Historians,* originally published in 1926, has recently been reprinted (New York: Russell & Russell, 1966) and is still illuminating. John T. Marcus, *Heaven, Hell and History: A Survey of Man's Faith in History from Antiquity to the Present* (New York: Macmillan, 1967), is actually concerned mostly with the Enlightenment. Carl L. Becker's famous essay, *The Heavenly City of the Eighteenth Century Philosophers* (New Haven, Conn.: Yale University Press, 1932), made luminously clear the nature of the transition toward historicism at the end of the Enlightenment. James W. Johnson, *The Formation of English Neoclassical Thought* (Princeton University Press, 1967), devotes a good deal of attention to history, as does Henry Vyverberg, *Historical Pessimism in the French Enlightenment* (Harvard University Press, 1958). J. H. Brumfitt, *Voltaire, Historian* (Oxford University Press, 1957), is a model study; there is also a useful chapter on Voltaire as historian in *Visions of Culture* by Karl J. Weintraub (University of Chicago Press, 1966); while Peter Gay has edited Vol-taire's *Philosophical Dictionary* (2 vols., New York: Basic Books, 1962) and *The Age of Louis XIV* appears in the Great Histories series (Wash-ington Square). Nellie M. Schargo, *History in the Encyclopedia* (Colum-bia University Press, 1947), provided additional insight into the *philo-sophe's* attitude toward history. Weintraub has an essay on "Toward a History of the Common Man: Voltaire and Condorcet," in Richard Herr and Harold T. Parker, eds., *Ideas in History: Essays Presented to Louis Gottschalk* (Durham, N.C.: Duke University Press, 1965). Montesquieu's

Considerations on the Causes of the Greatness of the Romans and Their Decline is a Cornell paperback. On Vico, A. R. Caponigri, *Time and Idea: The Theory of History in Giambattista Vico* (London: Routledge, 1953), and Benedetto Croce, *The Philosophy of G. Vico,* tr. by R. G. Collingwood (New York: Russell & Russell, 1964); Vico, *The New Science,* tr. by H. M. Fisch and T. G. Bergin (New York: Doubleday, 1961). A recent collection of essays to honor Vico's tercentenary has extraordinary scope and quality: *Giambattista Vico: An International Symposium,* ed. Giorgio Tagliacozzo (Baltimore: Johns Hopkins Press, 1969). A useful tool for closer study of the great Neapolitan is Elio Gianturco's *A Selective Bibliography of Vico Scholarship 1948-1968* (Florence: Grafica Tuscana, 1968). Eric W. Cochrane, *Tradition and Enlightenment in the Tuscan Academies* (Chicago: University of Chicago Press, 1962), indicates the role of history in the Italian Enlightenment. Richard H. Popkin has selected David Hume's comments on history in *Philosophical Historian* (Indianapolis, Ind.: Library of Liberal Arts, 1965); Ernest C. Mossner's excellent *Life of David Hume* (Austin: University of Texas, 1954) includes an appraisal of his historical work; Laurence L. Bongie, *David Hume, Prophet of the Counter-Revolution* (Oxford: Clarendon Press, 1965), notes the wide influence of Hume's *History.* Scottish "conjectural history" is discussed in Gladys Bryson, *Man and Society: The Scottish Inquiry of the Eighteenth Century* (Princeton University Press, 1945). The best recent book on Gibbon is Joseph W. Swain, *Edward Gibbon the Historian* (New York: St. Martin's Press, 1966), whose *Decline and Fall of the Roman Empire* is one of Washington Square's Great Histories; of considerable interest also is Gibbon's *Autobiography* (Meridian Books, 1961); cf. the alternate version, *Memoirs of My Life,* ed. George Bonnard (Chicago: Funk & Wagnall, 1969). (Vico's *Autobiography* perhaps began the practice of historians writing their intellectual memoirs; cf. among others Croce and Collingwood more recently.) H. Trevor Coulborn, *The Lamp of Experience: Whig History and the Intellectual Origins of the American Revolution* (Chapel Hill: University of North Carolina Press, 1966), an exciting study in the uses of history, and Thomas P. Peardon, *The Transition in English Historical Writing 1760-1830* (New York: Columbia University Press, 1933), are also worth mentioning in the area of British historiography. (See again J. R. Hale, *The Evolution of British History.*) In *Man on His Past* (Cambridge University Press, 1955, and Beacon paperback), Herbert Butterfield has an essay on the rise of the Göttingen school in the later eighteenth century. Kant's *On History* is available in a Library of Liberal Arts paperback. Herder's *Reflections on the Philosophy of History* is included in the Classic European Historians series (University of Chicago Press, 1968), ed. Frank E. Manuel. See also

G. A. Wells, "Herder's Two Philosophies of History," *Journal of the History of Ideas*, vol. XXI, October-December, 1960, and an essay on Herder by Isaiah Berlin in Earl R. Wasserman, ed., *Aspects of the Eighteenth Century* (Baltimore: Johns Hopins Press, 1965). Further on the Germans of the later eighteenth century, W. M. Simon, *Schiller: The Poet as Historian* (Keele, Eng.: University of Keele, 1966), and Deric Regin, *Freedom and Dignity: The Historical and Philosophical Thought of Schiller* (The Hague: Nijhoff, 1965). Another great transitional figure between the ages of Enlightenment and Romanticism is discussed by John C. Weston, "Edmund Burke's View of History," *Review of Politics*, vol. 23, no. 2 (April, 1961).

The Nineteenth Century

G. P. Gooch, *History and Historians in the Nineteenth Century* (Boston: Beacon Press, 1952), is a brave attempt to cope with the *embarras de richesse* of nineteenth-century historical writing. Georg G. Iggers, *The German Conception of History: From Herder to the Present* (Middletown, Conn.: Wesleyan University Press, 1968), is a recent work on a theme previously tackled by F. Engel-Jánosi, *The Growth of German Historicism* (Johns Hopkins Press, 1944), and still earlier by Friedrich Meinecke in a celebrated study, *Die Enstehung des Historismus*, unfortunately never translated into English, but reprinted by R. Oldenbourg of Munich as volume III of Meinecke's collected *Werke* (1965). In *Historical Essays* (Harper paperback), H. R. Trevor-Roper includes essays on Macaulay, Marx, Burckhardt, and other historians. Pieter Geyl, *Debates with Historians* (Meridian Books, 1958), contains essays on Ranke, Macaulay, Carlyle, and Michelet. Among studies of individual German historians, Theodore H. Von Laue, *Ranke: The Formative Years* (Princeton University Press, 1950), is outstanding in English; Roger Wines, ed. *A Ranke Reader* (Harper, 1970) facilitates direct acquaintance with one of the most famous of all historians. Andreas Dorpalen, *Heinrich von Treitschke* (New Haven, Conn.: Yale University Press, 1957), is equally good on another well-known German historian. Herbert Butterfield dealt with Ranke also in his *Man on His Past*; Meinecke's essay on "Ranke and Burckhardt" was translated by Hans Kohn in *German History: Some New German Views* (Boston: Beacon Press, 1954). Hegel's *Reason in History* (Library of Liberal Arts) or the Modern Library *Philosophy of Hegel*, ed. Carl J. Friedrich, can be supplemented by Walter Kaufmann, *Hegel* (Doubleday Anchor, 1965). Michael Grant, "A Great German Historian," *The Listener*, vol. 50, November 5, 1953, will serve to introduce Theodor Mommsen, whose *History of Rome* is a Meridian paperback. Werner Kaegi's massive biography of Jacob Burckhardt (3 vols., Basel: Schwabe,

1947-1956), has not been translated; there is a good essay on Burckhardt in Albert Salomon's *In Praise of Enlightenment* (Cleveland and New York: Meridian Books, 1963) and another in Karl Weintraub's *Visions of Culture,* where Michelet also receives a chapter. Burckhardt's *Civilization of the Renaissance in Italy* is readily available in paperback, and his *On History and Historians* has been edited by H. Zohn (Harper paperback). Michelet's *History of the French Revolution,* edited by Gordon Wright, has been included in the Classic European Historians series (University of Chicago Phoenix paperback), while his *Joan of Arc,* tr. and ed. Albert Guérard, is an Ann Arbor paperback. See also John Atherton, "Michelet: Three Conceptions of Historical Becoming," *Studies in Romanticism,* vol. IV, Summer, 1965. Further on French historians: F. Engel-Jánosi, *Four Studies in French Historical Writing* (Johns Hopkins Press, 1955); Douglas Johnson, *Guizot* (London: Routledge and Kegan Paul, 1963), dealing with the historian as well as the statesman; Jane Herrick, *The Historical Thought of Fustel de Coulanges* (Washington, D.C.: Catholic University Press, 1954); Edward T. Gargan, *De Tocqueville* (New York: Hillary House, 1965), which stresses the historical work of Tocqueville more than other studies of this great French writer. Alfred Cobban, "Hippolyte Taine, Historian of the French Revolution," *History,* vol. LIII, October, 1968, is hardly adequate but can serve to introduce another outstanding French historian. See also Stanley Mellon, *The Political Uses of History: A Study of Historians in the French Restoration* (Stanford, Calif.: Stanford University Press, 1958). Herman Ausubel and others, *Some Modern Historians of Britain* (New York: Dryden Press, 1951), contains essays on Hallam, Carlyle, Froude, and other nineteenth century historians as well as some twentieth-century ones. H. A. L. Fisher, *The Whig Historians* (1928), needs reprinting. There is an essay on Grote in Momigliano's *Studies in Historiography.* Duncan Forbes, *The Liberal Anglican Idea of History* (Cambridge University Press, 1952), deals with another group of British historians. Herbert Butterfield's *The Whig Interpretation of History* (Norton, 1965) is a celebrated essay. Among longer studies of great nineteenth-century British historians are Giles St. Aubyn, *Victorian Eminence: Life and Works of Thomas Henry Buckle* (London: Barrie & Rockliff, 1958); Gertrude Himmelfarb, *Lord Acton* (University of Chicago Press, 1952); W. H. Dunn, *James Anthony Froude* (2 vols., Oxford: Clarendon Press, 1961-64). On Acton see also Lionel Kochan, *Lord Acton on History* (London: Deutsch, 1954); essays by Herbert Butterfield in his *Man on His Past* and in A. O. Sarkissian, ed., *Studies in Diplomatic History and Historiography in Honor of G. P. Gooch* (New York: Barnes & Noble, 1962); and William H. McNeill, ed., Lord Acton, *Essays in the Liberal Interpretation of History* (University of Chicago

Press, Classic European Historians series). Joel Hurstfield has an interesting article on " 'That Arch-Liar Froude' " in *The Listener*, vol. 50, July 9, 1953. Josef L. Altholz, "Newman and History," *Victorian Studies*, vol. 7, March, 1964; David M. Fahey, "Henry Hallam: A Conservative as Whig Historian," *The Historian*, vol. 28, no. 4, (1966); and E. M. Yoder, "Macaulay Revisited," *South Atlantic Quarterly*, vol. 63, no. 4 (1964), are all worthwhile articles. Macaulay and Carlyle are major literary figures with a vast bibliography; from among many studies one might suggest, on the former, a chapter in Mario Praz, *The Hero in Eclipse in Victorian Fiction* (London: Oxford University Press, 1956), and one in W. C. Abbott, *Adventures in Reputation* (Harvard University Press, 1935). R. C. Firth's *Commentary on Macaulay's History of England* has recently (1965) been reprinted by Barnes & Noble. René Wellek wrote an article on "Carlyle and the Philosophy of History," in *Philological Quarterly*, vol. 23 (1944), pp. 55-76. Robert Preyer, *Bentham, Coleridge, and the Science of History* (Bochum-Langendreer, West Germany: H. Pöppinghaus, 1958), is interesting on some Victorian attitudes toward history, as also are portions of Walter E. Houghton, *The Victorian Frame of Mind* (Yale University Press, 1957), and John Holloway, *The Victorian Sage* (Norton, 1965); even more relevant is Jerome H. Buckley, *The Triumph of Time: A Study of Victorian Concepts of Time, History, Progress, and Decadence* (Harvard University Press, 1966). See also Olive Anderson, "The Political Uses of History in Mid-19th Century England," *Past and Present*, vol. 36, (1967), pp. 87-105. Donal McCartney, who is at work on a full study of the popular Victorian historian W. E. H. Lecky, has an article about him in *Irish Historical Studies*, vol. 14 (1964), pp. 119-41. Sir Llewellyn Woodward has commented on "The Rise of the Professional Historian in England" in *Studies in International History: Essays Presented to W. Norton Medlicott* (London: Longmans, 1967). A late Victorian professional is the subject of H. E. Bell's *Maitland: A Critical Examination and Assessment* (London: A. & C. Black, 1965).

Socialist and "Scientific" Historiography

M. M. Bober, *Karl Marx's Interpretation of History*, 2nd ed. (Norton, 1948); H. B. Mayo, *Introduction to Marxist Theory* (Oxford University Press, 1960); E. R. A. Seligman, *The Economic Interpretation of History* (Columbia University Press, 1907; paperback reprint); Benedetto Croce, *Historical Materialism and the Economics of Karl Marx*, a classic critique of Marxism reprinted in 1966 by Russell & Russell. See also Leo Loubère, "Louis Blanc's Philosophy of History," *Journal of the History of Ideas*, vol. XVII, January, 1956. Walter M. Simon, "Comte and Positivism," in *The Listener*, vol. 76, October 6, 1966, is a stimulating short essay. Frank

Manuel, *The New World of Henri Saint-Simon* (Cambridge University Press, 1956), and Simon's *European Positivism in the Nineteenth Century* (Cornell University Press, 1963) are standard works on their subjects. Robert L. Carneiro's introduction to *The Evolution of Society: Selections from Herbert Spencer's Principles of Sociology* (University of Chicago Press, 1967) is a useful summary of Spencer's evolutionary thought. See also Edward N. Saveth, "Scientific History in America: Eclipse of an Idea," in *Essays in American Historiography: Papers Presented in Honor of Allan Nevins,* ed. Donald Sheehan and Harold C. Syrett (Columbia University Press, 1960).

American Historiography

In addition to Sheehan and Syrett as just cited, useful general works include J. Franklin Jameson, *History of Historical Writing in the United States,* an older essay reprinted by Greenwood Press, 1969; Harvey Wish, *The American Historian: A Social-Intellectual History of the Writing of the American Past* (New York: Oxford University Press, 1960); H. H. Bellot, *American History and American Historians* (London: Athlone Press, 1952); John Higham, with Leonard Krieger and Felix Gilbert, *History: The Development of Historical Studies in the United States* (Englewood Cliffs, N.J.: Prentice-Hall, 1965); W. T. Hutchinson, ed., *The Marcus W. Jernegan Essays in American Historiography* (University of Chicago Press, 1937); Marcus Cunliffe and Robin W. Winks, eds., *Pastmasters: Some Essays on American Historians* (New York: Harper & Row, 1969). Among valuable studies of special areas are Peter Gay, *A Loss of Mastery: Puritan Historians in Colonial America* (New York: Vintage Books, 1968); David Levin, *History as Romantic Art* (New York: Harcourt, Brace & World, 1959), dealing with Bancroft, Prescott, Motley, and Parkman; George H. Callcott, *History in the United States 1800-1860* (Johns Hopkins Press, 1969); and Jurgen Herbst, *The German Historical School in American Scholarship* (Cornell University Press, 1965). The University of Chicago publishes in Phoenix paperback a series on Classics of American History which includes C. Harvey Gardiner's editing of Prescott's *Conquest of Mexico,* as well as volumes of Parkman, Motley, and Bancroft. Gardiner also has written a fine life of *W. H. Prescott* (University of Texas Press, 1969). Robert Wheaton, "Motley and the Dutch Historians," *New England Quarterly,* vol. 35, no. 3 (1962), has pointed out the inadequacies of Motley as historian if not as stylist. Later American historians: Lee Benson, *Turner and Beard: American Historical Writing Reconsidered* (Glencoe, Ill.: Free Press, 1960); William R. Jordy, *Henry Adams: Scientific Historian* (Yale University Press, 1952); Cushing Strout, *The Pragmatic Revolt in American History: Carl Becker and Charles Beard* (Yale University Press, 1959); Richard Hofstadter, *The Progressive Historians: Turner, Beard, Parrington* (New York: Knopf, 1968). The Turner school is dealt with in Wilbur Jacobs, ed., *Frederick Jackson Turner's Legacy* (San Marino, Calif.: The Huntington Library, 1965); Jacobs, J. W. Caughey, and Joe B. Frantz, *Turner, Bolton, and Webb: Three Historians of the American Frontier* (Seattle: University of Washington Press, 1967); David W. Noble, *Historians against History: The Frontier Thesis and the National Covenant in American History since 1830* (Minneapolis: University of Minnesota Press, 1965). Ray A. Billington has edited some Turner writings under the title *Frontier and Section* (Englewood Cliffs, N.J.: Prentice-Hall, 1961). James Harvey Robinson's *The New History* has been reprinted (Free Press paperback), with an introduction by Harvey Wish. *Detachment and the Writing of History: Essays and Letters of Carl L. Becker*, ed. Phil L. Snyder, is a Cornell University Press paperback (1958). There is a study of *Carl Becker: The Development of an American Historian* by Burleigh T. Wilkins (Massachusetts Institute of Technology Press, 1967). Charles Crowe, "The Emergence of Progressive History," *Journal of the History of Ideas,* vol. XXVII, January-March, 1966, is a good article, as is an older one by W. E. Bean, "Revolt among the Historians," *Sewanee Review,* vol. XLVII (1939), pp. 330-41.

Twentieth Century

Books with rather broad coverage include S. W. Halperin, ed., *Some Twentieth Century Historians* (University of Chicago Press, 1961); Bernadotte E. Schmitt, ed., *Some Historians of Modern Europe* (University of Chicago Press, 1942); F. M. Powicke, *Modern Historians and the Study of History* (London: Odhams, 1956); Fritz Wagner, *Moderne Geschichtsschreibung* (Berlin, Duncker & Humbolt, 1960), an outstanding German work. Hans Meyerhoff, ed., *Philosophy of History in Our Time* (Garden City, N.Y.: Doubleday Anchor Books, 1959), is a useful collection. Carlo Antoni, *From History to Sociology: The Transition in German Historical Writing* (Detroit: Wayne State University Press, 1959), is valuable. It includes the influence of Dilthey, on whom see William Kluback, *Wilhelm Dilthey's Philosophy of History* (Columbia University Press, 1956), and H. A. Hodges, *The Philosophy of Dilthey* (London: Routledge, 1952), as well as an article by Hajo Holborn, "Wilhelm Dilthey and the Critique of Historical Reason," *Journal of the History of Ideas,* vol. XIX, January, 1958 (reprinted in W. W. Wagar, ed., *European Intellectual History since Darwin and Marx,* Harper paperback.) Some of Dilthey's writings have been edited and translated as *Pattern and Meaning in History* by H. P. Rickman (Harper & Row, 1962). Nietzsche's *Use and Abuse of History* (Library of Liberal Arts) may be compared. There is a large literature on Croce, to which perhaps the best introduction is Hayden White's article, "The Abiding Relevance of Croce's Idea of History," *Journal of Modern History,* vol. XXXV, no. 2, (1963). His own book on historiography was translated as *History: Its Theory and Practice* (New York: Russell & Russell, 1960). H. Stuart Hughes wrote a serviceable appraisal of *Oswald Spengler* (Scribner's, 1952), whose *Decline of the West* is in a Modern Library edition. See also Huizinga's essay, cited in the text, from his *Dutch Civilization in the Seventeenth Century and Other Essays* (London: Collins, 1968). M. F. Ashley Montagu, ed., *Toynbee and History* (Boston: Porter Sargent, 1956), is a valuable collection of criticisms of Arnold J. Toynbee, whose great *A Study of History* appeared in 12 volumes between 1934 and 1961 and is now all in paperback (Oxford University Press). See also Edward T. Gargan, ed., *The Intent of Toynbee's History* (Chicago: Loyola University Press, 1961), and a forthcoming book on Toynbee by R. N. Stromberg (Southern Illinois University Press). Pieter Geyl's *Debates with Historians,* previously cited, has several essays doing battle with Toynbee, and his *Encounters in History* (Meridian Books, 1961) surveys other aspects of the contemporary historical scene. Franco Venturi, ed., *Historiens du XXe Siècle* (Geneva: Droz, 1966), is an interesting discussion of a number of European historians. In addition to this book, Halperin, and Schmitt (as above), individual historians are dealt with in many articles, of which the following list is a mere sample: Gerhard Masur, "Friedrich Meinecke, Historian of a World in Crisis," in Horace J. Weiss, ed., *The Origins of Modern Consciousness* (Detroit: Wayne State University Press, 1965); Rosalie L. Colie, "Johan Huizinga and the Task of Cultural History," *American Historical Review,* vol. LXIX, April, 1964; R. R. Davies, "Marc Bloch," *History,* vol. LII, October, 1967; Henry Winkler, "Sir Lewis Namier," *Journal of Modern History,* vol. 35, no. 1, (1963); Stanley G. Payne, "James Vicens Vives and the Writing of Spanish History," *Journal of Modern History,* vol. 34, no. 2, (1962). Paul Merkley, "Reinhold Niebuhr: The Historian's Theologian," *Queen's Quarterly,* vol. 71, no. 3, (1964), is a commentary on Niebuhr's *Faith and History* and *Nature and Destiny of Man* (Scribner paperback) which together with Karl Lowith's *The Meaning of History* (University of Chicago Press, 1949) and Rudolf Bultmann's *History and Eschatology* (Harper, 1957) may be taken as illustrative of post-World War I rejection of the idea of secular progress from a Christian perspective. The interesting subject of the uses of history in the USSR may be pursued in a variety of sources: M. Pundeff, ed.,

History in the USSR: Selected Readings (Stanford, Calif.: Hoover Institution, 1967); Klaus Mehnert, *Stalin versus Marx: The Stalinist Historical Doctrine* (London: Allen & Unwin, 1952); Pieter Geyl, "Soviet Historians," in *Encounters in History*; Valentine Giterman, "The Study of History in the Soviet Union," in *Science and Freedom* (Congress for Cultural Freedom; London: Secker & Warburg, 1955). See also Walter Laqueur, *The Fate of the Revolution: Interpretations of Soviet History* (London and New York: Macmillan, 1967).

Recent Trends

Boyd Shafer, Michel Francais, Wolfgang Mommsen, and A. Taylor Milne, *Historical Study in the West* (New York: Appleton-Century-Crofts, 1968), is a detailed survey of the state of the profession in the United States, France, Germany, and Britain. Walter Laqueur and George L. Mosse, eds., *The New History: Trends in Historical Research and Writing since World War II* was an issue of *Journal of Contemporary History* (vol. 4, 1968) which has been issued as a Harper paperback book. (These essays appear also in D. C. Watt, ed., *Contemporary History in Europe* (New York: Praeger, 1969). The special supplements of April, July, and September, 1966, on "New Ways in History" in the *Times Literary Supplement* (London) provide an abundance of ideas. Various academic exercises in the popular sport of evaluating the profession: Herbert Butterfield, *The Present State of Historical Scholarship* (Cambridge University Press, 1965); Geoffrey Barraclough, *History in a Changing World* (Oxford: Blackwell, 1956); R. W. Southern, *The Shape and Substance of Academic History* (Oxford University Press, 1961); J. H. Hexter, *Reappraisals in History* (Evanston, Ill.: Northwestern University Press, 1961); John Higham, ed., *The Reconstruction of American History* (Harper paperback, 1962); J. H. Plumb, ed., *Crisis in the Humanities* (Baltimore: Penguin Books, 1964), chapter on history by the editor. Some French trends were summed up in an article by the distinguished historian Pierre Renouvin, "Research in Modern and Contemporary History: Present Trends in France," *Journal of Modern History*, vol. 38, no. 1 (1966); see also Comité Francaise des Sciences Historiques, *La recherche historique en France de 1940-1965* (Paris: Editions du Centre National de la Recherche Scientifique, 1965). H. P. R. Finberg, ed., *Approaches to History* (Toronto: University of Toronto Press, 1962), is of some value in assessing recent fashions. Don K. Rowney and James Q. Graham, eds., *Quantitative History: Selected Readings* (Homewood, Ill.: Dorsey Press, 1968), brings together a number of articles in and on this recent fad; it does not reprint E. N. Hunt, "The New Economic History," *History*, vol. LIII, February, 1968, an examination of R. W. Fogel's econometric techniques. See also Douglas North, "Quantitative Research in American Economic History," *American Economic Review,* vol. LIII, no. 1 (1963), and "The State of Economic History," *ibid.,* vol. LV, no. 2 (1965). Asa Briggs, "The Victorian City: Quantity and Quality," *Victorian Studies,* vol. 77, summer, 1968, and articles on quantitative method by H. J. Dyos and A. B. M. Barker in Dyos, ed., *The Study of Urban History* (New York: St. Martin's Press, 1968) are also representative of the debate about quantification. Peter Laslett, *The World We Have Lost* (London: Methuen, 1965), is a plea for social history at the local level stressing demography. Other recent trends may be discerned in C. Vann Woodward, ed., *A Comparative Approach to American History* (New York: Basic Books, 1968), and Robert F. Berkhofer, *A Behavioral Approach to Historical Analysis* (Glencoe, Ill.: Free Press, 1968); also such works as Seymour M. Lipset and Richard Hofstadter, eds., *Sociology and History* (Basic Books, 1968), exploring relationships between history and other social studies. An issue of the *International Social Science Journal,* vol. 17, no. 4, (1964), was devoted to "History and Social Science," and many books appeared on this subject, for example, in addition to the sociology and history theme, I. M. Lewis, ed., *History and Social Anthropology* (Barnes & Noble, 1968), and Gordon Leff, *History and Social Theory* (Tuscaloosa: University of Alabama Press, 1969). But historians might also have been impressed by the thorough assault on all generalizing social sciences as fundamentally worthless in such books as A. R. Louch, *Explanation and Human Action* (Berkeley: University of California Press, 1966), or H. P. Rickman, *Understanding and the Human Studies* (London: Heinemann, 1967). Two articles on existentialism and history are Clarence J. Manford, "Sartrean Existentialism and the Philosophy of History," *Cahiers d'Histoire Mondiale,* vol. XI, no. 3 (1968), and H. B. Sharabi, "The Existential Approach to History," *The Historian,* vol. 26, no. 2 (1964)—hardly definitive studies, but ones that might lead the student to further research in this subject. "Newer Emphases in Jewish History" is the theme of an article by Salo W. Baron, in *Jewish Social Studies,* vol. 25, no. 4, (1963). There is a large number of such articles and books summarizing the state of scholarship in specific areas. For example, a number of them on British history are collected in the volume edited by Elizabeth C. Furber, *Changing Views on British History: Essays on Historical Writing since 1939* (Harvard University Press, 1966). Specialists in the various fields of history can guide the student to similar surveys in almost any subject area. Somewhat broader in subject matter is Beatrice F. Hyslop, "Trends in Historical Writing about Modern Europe in the Last Five Years," *The Annals* (American Academy of Political and Social Science), January, 1970.

Non-Western Historiography

Franz Rosenthal's *History of Muslim Historiography* has already been cited. The following Oxford University Press volumes provide basic orientation in their areas: B. Lewis and P. M. Holt, eds., *Historians of the Middle East* (1962); D. G. E. Hall, ed., *Historians of Southeast Asia* (1961); C. H. Phillips, ed., *Historians of India, Pakistan, and Ceylon* (1961); W. G. Beasley and E. G. Pulleybank, *Historians of China and Japan* (1961). John T. Marcus, "Time and the Sense of History: East and West," *Comparative Studies in Society and History,* vol. 3, no. 2 (1961), discusses basic philosophical themes; see also articles by Arthur F. Wright, "The Study of Chinese Civilization," *Journal of the History of Ideas,* vol. XXI, no. 2 (1960), and in Louis Gottschalk, ed., *Generalization in the Writing of History* (University of Chicago Press, 1963). Jacques Gernet, "L'histoire en Extreme-Orient," *Revue historique,* vol. 228, no. 1 (1962), discusses Beasley-Pulleybank and Hall. *Diogenes,* no. 42 (1963), devoted a whole issue to the theme of "Man and the Concept of History in the Orient." Albert Feuerwerker, ed., *History in Communist China* (Massachusetts Institute of Technology Press, 1968), may be compared with studies of Russian Communist historiography. Feuerwerker has also edited *Approaches to Modern Chinese History* (University of California Press, 1967).

On Latin America, see Stanley Stein, "The Tasks Ahead for Latin American Historians," *Hispanic American Historical Review,* vol. 40, no. 2 (1960), and "The Historiography of Brazil, 1808-1889," *ibid.,* vol. 41, no. 3 (1961); Robert Conrad, "Brazilian Historian" (Joao Capistrano de Abreu), *Revue de Historia de America* (Mexico), no. 59 (1965); Howard F. Cline, ed., *Latin American History: Essays on Its Study and Teaching* (2 vols., Austin: University of Texas Press, 1967), containing some essays on historians and trends in research. Two Latin American historians, Diego Barros Arana of Chile and Bartolome Mitre, Argentinian statesman and man of letters, are discussed in *The New Cambridge Modern History,* vol. XI (Cambridge University Press, 1962), 539-40.

An interesting category of historiographical literature traces the evolution of a particular controversy or concept or episode in the thought of historians. Pieter Geyl's *Napoleon: For and Against* (Yale University Press) is an outstanding example; there is no better guide to French historical literature of the nineteenth and twentieth centuries. Rushton Coulborn, *Feudalism in History* (Princeton University Press, 1956); Wallace K. Ferguson, *The Renaissance in Historical Thought* (Boston: Houghton Mifflin, 1948); and F. A. Hayek, ed., *Capitalism and the Historians* (University of Chicago Press, 1954) provide other examples, as does an essay such as J. H. Hexter's "Storm over the Gentry" in his *Reappraisals in History.*

2. BIBLIOGRAPHY ON THE CHALLENGE OF HISTORY

Much of the bibliography on the history of history also relates to the critical philosophy of history and need not be repeated here. Among the most relevant of the earlier citations are those on the German idealists, particularly on Dilthey, Burckhardt, Hegel, and Ranke; on the work of such Americans as Beard, Turner, and Becker; on Collingwood and Croce; and almost all the citations of books on contemporary history.

Two German philosophers not included in the preceding bibliography deserve special mention. The first, Heinrich Rickert, professed the critical bent of Kant. His major work on history, dating back in its origins to the turn of the century, has been translated into English as *Science and History: A Critique of Positivist Epistemology* (New York: Harper and Row, 1967). In it he explores, more elaborately than anyone else, the relation of value to history. Although most contemporary philosophers of history do not accept his idea of a higher or overarching system of values, they have often acknowledged the role of value in determining the subject matter of human history. The second major figure is Ernst Cassirer, whose book *The Logic of the Humanities* (New Haven: Yale University Press, 1960) has tremendously influenced the contemporary dialogue about history. In the book he tries to identify a logic of symbolic forms (or, more exactly, he argues for the existence of such a logic), which will provide the formal limits for all cultural studies, including history. By this approach, he tries to vindicate the distinctive nature of cultural phenomena and the critical importance of language.

Perhaps more than any other person, R. G. Collingwood incited and influenced the direction of the most recent controversies about history. In addition to his *Idea of History,* which incorporated essays written as early as 1935, a student should turn to his *Autobiography* (New York: Oxford University Press, 1939), which includes very provocative ideas on the use of history, and, as a supplement to the latter part of *Idea of History,* to his *Essays in the Philosophy of History* (Austin: University of Texas Press, 1965). The major works of Collingwood's greatest rival among idealists, Benedetto Croce, are cited in the first bibliography. With an even more humanistic, but existential, emphasis than these two giants, José Ortega y Gasset has argued for the distinctiveness of history and for its central importance to man, in *History as a System* (New York: W. W. Norton, 1941 and 1961).

In a 1942 article in the *Journal of Philosophy* ("The Function of General Laws in History"), Carl G. Hempel opened a complex debate over explanation in history. This article is included in Patrick Gardiner, ed.,

Theories of History (Glencoe, Ill.: The Free Press, 1959), and should be supplemented by a revised position taken in an article, "Explanation in Science and in History," in William H. Dray, ed., *Philosophical Analysis and History* (New York: Harper and Row, 1966). Hempel has consistently argued for the unity of all empirical inquiry and for the necessary equivalence of explanation in history and the generalizing sciences. His position was a direct challenge to idealists and thus provoked endless refutations. His position, often classified as a form of positivism, falls back on a general conception of scientific inquiry. Hempel's more general model of explanation is contained in his *Philosophy of Natural Science* (Englewood Cliffs, N.J.: Prentice-Hall, Inc., 1966). Perhaps Karl Popper has been even more influential among philosophers of science and has taken the same ground as Hempel. See his *Logic of Scientific Discovery* (London: Hutchinson University Library, 1968).

The problem of explanation, granting several levels of meaning in the word, has remained in the forefront of historiographical discussion for the past two decades. The most influential attack on the Hempelian model came from William H. Dray in *Laws and Explanation in History* (London: Oxford University Press, 1957). Dray, who fulfilled much of the intent of Collingwood, showed how often historians explain events, not by general laws, but by the reasonableness of behavior in a human agent. This position has been supplemented by a disciple of Collingwood, Alan Donagan, in *The Later Philosophy of R. G. Collingwood* (London: Oxford University Press, 1962), and in several articles.

A more balanced approach to explanation appears in Patrick Gardiner's *The Nature of Historical Explanation* (London: Oxford University Press, 1961). He carefully notes the actual language of historians and contrasts it with scientific language. Arthur Danto, in his *Analytical Philosophy of History* (London: Cambridge University Press, 1965), tries to clarify the various models of explanation and, by careful analysis, to dissipate the seeming conflict. He also brings a remarkable simplicity and clarity to several other historical problems. Some of the same balance and openness to actual historical language appears in William H. Walsh, *An Introduction to Philosophy of History* (London: Hutchinson University Library, 1951), and in Ludwig von Mises, *History and Theory* (New Haven: Yale University Press, 1958).

Problems of causation are often tied closely to explanation. Such is the case in by far the most extended analysis of causation, Morton G. White's *Foundations of Historical Knowledge* (New York: Harper and Row, 1965). In their *Causation in the Law* (London: Oxford University Press, 1959), H. L. A. Hart and A. M. Honore also explore this same issue.

Other subtle distinctions about causation are made by Michael Scriven, "Causes, Connections and Conditions in History," in Dray, ed., *Philosophical Analysis and History,* and by W. B. Gallie in *Philosophy and the Historical Understanding* (New York: Schocken Books, 1964). Causation, explanation, and other related problems are analyzed in William Dray's small, introductory text, *Philosophy of History* (Englewood Cliffs, N.J.: Prentice-Hall, Inc., 1964).

Much of the best literature on history has appeared in article form in scientific and philosophical journals. Fortunately, the best of this literature is now available in anthologies. The most thorough is the above-cited *Theories of History,* edited by Gardiner. This can be supplemented by the earlier cited anthology by Dray (*Philosophical Analysis and History*), by Alan and Barbara Donagan, eds., *Philosophy of History* (New York: Macmillan, 1965), and by Hans Meyerhoff, ed., *The Philosophy of History in our Time* (Garden City, New York: Anchor, 1959). A variety of theoretical articles are included in Hayden V. White, ed., *Uses of History: Essays in Intellectual and Social History* (Detroit: Wayne State University Press, 1968), and in Sidney Hook, ed., *Philosophy and History* (New York: New York University Press, 1963).

Since 1960, the international journal *History and Theory* (Wesleyan University Press) has provided the main medium for theoretical discussions about history. The offering has been exceedingly rich and on almost every conceivable issue. Short of exploring each volume, the student can best turn to an anthology of these articles, George H. Nadel, ed., *Studies in the Philosophy of History: Selected Essays from History and Theory* (New York: Harper and Row, 1965).

The expert will require more extensive bibliographies to supplement the short lists provided in this book. Again, he will be in debt to *History and Theory.* The Journal has already published three sections of a thorough and continuously updated bibliography: John C. Rule, "Bibliography of Works in the Philosophy of History 1945-1967" (*History and Theory,* Beiheft I, 1961); M. Nowicki, for 1958-1961 (Beiheft III, 1963); and Lewis D. Wurgaft, for 1961-1965 (Beiheft VII, 1967). For less extensive lists, one can turn to Ronald Thompson, "Selective Reading List on History and the Philosophy of History," in *Theory and Practice in Historical Study: Report of the Committee on Historiography* (Social Science Research Council, 1946); and to Martin Klein, "Bibliography of Writings on Historiography and the Philosophy of History," in Louis Gottschalk, ed., *Generalization in the Writing of History* (University of Chicago Press, 1963). The most complete guide to the abundant periodical literature on historiography is in *Historical Abstracts* (published quarterly since 1955).

The following is a selection of articles from the *Journal of the History of Ideas* (not elsewhere cited) dealing with historiographical topics; it will serve to suggest the range of interest by intellectual historians over the last thirty years:

W. Stull Holt, "The Idea of Scientific History in America," vol. I, no. 3 (1940)

Frederick J. Teggart, "Causation in Historical Events," vol. III, no. 1 (1942)

Richard B. Schlatter, "The Problem of Historical Causation in Some Recent Studies of the English Revolution," vol. IV, no. 3 (1943)

Eva Sanford, "The Study of Ancient History in the Middle Ages," vol. V, no. 1 (1944)

A. H. Johnson, "Whitehead's Philosophy of History," vol. VII, no. 2 (1946)

Jan Romein, "Theoretical History," vol. IX, no. 1 (1948)

Hajo Holborn, "Greek and Modern Concepts of History," vol. X, no. 1 (1949)

William R. Trimble, "Early Tudor Historiography," vol. XI, no. 1 (1950)

R. N. Stromberg, "History in the Eighteenth Century," vol. XII, no. 2 (1951)

Gerhard Masur, "Wilhelm Dilthey and the History of Ideas," vol. XIII, no. 1 (1952)

Lewis W. Spitz, "The Significance of Leibniz for Historiography," vol. XIII, no. 3 (1952)

Leonard Krieger, "Marx and Engels as Historians," vol. XIV, no. 3 (1953)

Jerome Rosenthal, "Voltaire's Philosophy of History," vol. XVI, no. 2 (1955)

Maurice Mandelbaum, "Concerning Recent Trends in the History of Historiography," vol. XVI, no. 4 (1955)

Buddha Prakash, "The Hindu Philosophy of History," vol. XVI, no. 4 (1955)

Philip J. Wolfson, "Friedrich Meinecke, 1861-1954," vol. XVII, no. 4 (1956)

Calvin G. Rand, "Historicism in Dilthey, Troeltsch, and Meinecke," vol. XXV, no. 4 (1964)

Flavia M. Alaya, "Arnold and Renan on History," vol. XXVIII, no. 4 (1967)

R. F. Hathaway, "Cicero's Socratic View of History," vol. XXIX, no. 1 (1968)

George Armstrong Kelly, "Rousseau, Kant, and History," vol. XXIX, no. 3 (1968)

INDEX

Acton, Lord, 38, 62, 74, 78, 125, 252, 263
Adams, Henry, 68, 84, 253, 263
Aeschylus, 10, 11
Alcuin, 22
Alison, Archibald, 78
Ambrose, St., 20
analogy and history, 229–230
Anderle, O. F., 99
Anglo-Saxon Chronicle, 22
anthropology, 68, 159–160, 238
Aquinas, St. Thomas, 23, 32–33
Aretino, Bruno, 34
Aristophanes, 11
Aristotle, 13, 16, 33, 175, 177
Arnold, Matthew, 73, 81, 272
Aron, Robert, 36
art and history, 124, 125, 139–141, 142, 144, 199, 208, 209, 210, 211, 212, 213, 215, 221–225, 237, 238, 245
Augustine, St., 20, 21, 22, 24, 253, 255–256
Aventinus, J., 257

Bacon, Francis, 54
Bancroft, George, 42, 73, 74, 263
Barnes, Harry Elmer, 6
Baronio, Cesare, Cardinal (Baronius), 35, 38
Barraclough, Geoffrey, 103, 105
Barth, John, 117
Barth, Karl, 93
Baudelaire, Charles, 121, 124
Baudouin, François, 37, 39, 258
Bayle, Pierre, 36, 45, 56

Beard, Charles A., 83, 85–86, 88, 141, 221, 263–264
Becker, Carl L., 85, 86, 88, 106, 263, 264
Bede, the Venerable, 20–22, 26, 256
behavioral theories, 161, 165, 180–181
Bentham, Jeremy, 76, 262
Bentley, Richard, 40
Berdyaev, Nicolas, 93
Berenson, Bernard, 123
Bergson, Henri, 83, 91
Berlin, Isaiah, 120, 121
Bible, 6, 7, 8, 38, 40, 78, 235
biology, 156, 173
Blanc, Louis, 57, 77, 262
Bloch, Marc, 83, 90, 265
Bodin, Jean, 37, 39, 258
Bolingbroke, Henry St. John, Viscount, 21, 47
Boniface, St., 22
Booth, Charles, 77
Bradley, A. C., 249
Briggs, Asa, 116
Bright, John, 78
Brogan, Denis W., 120
Browning, Robert, 73, 251
Bruni, Leonardo, 33
Brunner, Emil, 93–94
Buckle, Thomas, 66, 67, 68, 73, 100, 261
Bultmann, Rudolf, 93
Burckhardt, Jacob, 80–81, 83, 89, 123, 260–261
Burke, Edmund, 44, 57, 72, 260
Bury, J. B., 12
Butterfield, Herbert, 77, 100, 250

Camden, William, 41
Carlyle, Thomas, 64, 71, 72, 75, 76,
    260, 261, 262
Carr, Edward H., 36, 117
Casaubon, Isaac, 38
Cassiodorus, 20
Cassirer, Ernst, 158, 269
causation, 14, 18, 28, 48, 91–92, 109–
    111, 130, 131, 153, 168, 174–196,
    199, 200, 207, 208, 214, 215, 241
Charlemagne, 22
Cheyney, Edward P., 88
China, history in, 4, 106, 268
chivalry, 24–26
Christianity, 3, 4, 6–9, 20–21, 24, 38,
    72, 93–94, 255
Churchill, Winston, 73
Cicero, Marcus Tullius, 17, 18, 31,
    272
Civil War (American), 192–193, 203,
    204, 205, 231, 232
Clarendon, Edward Hyde, Earl of, 42
closed generalizations, 157, 165, 172
cognition, 141–143, 146, 197, 200,
    207, 208, 209
Cohen, Morris R., 125
Colet, John, 33
Collingwood, R. G., 16, 46, 52, 88–90,
    101, 124, 269, 270
Columbia University, 84
common sense, 143–145, 155, 170, 174
Comnena, Anna, 27
comparative history, 29, 70, 97–99,
    109–111, 116–117
Comte, August, 24, 53, 57, 66–68, 82,
    96, 100, 262
conception, 137–143, 147–148, 152,
    154, 157, 160, 198, 239, 246
Condorcet, Marquess de, 24, 55, 57,
    101, 258
Copernicus, Nicholas, 39
criticism and history, 235–239
Croce, Benedetto, 52, 88–90, 123, 216,
    265, 269
culture, concept of, 80–81, 136–137,
    156–157, 158, 159, 160, 161, 162,
    163–165, 168, 173, 178–181, 183–
    185, 196, 206, 236, 239, 241

Danto, Arthur, 168, 200, 270
Darwin, Charles, 65, 68–69, 79

De Quincey, Thomas, 245
Descartes, René; Cartesianism, 39, 44,
    45, 52, 151–152, 258
determinism, 162–164, 192–193, 211
Dewey, John, 86, 214
Dickinson, G. Lowes, 92
Diderot, Denis, 47, 49
Dilthey, Wilhelm, 88, 89, 264–265,
    272
Diodorus Siculus, 13
Disraeli, Benjamin, 72, 78
Döllinger, John I. von, 62, 78
Dray, William H., 185, 188, 270, 271
Dreyfus Case, 250
Duchesne, André, 51
Durkheim, Emile, 82

Einhard, 22, 26
Eliade, Mircea, 3–4, 51, 121
Eliot, George, 64, 73
Eliot, T. S., 102
Elizabeth (I), Queen; Elizabethan age,
    41–42
Elton, G. R., 108
Emerson, Ralph Waldo, 72
empiricism, 152, 248, 249
English (Puritan) Revolution, 41, 42–
    44
Erasmus, Desiderius, 32, 33
Eratosthenes, 40
esthetics and history: *see* art and his-
    tory
Euripides, 11
Eusebius, of Caeserea, 8–9, 20, 255
evidence (historical), 201, 202, 205,
    206, 207, 209, 211, 215, 216, 217,
    218, 219, 248
evolution, 68–69, 102
existentialism, 117–119, 267
explanation, problems of, 109–110,
    114–115, 130, 156–160, 166–169,
    183

Febvre, Lucien, 83
Fichte, Johann, 58, 62
final causes, 148, 160, 163, 176–179,
    181–187, 238
Fisher, H. A. L., 94
forces (historical), 195
free will, 125, 162
Freeman, E. A., 73, 74, 85

French Revolution, 46, 57, 60, 61, 64, 78, 131, 148
Freud, Sigmund, 82, 83, 91, 165, 170, 251
Froissart, Jean, 24–26, 256
Froude, J. A., 73–74, 75, 78, 125, 261, 262
Fustel de Coulanges, N. D., 79, 261

Galbraith, John Kenneth, 120
Galileo, 39, 151
Gardiner, Patrick, 172–173, 269, 270, 271
Gardiner, Samuel R., 73
generalization, 151–173; also 48, 125, 130, 133, 135, 138, 143, 144, 145, 147, 174, 176, 177, 179, 183, 187, 196, 202, 203, 210, 220, 231, 232
generalizing sciences: *see* sciences
Geoffrey of Monmouth, 22, 256
Geyl, Pieter, 74, 99
Gibbon, Edward, 45–46, 49, 51, 259
Gladstone, William E., 74, 79
Goethe, Johann W. von, 62
Göttingen, University of, 51, 61–62
Greeks, 3, 4, 5, 8–14, 16–17, 27, 113, 138, 253–254
Green, J. R., 73, 85, 107
Gregory the Great (Pope Gregory I), 20
Gregory of Tours, 20, 21, 26, 256
Grote, George, 73, 74, 261
Guicciardini, Francesco, 18, 34, 257
Guizot, François, 42, 59, 60, 63, 73, 74, 261

habit, 178, 180–181, 182, 190, 199
Hallam, Henry, 78, 262
Hammond, Mr. and Mrs. J. L., 86
Harbison, E. H., 32, 257
Hardy, Thomas, 94
Harrison, Frederic, 75
Hebrews (Jews, Judaism), 3–6, 7, 17, 93, 255
Hecataeus, 10
Hegel, G. W. F., 38, 52, 54, 58–59, 60, 62, 63, 64, 70, 71, 118, 149, 260
Heidelberg University, 35
Hempel, Carl G., 166–167, 168, 185, 269–270

Herder, Johann G. von, 52, 56, 62, 63, 259–260
Herodotus, 9, 10, 12, 13, 66, 254
Hess, Moses, 62
Hexter, J. H., 71
Hippocrates, 11
historicism, 57–64, 88–90, 98, 101, 118, 167
history
  in ancient times, 3–18
  and causation, 174–196
  comparative, 29, 70, 97–99, 109–111, 116–117
  critical philosophy of, 129–130
  definition of, 130–132, 143–144, 148–149
  during Enlightenment, 45–56
  and generalization, 151–173
  local, 106–107
  during Middle Ages, 19–30
  in nineteenth century, 57–81
  and objectivity, 197–219
  and policy making, 228–234, 244
  professionalism in, 73–77, 116, 220, 221, 224–225, 226, 262
  "radical," 86, 108–109
  during Renaissance and Reformation period, 31–39
  as a science, 65–70, 88, 89, 100–101
  speculative philosophy of, 94–99, 100, 101, 102–103, 125, 141, 149–150, 163, 166, 171, 206
  in twentieth century, 82–125
  in United States, 84–88
  uses of, 100, 130, 148, 180, 220–243
Hobbes, Thomas, 39–40
Holmes, Oliver W., Jr., 46–47
Homer, 9, 12, 23
Horace, 15
Huizinga, Johan, 81, 265
humanists
  recent, 116
  of Renaissance, 31–34
human nature, 141, 148, 165, 171–172
Hume, David, 45, 46, 47, 49, 51–52, 57, 72, 152, 259
Hundred Years' War, 24–25
Hus, John, 38
hypothesis, role of, 180, 203, 212, 214, 215, 216, 217, 248–250

idealism, philosophical, 57–64, 88–90, 135, 138, 162, 167, 178, 179
identity and history, 42, 234–235
imagination in history, 141–143, 212, 248, 249, 252
India, history in, 4, 268, 272
induction, 141–142, 214, 215, 216
inevitability in history, 192–193
inference, 198, 214, 215, 246, 247
inquiry, model of, 214–218, 233
intellectual history, 186, 238–239
interpretation in history, 218–219, 249
intuition, 183, 186, 197
Isaiah, 149
Isidore of Seville, 20
Islam, 4, 28–30, 256, 268

James, William, 83, 86
Jedin, Herbert, 38
Jenkins, Roy, 120
Jerome, St., 20
Joachim of Flora (Fiore), 23–24, 26, 38, 71
John of Salisbury, 22
Johns Hopkins University, 84
Johnson, Douglas, 250
Johnson, Edward, 8
Johnson, Samuel, 38
Joinville. Jean, Sire de, 24, 256
Jordan, Philip D., 252
Josephus, 11, 20, 32, 254–255
Joyce, James, 53, 99, 117
Jung, Carl G., 82, 91
Juvenal, 15

Kant, Immanuel, 52, 56, 58, 62, 63, 152, 153, 158, 259, 272
Kautsky, Karl, 77
Kennan, George F., Jr., 120
Kennedy, John F., 188–192, 194, 215
Kepler, Johannes, 39, 151
Khaldun, Ibn, 28–30, 32, 53, 256
Kingsley, Charles, 73
Kissinger, Henry A., 120
knowledge, definition of, 140–141
Kolakowski, Leszek, 58

Lafayette, Marquess de, 46
Lamartine, Alphonse de, 73
Lamprecht, Karl, 81

language and culture, 132–137, 139, 157, 180, 181
La Popelinière, Henri de, 37
Laslett, Peter, 107, 267
Latin American historians, 268
Law, and history, 37, 43
law-like explanation, 143, 148–149, 153, 155, 167–168, 169, 177, 179, 183, 184, 185, 197, 203, 220
learning theory, 161, 181
Lecky, W. E. H., 69, 73, 262
Leibniz, Gottfried W., 37, 40, 55, 272
Lessing, Gotthold E., 55
Levi-Strauss, Claude, 158
Leyden University, 35
life, concept of, 161–162
Lincoln, Abraham, 208
linguistics, 160
literature and history, 132, 142, 143, 207, 212, 238
Livy, Titus, 11, 14–15, 16, 18, 31, 32, 254
Locke, John, 40, 45, 47
logical analysis, 152, 157, 164, 167, 168–169, 215
Loria, Achille, 83
Lorsch, royal annals of, 22
Lovejoy, Arthur O., 48, 49
Lucian, 17
Luther, Martin, 31, 38, 39

Mabillon, Jean, 51
Macaulay, Thomas B., 38, 42, 60, 72, 73, 76, 78, 125, 262
Machiavelli, Niccolò, 18, 31, 32, 47, 257
Magdeburg Centuries, 35
Maitland, F. W., 44, 262
Malebranche, Nicolas, 40
man, distinctive attributes, 115, 133–146, 158–159, 173
Man, Henry de, 71
Marcellinus Ammianus, 20
Marcus, John T., 93
Maritain, Jacques, 7, 9
Marrou, H. I., 86
Marx, Karl; Marxism, 24, 38, 54, 57, 64, 66, 67, 69–71, 77, 79, 82, 88, 100, 118, 262

materialism, philosophical, 135, 151–152
mathematics, 142–143, 151, 152, 210, 211
matter, conceptions of, 151, 153, 155, 158, 162, 163, 173
McMaster, John B., 84, 85
mechanism, 163–164
Meinecke, Friedrich, 60, 265, 272
Mercier de la Rivière, 51
Meredith, George, 251
metaphysics, 115, 135, 138, 163
Michelet, Jules, 64, 73, 261
Michels, Robert, 83
Mill, John Stuart, 76
Milton, John, 38
mind-body problem, 135, 151, 162, 163
mind, concepts of, 151, 157, 159, 160–163, 164, 165, 173, 178, 181
Mommsen, Theodor, 64, 75, 76, 79, 260
Montesquieu, Charles Louis, 29, 30, 37, 45, 46–47, 48, 54, 100, 258–259
moral implications in history, 123, 222–223, 225, 226–227, 231, 237
moralism and history, 190–191, 192, 227
Morley, John, 73
motives and the historian, 220–221, 224, 225
Motley, John L., 73, 74, 263
Mueller, Adam, 58
Munich Conference, 229, 230

Nagel, Ernest, 195
Namier, Lewis B., 91, 107, 265
Napoleon I, 65, 78
narration and history, 28, 130–133, 151, 168, 198, 200, 201, 208–209, 210, 211, 212–213, 214, 215, 216
nationalism and history, 41–42, 59–60, 82, 233, 234, 235
natural history, 133–134, 147, 148
Nazi Germany, history, 92–93
Newton, Isaac, 39, 40, 45, 47, 48, 152
Niebuhr, Barthold, 64
Niebuhr, Reinhold, 93, 94

Nietzsche, Friedrich, 54, 69, 80, 83, 121, 265

objectivity and history, 197–219; also 85, 86–87, 125, 130, 140, 146
ontology, 135, 138, 139–140, 141, 149–150, 157, 162, 168
open generalization, 157, 166
operationalism, 217
Ortega y Gasset, José, 46, 103, 118, 120, 250, 269
Ostrogorski, M., 83
Oswald, Lee Harvey, 188–193, 215
Otto of Freising, Bishop, 24, 256
Owen, Robert, 66

Panikkar, S. K. M., 105
Pareto, Vilfredo, 82
Parkman, Francis, 73, 263
Pater, Walter, 80
Paul, St., 33
perception, 139–140, 147, 154
phenomenology, 118, 119, 124, 140, 142, 144, 163, 198, 211, 215, 240
philosophy, linguistic, 119
physics, 119, 121, 143, 145–146, 147–148, 149, 152, 153, 154, 156, 158, 161, 163, 210, 211, 214
Pirenne, Henri, 249
Plato, 4, 13, 16, 39, 138
Plumb, J. H., 104, 117
Plutarch, 18
poetry, 142, 144, 251
Polybius, 11, 13–14, 18, 31, 32, 95, 241, 254
Popper, Karl, 58, 100, 101–102, 214, 270
positivism, 67–68, 84, 88, 97, 166–167
Pound, Ezra, 93
Powell, York, 75
Praxiteles, 11
Prescott, William H., 73, 263
presentism, historical, 43–44, 85, 88, 197, 205, 218, 238
Procopius, 11, 27, 254
professionalism in history, 73–77, 116, 220, 221, 224–225, 226, 262
progress, idea of, 9, 38, 55–56, 59–60, 93–94, 101, 116–117, 240
Psellus, Michael, 27

psychology, 152, 161, 162, 164–165,
170, 182, 232

quantitative history, 111–116, 213
quantum theory, 158, 163

radical history, 108–109
Ralegh, Walter, 41, 65, 258
Randall, John H., Jr., 120
Ranke, Leopold von, 17, 61, 63, 64,
80, 84, 88, 260
reductionism, 135, 157, 162, 168
relativism, historical, 84–88, 197, 205,
218
Renan, Ernest, 42, 81, 272
research techniques, 112–113, 131,
201, 214, 216–217, 245–252
Rhodes, James Ford, 74
Ricardo, David, 77
Richelieu, Cardinal and Duke de, 51
Rickert, Heinrich, 269
Robinson, James Harvey, 85, 86, 264
Romans, 11, 13–17, 254
Rousseau, Jean-Jacques, 48, 50, 272
Rowse, A. L., 120
Ruskin, John, 73

Saint-Simon, Henri, 53, 57, 59, 263
Sallust, 11, 32
Santayana, George, 140
Sarpi, Paoli, 37–38, 43
Sartre, Jean-Paul, 71, 118, 257
Savigny, Friedrich, 60
Scalinger, J.-J., 40
Schelling, Friedrich, 58
Schevill, Ferdinand, 87
Schiller, J. C. F. von, 260
Schlesinger, Arthur M., Jr., 120
Schliemann, Heinrich, 65, 74
Schmoller, Gustav, 77
scholasticism, medieval, 23, 24, 28
Schorske, Carl E., 116
Schweitzer, Albert, 246
science
    method, 133, 142, 146, 151, 156,
    171
    organic, 155, 156, 161, 173, 214,
    236
    philosophy of, 152, 168–169
    physical, 141, 143, 145, 146, 147–
149, 150, 151–159, 160, 161, 164,
170–171, 176, 202, 210, 211, 214,
220, 228
    social, 82–83, 91, 104, 125, 147,
    148, 150, 164–165, 170–171, 232–
    233, 251
scientific revolution, 39–41
Scott, Walter, 73
Secret Service, 190, 194
Selden, John, 43
selection in history, 28, 198, 200, 201,
202, 203, 204, 205, 207, 227
Sempronius, Asellio, 18
Shakespeare, William, 41, 42
Shirer, William L., 248
Sidgwick, Henry, 105
Smiles, Samuel, 73
Snow, Charles P., 116
socialism, socialists, 7, 77, 86, 262–263
social sciences: see science
sociology, 67, 82–83, 104, 170, 251
Socrates, 33
Sophocles, 10, 11
Sorel, Georges, 71
sources, historical, 201, 216, 245, 248
specialization, 103–104, 107–108,
116–117, 120, 122
speculative philosophy of history, 94–
99, 100, 101, 102–103, 125, 141,
149–150, 163, 166, 171, 206
Spencer, Herbert, 66, 68, 69, 82, 100,
263
Spengler, Oswald, 94–95, 96, 98, 265
Spinoza, Benedict, 40
Stark, Johannes, 93
Stewart, Dugald, 55
Stubbs, William, 73
subjectivism, 85, 184, 186, 201, 207,
218
Suetonius, 11, 18, 254
symbols, 136, 139, 153, 157, 158, 161,
178, 180–181, 199, 201, 205–206,
216, 239

Tacitus, 11, 15, 16, 17, 18, 32, 254
Taine, Hippolyte, 68, 89, 261
Tawney, R. H., 83, 86
Taylor, A. J. P., 120
Thiers, Adolphe, 74

Thucydides, 9, 10, 11, 12–13, 16, 32, 96, 122, 254
Tillemont, Sebastien, 36, 43, 257
Tillich, Paul, 94
time and history, 146–147, 169, 198–202, 205, 211, 236
Tocqueville, Alexis de, 74, 261
Toynbee, Arnold J., 29, 53, 70, 75, 76, 88, 91, 94, 96–99, 100, 102, 106, 120, 122, 149, 251, 265
tragedy, 193, 240–244
Traill, H. D., 107
Treitschke, Heinrich von, 42, 60, 260
trend (historical), 195
Trevelyan, Charles, 78
Trevelyan, George M., 73, 75, 78
Trevor-Roper, Hugh R., 104, 120
truth, definitions of, 146
Turgot, A. R. J., 55, 56
Turner, Frederick Jackson, 84–85, 86, 263–264

universal history, 94–99, 100, 102–103, 105, 149–150, 163, 166, 171, 206
USSR (Soviet Union), history in, 92–93, 122, 265–266

Valéry, Paul, 100
Valla, Lorenzo, 33
value and history, 144–145, 147–148, 160, 166, 179, 193, 197, 199, 202, 206–210, 218, 227, 238, 239

Veblen, Thorstein, 82, 83
verification, 158, 214, 215, 216, 217, 247–248
Vico, Giambattista, 29, 37, 45, 46, 52–55, 88, 259
Villehardouin, Geoffroi de, 24, 256
Virgil, 15
vitalism, 135, 162
Voltaire (François-Marie Arouet), 45, 46, 49–51, 54, 56, 66, 79, 94, 107, 121, 253, 258, 272

Wallace, Henry A., 182
Wallas, Graham, 83
War of 1812, 175
Webb, Sidney and Beatrice, 79, 86
Weber, Max, 82, 83
Wells, H. G., 94–96, 98, 99
Westermarck, E. A., 69
Whalley, Peter, 49
White, Morton G., 194, 270
Woodward, E. L., 101
World War I, 83, 91–92, 96, 97
World War II, 91, 92, 97, 167, 233, 234
Wright, Arthur F., 106

Xenophanes, 10
Xenophon, 11, 13, 254

Zola, Emile, 94